Nonprofit Boards

by Jackson Cooper and
Caitlin Pontrella

for dummies®
A Wiley Brand

Nonprofit Boards For Dummies®

Published by: **John Wiley & Sons, Inc.**, 111 River Street, Hoboken, NJ 07030-5774, www.wiley.com

For general information on our other products and services, please contact our Customer Care Department within the U.S. at 877-762-2974, outside the U.S. at 317-572-3993, or fax 317-572-4002. For technical support, please visit https://hub.wiley.com/community/support/dummies.

Wiley publishes in a variety of print and electronic formats and by print-on-demand. Some material included with standard print versions of this book may not be included in e-books or in print-on-demand. If this book refers to media that is not included in the version you purchased, you may download this material at http://booksupport.wiley.com. For more information about Wiley products, visit www.wiley.com.

Library of Congress Control Number is available from the publisher.

ISBN 978-1-394-41353-9 (pbk); ISBN 978-1-394-41355-3 (epdf); ISBN 978-1-394-41354-6 (epub)

SKY10165745_082026

Table of Contents

Introduction

Every year, thousands of people say yes to serving on a board. They may do so as a favor to a friend or to support a cause they believe in, but the role goes beyond just a favor. It's a serious responsibility to serve as a strategic thinker, executive partner, and public ambassador for a mission.

Some know what they're signing up for. Many don't. *Nonprofit Boards For Dummies* is for both.

Serving on a nonprofit board can be one of the most meaningful experiences of your life — and one of the most frustrating, especially if you don't understand the role you're stepping into and what you're going to be asked to do. You become one of the foremost catalysts of change for your community, but you also hold an immense legal responsibility and an expectation to drive strategic direction through your leadership.

Fear not! Our goal in writing this book is to give you the knowledge, language, and tools to show up as the kind of board director your organization needs. Whether you're brand new to board service or a seasoned veteran, you can always discover more about governing well.

About This Book

Great boards take an active role in learning about what governing well means. They listen intently and ask questions during meetings; they participate in committee work, support staff and their executive, and, yes, even read books like this one to find out more about what nonprofit boards do.

In this book, we distill our combined 30-plus years of working with nonprofits and their boards into a practical guide to help current and potential board directors serve their nonprofits to the best of their abilities. We see the book as a start for those interested in serving on a board, as well as a resource to even the well-seasoned leader. Although guides and resources about nonprofit boards abound, we haven't found a central book on the basics of being a board director to point people toward.

We outline topics and considerations to be aware of when you begin to serve on a board, such as the following:

- What nonprofit boards do, how they're structured, and who's ultimately responsible (and liable) for governing an organization
- What legal duties, core responsibilities, and leadership practices make a board effective
- How to recruit, onboard, and keep the board engaged
- How to run meetings and committees that get things done
- What the standards are for big-picture governing work, including strategic planning, financial oversight, fundraising, advocacy, and risk management
- How boards and staff work together, including with an executive leader, to make the mission come true

If you have yet to serve on a board, this is the ideal book!

If you have significant board experience already, allow this book to be a resource you give to incoming board directors or, perhaps, to remind you of topics and issues that may arise.

No one nonprofit board is the same. The more you can understand and identify how to handle crises, mitigate risks, align values, and set strategic direction, the better prepared you are as a board director.

Foolish Assumptions

In writing this book, we had to make a few assumptions about who our readers are. Over 90 percent of nonprofits in the United States operate on a budget of under $1 million, so there's a good chance your organization falls in that category. That said, the knowledge and best practices in this book are the same ones boards with much larger budgets and more complex operations rely on. We want you to have the best regardless of where you are.

We also assume you may be in one or more of these situations:

- You're interested in serving on a board to meaningfully use your skills, meet new people, and contribute to a cause you care about.
- You're new to a board and finding your footing in governance.

- You've served on a board before but felt thrown in without real training or mentorship.
- You're running into a challenge with your board and aren't sure what to do next.
- You're an executive leader trying to strengthen your relationship with your board and get more out of the partnership.
- You're a nonprofit staff member trying to better understand how your board works and how to work alongside it well.
- You're a community member just curious about how your neighborhood friendly nonprofit works and what getting involved may look like.

Icons Used in This Book

For Dummies books use little pictures called icons to flag parts of the text that stand out from the rest for one reason or another. Here's what those icons mean so you know what to look for.

TIP

Tips show off tried-and-true wisdom, drawn from our own experiences on boards, advice we've received from fellow nonprofit colleagues, and verified resources for boards. Keep them in your back pocket and put them to use when the time calls for it.

REMEMBER

This icon flags bits of information that are particularly noteworthy or interesting — the stuff you shouldn't forget.

WARNING

This icon is a heads-up to help you avoid compliance mistakes, risks, drama, and traps.

Beyond the Book

In addition to the abundance of information and guidance we provide in this book, you get access to even more help and information online at `Dummies.com`. Check out this book's online Cheat Sheet. Just go to `www.dummies.com` and search for "Nonprofit Boards For Dummies Cheat Sheet."

The Online Appendix serves as a practical toolkit of supplementary resources to support you and your board as you strengthen your governance practices. It includes reference materials, templates, checklists, and guidance that you can use alongside the book. Two Bonus Chapters provide insight into ten types of board personalities and key questions to ask your Executive Director. You can access the Online Appendix and Bonus Chapters at `www.dummies.com/go/nonprofitboardsfd`.

Where to Go from Here

Because we wrote each chapter of this book as a standalone, you have some options. Everything is organized so you can jump right in and read this book cover to cover or use it as a reference tool and flip directly to what you need when challenges arise.

If you're brand new to serving on a board, or even just considering it, we highly recommend you start with Part 1.

If you're unsure of where to start, check out this governance quiz! Take a few minutes to think about each question. If you mark No or Unsure, check out the associated chapter(s) to round out your gaps in knowledge.

If you want to. . . .	Then flip to Chapter(s). . . .
explain the difference between governance and management/Are clear on what falls under staff versus board authority	2, 19, 21
know who your organization is legally accountable to	2
learn the three legal duties of all boards	3
define what a conflict of interest is, and if your organization discloses them	3, 16
know what decisions require full board approval	8
know the specific roles and responsibilities of board officers	5
be familiar with how committees are structured and what different committees (like executive, finance, governance, and fundraising) do	11
understand your organization's bylaws	8
create a strategic plan, and understand how to use it	12
understand the organization's financial statements enough to ask questions in board meetings	15
learn more about your role, if any, in fundraising	13

If you want to....	Then flip to Chapter(s)....
understand what policies your board needs to protect itself and the mission	17
your organization to participate in advocacy work, and are not yet familiar with the legal implications	14
understand the board's relationship with the executive	19
know what to do if your executive leader underperforms or suddenly resigns	20
your board to regularly evaluate its own performance	18
feel engaged and clear on your personal contribution to the board	3, 4, 13
To know if a decision feels wrong or that you don't agree with the board, and understand what to do next	20
understand how to be recruited and onboarded in a way that made you confident and ready	6

Bottom line? The only right way to use this book is what works best for you. Skip ahead, go back, reread, read three times — however you need to use the book, we hope it empowers you and your fellow board directors to align on what keeping drama outside the boardroom and creating real change, together, means. It starts with you.

We're always interested in your questions, suggestions, or comments, so get in touch! Send Caitlin and Jackson an email at `nonprofitboards.fd@gmail.com`. You can also visit `nonprofitboards.org`, where you can keep up-to-date, see new content, and stay in touch!

1 Introducing Nonprofit Boards

IN THIS PART . . .

Check out what governing with integrity, excellence, sustainability, and equity front of mind means.

Identify your organization's current stage of maturity and what that means for how your board works.

Understand the internal and external stakeholders, aside from the board, who help your nonprofit remain accountable to its mission and community.

IN THIS CHAPTER

» Introducing the four aspects of good governance

» Exploring key characteristics of a nonprofit

» Touching on board function and makeup

» Figuring out your board's stage of maturity

Chapter 1 Defining Nonprofit Governance

The United States has more than 1.8 million registered nonprofits in all sorts of fields: hospitals and shelters, schools and food banks, theatres and museums. They fill gaps the government can't and private companies won't, and at the helm of every single one is a board.

In this chapter, we define what makes for good governance. We explain what nonprofits are and what boards do and share a framework for understanding how the board's role evolves right alongside the organization.

Defining Governance

Governance is one of those words that gets used a lot but is rarely defined. Despite the many definitions the Internet or textbooks can provide you, no one agrees on a single explanation. Here are just a few:

- "The act or process of governing or overseeing the control and direction of something." —Merriam-Webster

- "The way the rules, norms, and actions [of a nonprofit] are structured, sustained, regulated, and held accountable." —Nonprofit Quarterly
- "Nonprofit governance simply means how your nonprofit is administered." —Harbor Compliance
- "Nonprofit governance is defined as the process of providing strategic leadership to a nonprofit organization. It entails the functions of setting direction, making policy and strategy decisions, overseeing and monitoring organizational performance, and ensuring overall accountability." —`Boardable.com`

REMEMBER

We define *governance* as the systems of rules and processes by which decisions are made, power is exercised, and accountability ensured at your organization. Good governance is the difference between an organization that struggles and one that thrives.

The rest of this book talks about the many aspects of governance, from the big picture elements of strategic planning and financial oversight to the day-to-day details of running effective committee meetings and writing policies that protect. In this section, we offer a framework to understand what *good* governance means: integrity, excellence, sustainability, and equity (see Figure 1-1).

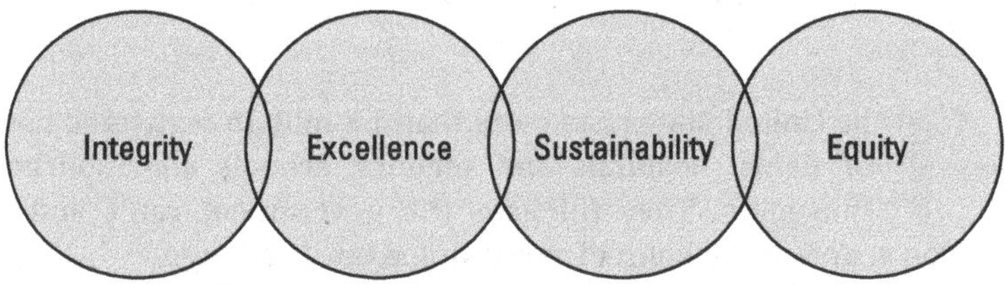

FIGURE 1-1: The elements of governance.

Doing right: Integrity

Good governance starts with integrity — doing the right thing — even when it's inconvenient or hard. Boards always need to operate with the highest level of integrity because it's the underlying foundation of your three legal duties. See the Online Appendix for characteristics of boards that operate with a high level of integrity.

Doing well: Excellence

Boards have a responsibility to their communities to set high standards for performance, hold leadership accountable, and ensure the organization does its very best in pursuit of its mission. See the Online Appendix for characteristics of boards that aim for excellence.

Thinking long-term: Sustainability

Great boards resist short-term pressures, keep their eyes on the horizon, and recognize that the future relies on looking past the current budget cycle. Wishing for mission success one thing; marrying it with organizational stability and sustainability is another. See the Online Appendix for characteristics of boards that care about sustainability.

Being inclusive: Equity

Diverse perspectives lead to better decisions and more resilient organizations. Boards that center equity as an everyday practice are better positioned to serve communities because they become a more responsive partner. See the Online Appendix for characteristics of boards that value and practice equity across the organization.

Understanding What Defines a Nonprofit

What makes a nonprofit a nonprofit? Is it simply having a mission statement? Creating programming? Being run by a team of volunteers? The focus on community? Most people have a sense of what they think a nonprofit looks like, but a specific legal and tax reality lives behind the label. In the most basic and generalized sense, *nonprofit organizations* are typically *corporations* with a *special tax status* serving the *public good*. The following sections dig into each piece of that puzzle to help you understand a bit more.

REMEMBER

We want to emphasize that *nonprofit* is a tax status, not a business model. Nonprofits still need to make money, invest in their people and infrastructure, and operate with the same financial discipline as any healthy business.

Being formed as a corporation

The vast majority of nonprofit organizations are formed as corporations (sometimes they also choose to be unincorporated associations, trusts, or LLCs). That's because *corporations*, legal entities formed at the state level, provide liability protection and continuity benefits.

A corporation is legally separate from its owners and considered a distinct "person" in the eyes of the law. That means that if the organization faces a lawsuit or ends up with bad debt, board directors are generally shielded from personal liability. The organization (corporation) is responsible, not you individually.

It also means the organization can outlast any one person. Directors can rotate off or change leadership easily, making passing the mission on to future generations much easier. That's the continuity benefit.

REMEMBER

Unlike for-profit corporations, which are legally accountable to shareholders, nonprofits don't have an automatic legal obligation to donors in the same way. In nonprofits, no one owns it. But that doesn't mean anything goes. Organizations still need to operate transparently and as good stewards of public money, and risk can quickly rise in the form of misusing funds, misrepresenting how donations will be spent, or violating terms of grant agreements. Check out Chapter 17 to find out more about organizational risk.

Receiving a special tax status

Nonprofit organizations are distinct from their for-profit counterparts thanks to a special tax exemption status granted under Section 501(c) of the IRS tax code, which relieves them from having to pay federal income taxes on revenue earned in service of their missions. The exemption is in place because nonprofits exist to serve the public good rather than generate profits for private individuals.

Organizations typically need to secure tax exemption at the federal and state levels, which requires two separate processes. Interestingly, the United States has more than 30 categories of tax-exempt organizations, spanning missions serving religious, educational, scientific, advocacy, and more causes.

WARNING

Nonprofit organizations aren't free from paying *all* taxes. They're still responsible for payroll taxes, unemployment taxes, and, in many states, business and occupation taxes. Chapter 15 has details on taxes and other financial concerns.

Serving the public good

A nonprofit exists to serve the public good. *Public good* means providing programs and services that improve people's well-being, expand freedom of thought, enhance public life, and build stronger communities.

UNDERSTANDING THE TWO TYPES OF 501(C)(3)S

By far, the most common type of 501(c) organization is the 501(c)(3), with approximately 1.5 million registered in the United States as of the writing of this book. This category includes public charities, like your local food bank and art museum, as well as private foundations. Chances are the organization you serve, or are considering serving, falls into one of these two groups.

- **Public charities:** *Public charities* make up most of the registered 501(c)(3)s. The groups are focused on delivering programs and services directly to the community. They actively engage in running programs, providing health care, and offering other social services, and they need to demonstrate broad-based public support in their mission.
- **Private foundations:** *Private foundations* are established by a single individual, family, small group, or business and have a requirement to distribute a portion of their funds every year. You can find two types of private foundations. A *non-operating foundation* supports public charities' work by grantmaking. That is, it funds other nonprofits to do the work instead of running the programs itself. An *operating foundation* is a hybrid model that both delivers programming the way a public charity may and engages in grantmaking but doesn't have to demonstrate public support.

Identifying What a Board Is

A *board* is a group of individuals who've been appointed or elected to govern and oversee the operations of your nonprofit. Together, they're the legally accountable body responsible for the organization's integrity, finances, and direction. In brief, they're the volunteers with a fiduciary responsibility to the mission and the community.

REMEMBER

Boards are legally obligated to act in the organization's best interest. That means they must act with care and do their due diligence when making decisions, put the organization's interests above their own, and ensure the organization stays true to its mission and complies with the law. We break down everything you need to know about being a first-rate fiduciary in Chapter 3.

Board service also tends to be volunteer work. That may surprise you considering the serious nature of the work and the level of time, responsibility, and commitment it requires. Yet the nonprofit sector has thrived, with millions of people freely giving their time, energy, and expertise to improve their communities and causes.

WARNING

Board service isn't the same as general volunteering. Don't join a board if you're just hoping to be more involved in events or want to be on the ground with programming. Boards govern at the 10,000-foot level and are responsible for strategy, financial health, and other legal obligations. Though they're technically volunteers, they're *not* like the ones on the ground day-to-day.

Looking at who's qualified to serve

No single standard dictates who can serve on a board. Generally, directors need to be at least 18 years old, be of sound mind, and meet any other requirements the organization's bylaws set forth. Board directors aren't required to be U.S. citizens or residents, may live outside the state you're operating in, and don't even need to have a personal connection to the mission. See Chapter 6 for more information about how to recruit the best board for you.

Getting a handle on how boards govern

Boards govern by setting mission and direction while ensuring the organization has the resources needed to carry out those aspirations. They also are responsible for stewarding those resources and safeguarding the reputation and public image of their organization. We explore the legal responsibilities and duties of each director in Chapter 3 and then in Chapter 4 review other things boards may do, depending on the scale, complexity, and nature of their work.

TIP

Many groups participate in governance beyond the board of directors: the IRS, state regulators, volunteers, staff, and more all get a say. We look at the greater governance ecosystem, including how all the different internal and external stakeholders participate in accountability, in Chapter 2.

Governing Differently as You Grow

Many nonprofits start with a passionate founder or a small group of committee community members willing to do whatever is necessary to get things off the ground. The board is likely hands-on and in the weeds, and that's perfectly fine. But as your organization grows, the way your board governs must grow, too. What worked when you were scrappy and small is no longer sustainable, or appropriate, after you have paid staff, multiple program sites, millions of dollars in donations, and facilities under the banner of your mission.

TIP

Ask yourself, where's my board currently? We don't mean location-wise or in size but in its maturity. Just like people, boards grow and mature over time. Answering this question helps you understand how to adapt our advice to your current situation.

In the following sections, we look at a simple framework, first created by Karl Mathiasen III, for understanding where your organization is in its governance journey. We also add some context to help you better understand the friction your board may encounter as you continue to grow.

REMEMBER

Board growth isn't a race. Some boards spend years (even decades!) in the organizing stage. Growth looks different for every nonprofit, and moving slowly isn't a sign of failure. What matters more is that your board is self-aware and functional.

Figure 1-2 shows the three stages of nonprofit maturity, from organizing to institutional governance.

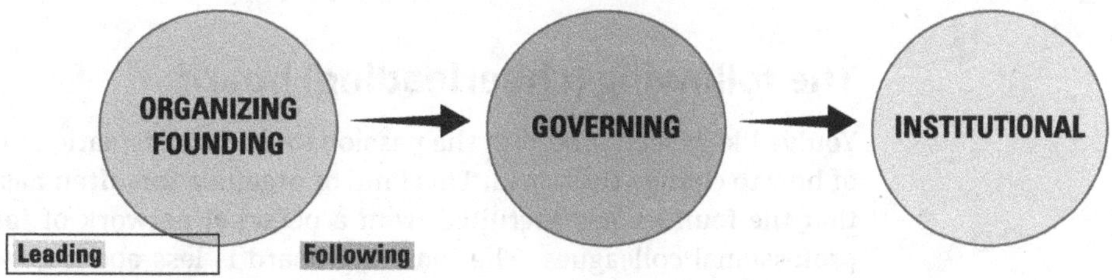

FIGURE 1-2: The three stages.

Stage 1: The organizing board

Though every story starts here, no two stories are exactly the same. Some boards are built around a visionary founding leader who fills the board full of friends, family, and folks from their personal network, and others emerge from a group of community members or neighbors who see a need and come together to act.

In this organizing stage (Figure 1-3), governance is more informal, relationships are close, and the energy is high, with everyone in the trenches figuring it out together.

The two most common flavors of organizing board are these:

- **Following boards (cheerleading):** Where the organization was built around the vision of a central leader, with the board largely following their lead and cheering the founder on
- **Leading boards (working):** Where the organization was built through effort, with the board sharing ownership of the vision from the start and working to bring the mission to life

We dig into these options in the following sections.

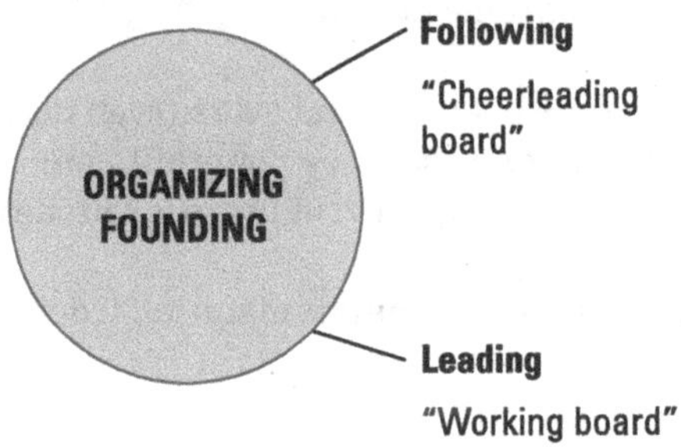

FIGURE 1-3: The two types of organizing boards.

The following (cheerleading) board

You've likely seen it before: the passionate and charismatic founder with a vision of how to change the world. This kind of organization often has a following board that the founder has recruited from a personal network of family, friends, and professional colleagues. The founding board is less about governance and more about belief — belief and trust in the founder. Board directors' whole job revolves around encouraging and validating (and sometimes resourcing) the founder's vision. There's little to no independent oversight or accountability of the executive, and the board trusts the founder implicitly.

Here are the signs you're on a founding board:

- The board is small and composed primarily of people the founder knows well and trusts personally.
- Everyone is fully committed to the leader and their vision — but not necessarily to the mission itself.
- Meetings are less frequent, informal, and focused on operations. The board sits and listens to the founder and then offers advice and encouragement.

- Directors aren't involved in the organization, aren't task-oriented, and don't hold the founder accountable.
- The board doesn't typically play a significant role in fundraising.

If you're serving on a following board, you need to watch out for some blind spots in governance:

- Higher risk of compliance errors, financial mismanagement, and ethical lapses because no one is really asking hard questions
- Lack of expertise in critical areas because of nonstrategic recruitment
- Likelihood of conflicts of interest that may compromise the organization
- Mission drift as the organization falls to the whims of the founder's evolving interests or personality
- The founder as the single point of failure (their burnout, illness, or departure leaves no depth to back fill)
- Organization growth that outpaces the founder's skill set, putting the board in the awkward position of having to performance manage a personal relationship

WARNING

Following boards face an inevitable reckoning: the moment the founder steps away. When that transition comes, planned or not, the board is forced to grow. Without proper succession planning, the moment can be deeply destabilizing. Don't wait. Head to Chapter 20 to get started on succession planning.

To transition to the next stage (governing), the board must do the following:

- Step up and educate itself on what good governance at a mature organization looks like.
- Self-structure and self-direct by creating a workplan, forming committees, engaging with finances and strategy, and assisting with fundraising.
- Adopt foundational governance policies and financial controls, and update bylaws to reflect on the organization's needs to operate into the future.
- Add new, independent voices with no relationship to the founder into the mix.
- Redefine the line between governance and management and adopt a more neutral board-executive relationship.
- Hold an honest conversation with the founder about the future and succession.
- Exit directors who are unable or unwilling to make the shift.

REMEMBER

Shifting away from being a following board can painful. It means asking directors to give more time and take on more responsibility, which can feel uncomfortable. They may say things like "I didn't sign up for this" as the original informal agreement of their service shifts from supporting a friend to taking on fiduciary authority. This shift can lead to conflict or disengagement, and at least a core committed group of directors has to be willing to navigate this friction.

The leading (working) board

The leading board is one built on shared ownership from the start. Not every organization forms around a single founder. Some of the most impactful nonprofits have been started by a group of community members or concerned neighbors who saw a need and bound together to make a difference. The vision, not a person, sits at the center. The work, the strategy, and responsibility belong to everyone in the room.

You may be on a leading board if:

- » The board is a bit of a hive mind, connected by similar values and ideas and a passion for the mission
- » Directors share a strong sense of ownership and a personal level of investment in the organization's success
- » Board work is very hands on and involved with the nonprofit's operations, and directors are willing to do whatever it takes to keep things moving
- » Meetings are operationally focused, with board directors reporting their work and tasks being assigned
- » The board is apprehensive or resistant to hiring staff, or only a limited number of non-executive staff members are in place

If you're serving on a leading/working board, keep an eye out for these governance issues:

- » Higher risk of compliance errors and financial mismanagement because the board is too focused on doing the work to properly oversee it
- » Mission and strategy stagnation as the organization keeps doing what the board knows and loves rather than what the community has evolved to need
- » Governance bad behaviors, like side conversations, group chats, water-cooler decision-making, and general conflict avoidance, that make decisively addressing dysfunction or ethical concerns difficult

- Directors feeling overwhelmed as they struggle to keep up with increasing assignments and operational demands as the organization grows ("I'm just a volunteer!")
- A power struggle emerging around ownership/authority after staff members are hired
- Board leadership determined by popularity contest or availability rather than by expertise and ability

WARNING

The catalytic event that forces a leading/working board to grow up is the moment the organization hires its first paid staff. What follows can drag on for years: a prolonged power struggle between the board that built everything and the staff now being asked to lead. This muddy middle can be a dark age for an organization. But the reality is that you can't really expand your impact and reach with a working board. You'll always be capped by volunteer capacity. If you really want to grow, you have to let go.

To transition to the governing stage, the board needs to:

- Step up and educate itself on what good governance at a mature organization looks like
- Hire staff and trust it! Get out of the work of *doing* the work day-to-day, delegate operational authority, and build a professional relationship with clearly defined lanes
- Restructure the board by sunsetting operational committees, updating charters, and creating a workplan focused on strategy, oversight, and policy development rather than operational and programmatic execution
- Actively recruit new, independent voices from outside the founding circle to break the insider/outsider dynamic
- Check egos at the door and accept that no one owns your nonprofit; it's going to change, and you need to change with it
- Exit directors who are unable or unwilling to make the shift

Moving from a leading/working board calls for a fundamental shift of identity. Many directors join boards because they want to be hands-on, running programs, organizing events, and working alongside volunteers day in and day out to deliver on the mission. As staff take over that work, those directors are no longer needed in the same way, and the shift can feel like a real and unbearable loss. Resentment follows, and trust nose dives. The boards that make it through are the ones who recognize what they're going through and embrace the change.

Stage 2: Governing

The governing board is the adult form of the organizing board, where the chaos of the early days has settled into something more intentional, structured, and sustainable. Governance is no longer informal or accidental. The board knows its role, respects the line between governing and managing, and has built the relationships and systems to back it up.

Signs that you're on a governing-stage board include the following:

- » The board is focused on strategy and oversight. It stays out of the weeds of operations, and directors respect the line.
- » A balance of power exists between board and staff, with the executive leading day-to-day operations and the board holding them accountable for results.
- » The board president and executive have a healthy, professional relationship and work together effectively to keep the organization on course.
- » Committees are in place and functional, regularly reporting progress against an overarching workplan for the board.
- » The board is diverse and intentionally recruits new directors with different skills and perspectives.
- » Fundraising is a normalized part of the work, and directors are actively, even if imperfectly, engaged in securing resources for the organization.
- » Essential governance policies are in place, bylaws are up to date, and directors have a shared understanding of the legal and chosen responsibilities of the board.
- » Self-assessment is a standard practice, as is ongoing education.

REMEMBER

Organizations who have reached this stage aren't homogenous and show varying levels of maturity. Rare is the governing board that's good at everything. What they all share is a strong foundation and a commitment to doing better.

If you're serving on a governing board, the danger is more angled toward complacency and blind spots that happen when things are going well enough. Here are some things that you may find you need to mitigate:

- » Governance that drifts into theatre, with the board going through the motions
- » Strategic drift or complacency, with the organization doing what it's always done without questioning whether that's still working
- » Committees that meet but don't produce anything

- Policies that exist but either go without updating or aren't followed
- A board that stops self-assessing, skips orientation for new directors, or deprioritizes education for other projects
- Overreliance on a successful executive, rubber-stamping whatever they bring
- Failure to keep the board's expertise in line with rapid growth in complexity
- Allowing the same people to drive every conversation, leaving fresh perspectives unheard even when new voices are welcome
- Long-tenured directors (nine or more years) with no term end in sight, stuck in how things used to be when you were still a working board (more on those boards in the earlier section "The leading (working) board")

Most nonprofits never need to move beyond the governing board stage. For the vast majority, it's the destination, not a steppingstone to something better. That said, sometimes an organization finds itself being pushed toward something bigger. A few things that signal you need to evolve include the following:

- Becoming a significantly public institution, where a higher level of public scrutiny requires more formalized oversight
- Crossing into enterprise-level operations, meaning you have 250-plus employees, budgets over $25 million, and/or programs or services being delivered across multiple sites or states
- Managing multiple entities, subsidiaries, affiliates, or chapters under the same banner
- Securing large government contracts or operating in a highly regulated environment
- Competing for, or dependent on, major philanthropic investments that require a more credentialed or connected board
- Increasing liability and risk exposure to a level that demands more sophisticated legal and financial oversight
- Being unable to provide the financial capacity, expertise, or prestige from the board that the organization needs to compete at its level

REMEMBER

The question isn't "How do we become an institutional board?" It's "Is our current governance adequate for the organization we are today?" If the answer is yes, stay the course and govern well. If the answer is no, here's how to move from a governing board to an institutional one:

- Formalize and professionalize your board structure, updating committees to reflect the risks you need to manage.

- Bring on dedicated, paid staff to provide board support. Volunteer-driven governance is no longer sufficient.
- Be more intentional about recruitment, assessing and addressing gaps in financial capacity, legal expertise, risk management, and public representation.
- Transition directors on who no longer can support the organization at this level.
- Formalize evaluation of both board and executive leadership, including annual reviews with metrics for performance.
- Be ready for stakeholder activism. Employees, community members, funders, and many more people will have an opinion about the organization and will not hesitate to speak up.
- Anticipate regulatory attention. Large nonprofits operating across multiple states face increased compliance and operating requirements.
- Review and update all governing documents to support and reflect the complexity you need.

Stage 3: Institutional

The institutional board is the enterprise form of governance, where the organization has become a large scale or serious public institution. The shift typically begins after an organization approaches and crosses $25-million-plus in operations and where the complexity of asset management, the scale of risk exposure, and the level of public accountability demands a much higher standard of professional expertise at the board level. Think hospital systems, large universities, international human services organizations, national disaster relief entities, and so forth. At this scale, the consequences of getting things wrong are public and can be life-threatening.

You may be on an institutional-stage board if:

- The board is large and formally structured, with directors who bring substantial financial capacity, executive-level professional expertise, and public influence
- Service carries public prestige and attracts civic, industry, and philanthropy leaders whose association gives the organization greater credibility

- Fundraising is professionalized and fully led by staff, with sophisticated major gift programs, capital campaign plans, and board activation
- Committees are fully functional and independently operational across all domains (finance, audit, governance, compensation, risk management, and so on), with a high level of vested authority
- Performance expectations are set and proactively managed for board and executive leadership
- The board-CEO relationship is defined by professional distance, with clear mechanisms for evaluation, escalation, and termination
- Governance infrastructure is supported by dedicated staff, legal counsel, formal board management systems, and up-to-date policies and procedures

Here are some areas of risk exposure:

- Directors who are there more for prestige and expect influence disproportionate to their role
- Committees that operate too independently such that they create silos and the board loses visibility into critical decisions
- Overly bureaucratic and rigid policies and processes that slow down the work beyond what's reasonable
- Organizational growth so complex that no director really understands the whole picture
- Such a wide gap between the board and the communities being served that the board loses touch with the mission

Reflecting on your growth

However your board is structured today — whether you're in the thick of organizing around your mission, coming into your own as a governing board, or navigating the complexity unique to institutions — the most important thing is to be honest about where you are. Not where you wish you were or where you think you should be, but where you actually are. Honest self-assessment helps you spot problem patterns faster, leverage expertise you find, and make better decisions.

IN THIS CHAPTER

» Thinking of governance as a large ecosystem of stakeholders

» Seeing the difference between direct authority and softer influence in nonprofits

» Identifying ways your organization can engage with groups to govern more effectively

Chapter 2
Understanding Who's in Charge

Governance is the practice of who has a voice in making decisions, how decisions are made, and who is accountable. With that understanding, the board of directors is only one part of a larger ecosystem of internal and external groups that govern the nonprofit sector.

Some of these groups — such as state regulators and federal agencies that set tax policies or oversee the power dynamics involved in fundraising and donations — hold the authority to directly influence a nonprofit's culture and operations. And because of their direct impact in local communities, nonprofits often must respond to pressure from nongovernment organizations.

For example, watchdog organizations and media outlets help shape the public perception of nonprofits, pushing them to deliver on their promises and fulfill their mission. Even those who work at nonprofits — including volunteers — hold daily decision-making power that determines how governance functions.

This chapter explores the broader landscape of governance and how it shows up in your organization, and provides guidance on how to manage toward making sound, impactful decisions that stand up to scrutiny inside and outside the organization.

Answering to Regulatory Bodies

A wide array of governmental bodies, from the federal level all the way down to county and local agencies, directly inform the governance practices at your organization. Each of these regulators places unique requirements on nonprofits, as well as offering resources to help you practice good governance. In the following sections, we look at some of these regulatory bodies.

Internal Revenue Service

The Internal Revenue Service (IRS) is the federal tax authority that grants, monitors, and revokes the 501(c) exemption status for nonprofit organizations in the United States. There are 29 types of 501(c) status, each designated for a different purpose. An organization granted this status is relieved from paying federal income taxes and in turn required to file an annual public tax return, the Form 990 (990-N, 990-EZ, 990), which provides a transparent look into its financial performance, governance activities, and program outputs.

Under public inspection laws, any member of the public has a right to obtain a copy of your current and previous three years of 990s, as well as your organization's application for tax exemption (which may include your articles of incorporation and bylaws). This is one of the key ways your nonprofit demonstrates overall trustworthiness and accountability.

REMEMBER

Your board needs to ensure proper financial oversight, accurate filings, and fiscal policies that meet IRS standards to maintain exempt status. Getting this wrong may result in a federal audit, fines, or revocation of your exempt status.

Federal Election Commission

The Federal Election Commission (FEC) oversees and regulates campaign financing and enforces limits on political contributions and spending. Most nonprofit organizations are prohibited from participating in political campaigns or endorsing candidates. But even nonprofits that *can* engage in some political activity — like *501(c)(4)s*, which include social welfare organizations such as the American Civil Liberties Union — must adhere to rules around disclosure and spending limits.

WARNING

If your organization operates anywhere near the political arena, the board needs to establish clear boundaries for lobbying and political activity, and ensure staff receive the necessary training to meet federal regulatory requirements. FEC violations can trigger investigations, heavy fines, and further legal action.

Federal Trade Commission

The Federal Trade Commission (FTC) protects consumers from deceptive or unfair business practices. Though FTC guidance and oversight typically doesn't apply to most nonprofit organizations, it may become relevant if your organization generates any unrelated business income, partners with for-profit entities, or operates in commercial arenas (such as health care).

REMEMBER

Even as a nonprofit, your organization is expected to be truthful in its fundraising solicitations and advertisements. If you're doing anything that looks like commercial activity, make sure the board is paying attention.

State Legislature

State legislatures establish the legal framework that all nonprofits must follow to exist. First and foremost, they set the minimum requirements to register as a charity in the state and determine which taxes nonprofits must collect and pay (such as sales or property tax) and which taxes nonprofits are exempt from. They also may establish rules for the minimum size of the board, required officers, meeting structure and procedures, recordkeeping, and reporting. Oversight and compliance is then delegated to the state's attorney general and Secretary of State.

TIP

Organizations should monitor state legislative activity, because new or amended laws can directly affect governance, operations, and sometimes programming. Consider joining a service organization or a coalition of similar nonprofits to stay informed.

State Attorney General

The state attorney general (AG) is an elected official whose duties include overseeing nonprofits in your state. They're responsible for protecting the public's interest in charitable assets and helping keep nonprofits accountable to their mission. One of the key ways the AG does this is by auditing and investigating nonprofit activity, enforcing compliance with solicitation laws, and taking action against fraud or mismanagement. In extreme cases, they can sue individual board directors, remove members from the board, or dissolve the organization.

REMEMBER

As a board director, you must understand and uphold your fiduciary duties (more on that in Chapter 3) and ensure your organization is properly registered with the state, files annual reports with the Secretary of State on time, and maintains accurate records.

Secretary of State

The Secretary of State (SOS) oversees the registration process for incorporation and solicitation, which is your permission slip for fundraising in the state. The SOS processes incorporation applications (the first legal step to founding a nonprofit), maintains official records, and requires annual filings to keep your organization in good standing.

WARNING

Board directors should ensure these filings happen on time. Missing a deadline can result in penalties, loss of good standing, or administrative dissolution of your organization. Check your local SOS, because every state has different requirements and thresholds for reporting and registration.

State Labor Department

Your state's labor department is responsible for enforcing workplace safety, health, and employment standards. Just like any for-profit business, if your organization has employees, it needs to comply with employment law. This includes properly classifying employees (as exempt or non-exempt), keeping the employee handbook up to date, and monitoring the changing labor law landscape. Violations of these standards can lead to serious fines or lawsuits.

Working with Funders

Beyond regulatory bodies, nonprofits must navigate relationships with external groups that fund their work. Government agencies, private foundations, corporations, and individual donors each come with their own expectations and potential influence over organizational decisions. The following sections explain the role these groups play in directing your mission.

TIP

Your board should establish a clear gift-policy to ensure your organization only accepts gifts from funders and institutions that align with your values and goals. You'll want to watch out for conflicts of interest, spending restrictions, and funder influence over strategy, all of which can compromise your board's independence. See Chapter 16 for more on that.

WARNING

Any funder can place a *restriction* on how their gift is used, meaning they specify how, when or where the funds may be spent. When they do, your board is legally responsible for honor those conditions. Mismanaging restricted funds can result in legal liability and reputational harm. Read more in Chapter 17.

Governmental grant-making agencies

Federal, state, and local governments collect tax dollars from individuals and businesses to fund public services and initiatives, redistributing a portion to nonprofits through competitive grant programs. Grants are typically awarded through a competitive application process and open to any eligible nonprofit registered with the IRS as a 501(c)(3).

REMEMBER

Governmental grants can be a prestigious and significant source of funding, but they often come with strings attached, including complex reporting, auditing, and governance requirements. This can steeply increase the administrative workload and costs for your team. Make sure your board understands these obligations, and the impact on your staff and budget, *before* you apply.

Grant-making foundations

Private grant makers and foundation — funded through endowment or investments from major donors, family estates, or trusts — set and pursue their own philanthropic goals by providing grants to aligned nonprofits. Like governmental funders, their grants usually involve an application process and can come with specific requirements or restrictions for spending funds and reporting requirements, which may influence how your organization operates. For exceptionally large gifts, foundations may even request a seat on your board or advisory committee to stay closely involved.

Corporate giving

Corporate giving has grown steadily over the last decade, with businesses of all sizes looking to elevate the social impact of their brand. It consists primarily of marketing sponsorships (such as funding a gala or program), and employee giving programs, where corporations match employee donations dollar for dollar and encourage volunteering.

However, larger corporations may even go as far as establishing their own foundation (for example, The Walmart Foundation or The Coco Cola Foundation) to advance philanthropic their goals separate from their corporations' interests. These foundations may either directly provide programming or make grants to other nonprofits.

TIP

If you work for a for-profit company, check with your HR department about employee giving or volunteer, including whether board service or event volunteering can be matched for a donation!

REMEMBER

Corporate partnerships can bring big bucks but also invite public scrutiny. Evaluate each partnership carefully to ensure their ethics and values align with your nonprofits mission before accepting.

Individual donors

Individual giving is the backbone of the nonprofit sector. Through their donations, everyday people determine which missions move the world forward. Think of your donors as a built-in focus group that want you to succeed. They can offer valuable feedback on programs and community engagement. However, as gifts grow larger, so can a donor's expectation of influence over the way the organization is run. Boards must ensure individual interests don't outweigh the needs of the broader community and that no donor uses their gift as leverage over how things are done.

Responding to External Voices

Watchdog organizations and media outlets may not fund your organization but they can influence who does. By evaluating performance and reporting on compliance issues, they can amplify your organization's successes and failures. In this section we are going to look at just how their voice shapes the public perception of your nonprofit, and influence where and to what degree donors, foundations, and corporations give.

Watchdogs and rating agencies

While the term *watchdog* may sound scary, these organizations play an important role in keeping nonprofits honest. Similar to the Better Business Bureau (BBB), organizations such as Charity Navigator, Candid, CharityWatch, BBB Wise Giving Alliance act as independent evaluators, monitoring and grading nonprofit health and performance. They look at mission impact, financial health, executive compensation, and governance transparency, and translate complex information into something more digestible to the public. While they have no direct power over nonprofits, their evaluations can significantly influence a nonprofits reputation and, by extension, donor behavior.

TIP

Pay attention to these groups because they may surface critical compliance issues you've missed. If a rating agency flags a problem before you've addressed it, that's a reputational hit you could have avoided. Most watchdog agencies maintain a public profile for every registered nonprofit, so make sure your organization has claimed its profile on each platform and monitors its ratings.

Mass media

Mass media refers to all communication channels that reach a large public audience. This includes traditional outlets like television, newspapers, and magazines, but also digital platforms and social media. Altogether, the stories shared through these channels shape how the public sees your organization, which directly affects whether donors give and whether people participate in your programs.

Nonprofits should use mass media to build trust, promote transparency, engage with the public, and amplify their impact. From a governance perspective, boards are responsible for ensuring that there's clear authority about who can speak on behalf of the organization, that public messages are aligned with the organization's strategy and brand, and that confidential or sensitive information is being protected.

REMEMBER

Media coverage can make or break an organization's reputation in ways that used to take years but now can happen in hours. A well-placed success story can bring in funding and volunteers, whereas a poorly handled crisis can lead to the nonprofit being shut down. As your organization grows in complexity and size, so will the risks that come with media engagement. You must ensure that your board establishes appropriate oversight mechanisms without drifting into day-to-day management.

Listening to Internal Voices

Beyond external stakeholders, nonprofits need to pay attention to people closest to the work, including voting members, management, and staff.

Governance members

Governance members are people or groups who are given formal voting rights through your bylaws. In most nonprofits, board directors fill this role, but in some organizations, like a co-op or a union or a neighborhood association, voting rights are extended more broadly, where members may have the power to elect board directors, vote on bylaw changes, or even weigh in on strategic decisions. Your board needs to understand who is a *member*, take their right seriously, and follow the processes outline in your bylaws . . . otherwise decisions your board makes may be challenged as invalid or unenforceable.

Executive leadership

As your organization grows, the board may hire staff an executive director or CEO and delegate day-to-day operational authority to them. This executive leader serves as a bridge between the board and organization, ensuring that board-approved policies are implemented and keeping the board informed with the strategic, financial, and operational information it needs to make informed decisions. Flip to Chapter 19 to learn more about how to build a healthy board-executive partnership.

REMEMBER

Hiring an executive doesn't alleviate the board of its legal duties. The board remains ultimately accountable for the organization and must maintain clear lines of communication and reporting with its executive leader to fulfill its responsibilities.

Affiliated entities

In some cases, your organization may be formally affiliated with another entity — whether that's a government agency, private business, or fellow nonprofit — in a relationship that goes far beyond a typical partnership. Unlike a program partner or a vendor, these arrangements are usually legally entangled, meaning each organizations governance decisions can directly affect the other. Common examples include a public city library and its nonprofit foundation or a public market and its nonprofit arm, where both groups work together to deliver a service to the community. These arrangements exist for many reasons, but the governance implications can be significant. Your board may need to adopt and follow the requirements of your affiliated entity, including stricter financial oversight or reporting requirements.

Accounting for the Interests of Other Stakeholders

Rounding out the governance ecosystem are the groups who help implement your programs or are directly impacted by your services. Ancillary boards, partners, beneficiaries, and professional oversight bodies. Their influence on your governance may be less formal but still very real.

Advisory groups

An *advisory group* is something formed by the organization to bring together a specific set of voices to help inform decision-making. Common examples include a youth board, an artist advisory council, or an emeritus board. These specially formed groups are often asked for input on major decisions that directly affect the communities or constituencies they represent, and can help the board be more effective stewards of their mission. You can read a little more about this in Chapter 11.

Program partners

A *program partner* works alongside you to deliver your services and programs. Some relationships are loose collaborations while others involve complex contracts, strategic plans, and shared legal and financial obligations. Partners may ask you to adopt more stringent employment practices, carry additional liability coverage, or meet other conditions that affect how your organization operates. The more complex a partnership, the more likely it is to influence your governance.

Beneficiaries

Anyone who participates in and benefits from one of your services or programs is considered a *beneficiary*. This may include a patron or donor attending a theatre performance, a student participating in an educational workshop, a veteran receiving support services, or a family receiving food assistance.

REMEMBER

People don't often think of these folks as having an influence on organizational governance, but in fact they should be at the center of it. Your organization exists to serve them, and their insights should help shape your mission.

Your board can govern better by engaging beneficiaries in many ways, from sharing feedback on lived experiences to filling seats on the board or participating in an advisory group. These approaches help ensure that programming decisions and policies are shaped by the real experiences and needs of the people you serve, making your work more relevant and impactful.

TIP

Regularly gather feedback from your community about who participates in your programming, fundraising events, and volunteering so that you can understand whom your programs are impacting. Staying receptive to feedback from your community will also help you shape policies and programs that represent your community best.

Professional oversight organizations

Nonprofit organizations, particularly sector-specific ones such as higher education, health care, and social services nonprofits, may have additional influences on their governance and operations. In fields such as these, you're likely to encounter accrediting bodies, review boards, and licensing advisory boards designed to ensure your organization is meeting a minimum standard of quality in program delivery.

2

Organizing and Energizing People

IN THIS PART . . .

Explore the many ways boards fulfill their legal obligations, from safeguarding the mission and setting strategy to hiring an executive leader and fundraising.

Get a practical orientation into how the roles of board president, treasurer, and secretary work and what you can do to successfully serve in them. Understand how to put together a board that can lead effectively.

Create a board recruitment process that attracts top talent and helps build the board you need.

Find ways to fire up your board that keep it excited and engaged in the mission year-round.

IN THIS CHAPTER

- » Defining board directors' legal and ethical obligations
- » Understanding the three duties of a board director
- » Looking at examples of your rights and duties in action

Chapter 3

Breaking Down Your Legal Duties

So, you're about to join a nonprofit board. First, congratulations — this is a major milestone in anyone's career and life. Board directors take on the rewarding responsibility for stewarding the mission of an organization and serving their community. But although board directors are volunteers, the role comes with significant legal duties and obligations.

In this chapter, we'll walk you through the three core legal duties that every board, everywhere, is responsible for fulfilling, including what they look like in practice, what you need to do to protect the organization and yourself, and what rights you have as an individual and board in turn. Consider this the foundation for everything inside this book.

Looking at the Legal and Ethical Responsibilities of Board Directors

A fundamental aspect of board directorship is the concept of being a *fiduciary*, which means you are legally and ethically responsible for acting in the best interests of the organization. The fiduciary obligations of all board directors can be divided into three broad categories:

- **Duty of care:** Act in good faith and with reasonable care when making decisions on behalf of the organization.
- **Duty of loyalty:** Always put the best interests of the organization first.
- **Duty of obedience:** Ensure the organization complies with all relevant laws and regulations and stays true to its charitable mission.

These responsibilities exist to protect the public's interest, keep the organization focused on its mission, and ensure that charitable resources are being used appropriately. They are further defined by federal and state law and apply to all nonprofit leaders.

WARNING

Because the board is a collective entity, every director shares responsibility for the actions taken by the board as a whole or by individuals acting on behalf of the organization. It's worth noting that failure to uphold any of these duties can expose you to personal liability, including legal fees or charges, depending on your bylaws, insurance coverage, and the nature of the situation. Let's dive in.

Duty of care

The *duty of care* is just as it sounds: *take care* of the organization — its mission, assets, people, and goodwill from the public — the same as you would anything you personally value. This means showings up, actively participating, and when making decisions, ensuring you're as informed as you can reasonably be. This doesn't mean you're expected to run the organization's day-to-day operations. That's the job of the staff. But you *are* responsible for oversight, making sure the organization is being run well and in alignment with its mission.

Board directors can act in the following ways to establish that they have fulfilled their duty of care:

- **Actively participate.** Attend board meetings. Ask questions (even the so-called dumb ones). Serve on a committee.

- **Do your homework.** Understand the organization's mission. Read all materials provided ahead of meetings. Review organizational policies and plans.
- **Monitor the organization's performance.** Board directors need a way to effectively monitor the overall health and success of the organization, especially because they aren't involved in the day-to-day operations. Review the nonprofit's impact numbers, financial reports, and other key performance indicators.
- **Make your own decisions.** You should understand the risks and benefits associated with major decisions. Ask for more information or seek additional expertise if needed. You should never cast a vote you're uncertain about or just go with the flow. Perhaps most important, don't be afraid to say *no* if you feel you don't have enough information or are uncomfortable with an action or decision.
- **Document your diligence and how decisions were made.** The board and its committees should keep minutes of all meetings, including the high points of what was discussed, as well as any dissent and a complete record of any votes. When done well, these notes not only serve as a useful historical resource for your organization but also offer invaluable protection if an issue arises in the future. Chapter 10 provides detailed guidance on how to take minutes that are useful.
- **Create a good information-sharing system.** Ensure all directors have access to all relevant documents by creating a centralized hub and maintaining it.

REMEMBER

You won't get every decision right . . . and that's okay. A legal precedent extended to nonprofit board directors and officers called *the business judgment rule* protects you from personal liability for bad decisions, so long as you can show that you were adequately informed and acting in good faith when making those decisions.

REMEMBER

Every board director brings different personal and professional experiences to the table. If you have specialized expertise — such as a background in finance, law, or human resources — you're expected to use that knowledge when making decisions. This doesn't mean you have more responsibility than others, but that your board will look to you to help them meet their duty of care as well.

On the other hand, it's not reasonable to expect any board director to be an expert in a wide array of professional areas. Many legal statutes provide that the board should be able to rely in good faith on information presented by the organization's officers and employees, legal counsel, or other professionals they believe to be competent.

THE COST OF FAILING TO CARE

Sometimes it's easier to understand a concept when you see it in action. Here are a couple scenarios where lack of preparation or attention creates real legal risk for a board.

Scenario A: It's the end of the year and the proposed budget for next year is up for approval. You didn't have time to read through the board packet because you've been busy with the holidays. When you get to the board meeting, there aren't many questions and most of the group seems okay with passing the budget proposal. When the vote is called, you raise your hand along with everyone else.

Why this is risky: If something goes wrong, you may be held personally liable. You can't claim you didn't know about the issue because you had access to the information but never looked at it and then voted without being adequately informed. The business judgment rule won't protect you.

Scenario B: During a board meeting, the treasurer mentions finding some irregularities in the financial reports. You don't really understand what that means, but, hey, you're not a finance professional. You don't ask any questions, and neither does anyone else.

Why this is risky: You don't have to be a financial expert, but you do have to ask questions when something doesn't sound right. Silence in the face of a red flag will be viewed as a lack of care and open you up to personal liability.

Duty of loyalty

The *duty of loyalty* means that when you agree to serve on a board, you are there to serve the organization and its mission first and foremost. You're not there to advance your personal interests, or those of your family or a business you own. Let's look at this a little closer:

First, you shouldn't use your board service as a means for personal or commercial gain. You need to proactively disclose conflicts of interest, as well as avoid situations that just *look* like a conflict of interest. And, when decisions come up where you have a personal stake, you must step back and let others decide. See Chapter 16 to learn more about how to effectively navigate this situation.

Second, you must protect confidential information, including financial data, personnel matters, and strategic plans entrusted to you. This extends to protecting the confidence of your fellow directors, who need to be able to *speak in draft* and think out loud as you work through difficult issues.

Third, you should never speak on behalf of the organization unless you've been authorized to do so. This can accidentally happen if you're approached by the media or invited to professional events. Be sure to keep your remarks general and defer any questions to the leadership of the organization — either the executive or the board chair.

Finally, you must not push the organization toward offering certain services or programs simply because they align with your personal interests. Your job is to serve the mission, not to use the organization as a platform for your own causes or hobbies. Here's how to get it right:

- **Ensure your board is ready to handle conflicts of interest.** Conflicts will happen, especially with a well-connected board. The policy should detail how to handle a conflict and a process for regularly reviewing disclosures. See Chapter 16.
- **Proactively disclose your professional connections.** Everyone on your board has different personal and professional ties, and that's a good thing. But conflicts aren't always obvious until you're already in the middle of a discussion, which is why proactive disclosure helps.
- **Recuse yourself when appropriate.** Step out of the room and don't participate in discussions or decisions when you think your impartiality may be compromised or you have a personal stake in the outcome, whether it's financial, relational, or something else.
- **Don't use your board position for credibility or access.** It can be tempting to name-drop your affiliation with the board to open doors for yourself or enhance your opinion during a conversation. But using the organization to boost your personal or professional interests crosses a line.
- **Be clear that your views are your own.** If you're posting on social media or speaking at an event, make it clear that you're sharing your personal views. A simple "these views are my own" disclaimer goes a long way. You don't want your hot take to end up in a headline with your organization's name attached.

THE COST OF PUTTING YOURSELF FIRST

Breaching your duty of loyalty doesn't require bad intent. Here are two scenarios where someone crossed the line and opened the organization up to liability.

Scenario A: You own a catering company. At a board meeting you learn that the organization is looking to serve food at their fall gala. You suggest that they hire your company and you even offer a discount. After some discussion with you in the room, they vote to hire your company without getting other bids.

(continued)

(continued)

Why this is risky: Even if you are well-intended, you're putting yourself in a position to personally profit from your board service. It's not necessarily wrong for an organization to hire a board director's company. However, the process matters. You should remove yourself from the discussion and vote, and the board should demonstrate that the price of your services is reasonable by getting other competitive bids.

Scenario B: A board director is passionate about young people's mental health and suggests that the organization start a new program focused on it. It's not quite aligned with the mission or strategic plan, but everyone agrees that it's important work and you have some extra funds, so why not? The board approves the proposal.

Why this is risky: The board's job is to serve the nonprofit's mission, not pursue every good cause. No matter how good an idea sounds, if it doesn't align with what the organization exists to do, it's not the right fit. Your donors didn't give money to support individual board directors' pet projects and interests that don't sync with the mission.

Duty of obedience

The *duty of obedience* is about keeping promises: The promise to the government to follow the law; the promise to the community to provide a public good; the promise to donors to ensure their gifts are to advance the mission; the promise to your volunteers and staff to treat them well; and so on. In practice, this means:

- **Honor the mission.** Make sure every major decision about programming and every use of funds is tied back to why the organization exists. If the mission needs to evolve, engage in a thoughtful process to make the necessary changes.
- **Read and follow your bylaws.** They are your organizations rulebook and the board is expected to follow them consistently. If they're outdated or unclear, amend them rather than work around them. The more time you spend with your bylaws, the more comfortable you will be navigating them.
- **Ensure your organization meets its legal and regulatory requirements.** Keep a checklist of critical federal and state filing requirements, including your Form 990 filing (your tax return), solicitation registration, and other annual reporting obligations, as well as a list of key materials you need to have in place, such as policies and handbooks. See Chapters 16 and 17 for more on this!
- **When in doubt, ask.** You're probably not a lawyer, and you aren't expected to know everything. But you *are* expected to ask questions. If you're unsure whether something is legal or in line with the bylaws, speak up.

THE COST OF BREAKING THE RULES

The following scenarios can help you understand the duty of obedience.

Scenario A: The board president needs a quick decision on a new lease, so she emails the board and asks everyone to reply with a yes or no. A majority say yes, and the lease gets signed. However, the bylaws don't allow for electronic voting.

Why this is risky: Even if the vote was unanimous, the decision wasn't made properly. If something goes wrong with the new lease, the board may be exposed to liability for not following its own rules.

Scenario B: Ahead of the holidays, your organization rushes to sign up and start raising money online, hoping to reach new donors in several different states through an end-of-year campaign.

Why this is risky: Most states require nonprofits to register before soliciting donations from their residents. Rushing into fundraising in a new state without doing your due diligence opens your organization up to liability. Ignorance of the law isn't a defense, and the organization can face penalties that include fines, forced refunds, and even being barred from fundraising in that state.

Breaching Your Fiduciary Duties

Directors most commonly breach their fiduciary duties when they act in a way that isn't in the best interests of their nonprofit. While this may sometimes happen intentionally, for the most part, people fail to meet their duties due to carelessness, inattention, or just plain ignorance (that is, not knowing any better).

REMEMBER

Not every mistake is a major problem. From a legal standpoint, a breach only becomes serious when it's connected to actual harm, such as financial loss, legal liability, or reputational damage. That said, even small lapses create risk over time. Patterns of inattention add up, and what started as "no big deal" becomes a real liability.

WARNING

Watch out for these common ways board directors breach their fiduciary duties:

- Regularly missing meetings or failing to stay informed.
- Failing to ask questions about things you don't understand or know. If you don't know what you're voting on, you're making uninformed decisions.

- Approving financial decisions without asking questions or understanding background or reference data.
- Ignoring warning signs such as recurring deficits, cash flow problems, and delayed reporting.
- Allowing conflicts of interest to go unreported or unmanaged.
- Participating in conflicted decisions, including voting on matters involving personal, family, or business interests, or steering contracts to friends.
- Approving things that don't align with the mission, such as new programs or partnerships.
- Inserting yourself into day-to-day operations or giving directions to staff.
- Avoiding executive accountability, failing to conduct performance evaluations, or not addressing leadership concerns in a timely fashion.
- Not following the bylaws.
- Failing to act when something is clearly wrong, including tolerating unethical behavior or avoiding hard conversations.

REMEMBER

Board service is a serious responsibility. You won't always get every decision right, and you're certainly not expected to be perfect. But you are expected to show up, try your best, and ensure the right checks and balances are in place. If you do that consistently, you're doing your job and will likely be protected.

Knowing Your Rights

Just as you have obligations to your organization, your organization has obligations to you. Although the board ordinarily can only act collectively, the rights you have as an individual are designed to give you the information and authority necessary to govern effectively and ethically and fulfill your three legal duties.

Your right to information

As a member of the board, you have an absolute right to view the corporate books and records kept by the organization, and to communicate with management to gather the information you need to fulfill your responsibilities. However, these rights come with boundaries. Requests should be made in good faith, for a proper governance purpose, and should always be documented. This is especially important when it comes to personal data. Access personal information only when you have a clear, documented governance reason to do so, as misuse of personal data creates liability for both you and the organization.

REMEMBER

In general, you have the right to access the following records:

- Governance documents such as the articles of incorporation and bylaws.
- Board and committee meeting minutes, as well as any record of actions taken by the board.
- Insurance policies, long-term contracts, and lease agreements.
- Accounting records, including annual and audited financial statements.
- Strategic plans or business plans.
- Internal policies and personnel policies.
- Aggregate and anonymized data (for example, number of donors or donation amounts) to understand demographics and program performance.

On the other hand, you are not entitled to these records:

- Communications protected by attorney-client privilege, unless they've been shared with the full board.
- Confidential personnel files, including employees' medical information, to protect privacy.
- Whistleblower complaint details, unless you're conducting the investigation.
- Donors' protected information, such as specific personal data or individual donation details, if not necessary for fundraising oversight.
- Contact details of donors or community members, especially for unrelated outreach.
- Any records unrelated to your fiduciary duties.

Your right to rely on experts

It isn't reasonable to expect one individual alone to have the depth of expertise to provide sufficient oversight over every facet of an organization. Thus, you may legally rely on information, opinions, and reports from experts, including the officers or employees of the organization, legal counsel, accountants, and other professionals, so long as you think they are competent and acting in good faith. Just make sure you collect and retain documentation related to their provided expertise.

Your right to participate and vote

You have the right to attend and participate in board meetings, including being notified of meetings within a reasonable amount of time. You have the right to know what's on the agenda and to speak and ask questions on any matter under consideration. You have the right to engage in setting the organization's strategic direction. And, above all, you have the right to cast your vote, one way or the other, and have your vote put on record.

Your right to due process and protection

While it's not a "right" in the traditional sense, you have the right to ask the organization to carry directors and officers' insurance and to have an indemnification clause in the bylaws to protect you from personal liability for board decisions. And you have the right to expect that fair processes, as outlined in the bylaws, are followed if there are conflicts of interest or issues with your board service.

These requests should go to the designated board officer or executive leadership. In very serious situations, you may have a duty to escalate any concerns, but this is rare and should only happen after discussion with legal counsel.

Your right to dissent or leave

If at any time you don't agree with a major decision or the direction of the organization, you have the right to dissent and have your dissent recorded in the minutes of the meeting. If you are truly at odds with the rest of the board and cannot resolve the disagreement — for example, in extreme cases of consistent bias, adversity, or just plain injustice — you can and *should* resign from the board. If you feel you cannot get behind the decision or the ethics surrounding it, it's time to move on.

We recommend leaving if you feel unsafe, suffer actual harm, or anticipate damage from any decisions made by the board. You are in control of your service on the board because you are first a person and then a volunteer.

IN THIS CHAPTER

» **Understanding your organization's values**

» **Knowing the board's primary responsibilities to the organization it serves**

» **Remaining accountable to your legal and volunteer duties as a board director**

Chapter 4
Considering Common Board Responsibilities

Being a board director means more than being "just" a volunteer. It comes with serious legal obligations, as you discover in Chapter 3, and a wide array of responsibilities to fulfill over the course of a year to help the organization meet its goals and ensure its mission serves its beneficiaries. This includes everything from setting the organization's strategic direction and monitoring finances, to hiring and possibly firing an executive leader.

It's crucial to identify what your board is responsible for and revisit your duties as you grow. Without clarity on this front, you risk missing something important, creating legal or financial exposure, failing to catch risks before they become crises, or overstepping into areas that belong to the organization's staff. Any one of these mistakes can hurt trust and distract from your goals.

When everyone around the table knows what's expected of them to support the organization's success, the board can more effectively function as a team. In this chapter, we cover the common responsibilities a board may need to fulfill to meet its legal duties and recommended practices for how to get things right.

Laying the Foundation for Success

Every board starts in the same place: with three legal duties that are fixed obligations, regardless of your size, mission, or how long you've been around (see Chapter 3 for more on these duties). But how your duties of care, loyalty, and obedience show up in practice looks different for every board, shaped by who you are, what you value, and what your organization is navigating in its present moment.

Before diving into the most common responsibilities boards take on, you need to do a little self-examination. Great boards know themselves well, including what they value and stand for, the context they're operating in and how it influences their governance choices, and how to adapt the best practices, tools, and templates they find to their unique needs.

TIP

Speaking of tools, you bought this book. Congratulations! You're already one step ahead in the self-reflection process. Check out the appendix for a complete list of resources to help you strengthen your board and do better work.

Knowing your values

Your organization's core values are one of the first places to look when figuring out what your responsibilities will look like in practice. Your legal duties tell you what laws and regulations you're obligated to uphold, but your values will tell you how to create the greatest impact with your governance.

Does your organization value transparency? Inclusion? Innovation? Sustainability? These aren't just buzzwords on your website; they're a lens through which your board can assess which practices are truly best for your mission and its context. For example:

- If your board values transparency, you can hold town halls or publish accessible summaries of board decisions and organizational finances.
- If your board values sustainability, you can adopt regular strategic planning, explore financial practices that support long-term resilience (like reserve funds or endowments), or invest in succession planning to ensure continuity of leadership.
- If your board values inclusion, you can undertake practices that embed it across your work, such as conducting board equity audits, adopting organizational policies oriented toward inclusion, or utilizing decision-making processes that give voice to a diverse group of stakeholders.

Understanding your context

No two organizations are alike, and the boards that govern them shouldn't be either. A board that takes time to understand its context will always make better decisions and more effectively govern its organization than one that simply borrows practices from elsewhere. The following sections cover some variables that can inform the responsibilities that fall to your board.

Organizational maturity

Where your organization is in its life cycle has a big influence on how active your board needs to be. Younger nonprofits tend to have more hands-on boards, with frequent meetings, operational responsibilities, and project-based committees. As operations mature, boards typically step back into a more strategic and governance-focused role. Neither is wrong; they just reflect where the organization is in its journey.

Operations

The degree to which your organization relies on volunteers or paid staff to get the work done makes a significant difference in what the board is asked to do. In a volunteer-run or volunteer-driven organization, board directors are usually asked to roll up their sleeves and help with operational tasks (such as writing marketing copy or teaching classes or doing the bookkeeping).

Once an organization can hire employees, these activities tend to be delegated to staff, enabling the board to focus on governance and strategy. It's one of the clearest signs of organizational growth.

Finances

How much money you have access to will directly affect the level of responsibility your board carries. A smaller organization may find itself keeping a close eye on cash flow and requires only basic nonprofit financial literacy, while a larger organization will need to set up dedicated committees to oversee auditing, investing, or budgeting, or go as far as paying for added expertise.

Situational factors

Periods of rapid growth, crisis, or leadership transition will demand different things from a board than periods of stability. When your organization is facing significant change or challenges, your board may need to take a more active role: maintaining closer oversight of leadership, collaborating on operational decisions, or even taking charge during gaps in leadership. Depending on the situation, you may find your responsibilities expanding significantly until things are steady.

REMEMBER

Risk tolerance is also a factor. Every board has its own comfort level with uncertainty and innovation, and that mindset determines how it approaches governance. Boards with a higher tolerance for risk may adopt more flexible strategic plans or seek to streamline approval processes to enable quicker decisions. Boards that prefer stability may emphasize stronger internal controls, more frequent financial reviews, and detailed risk-management frameworks to safeguard continuity.

TIP

No two nonprofits are alike, but many organizations working toward the same cause share similar budget size, operational practices, and programming. Seek out organizations in your space and become friendly with them; you can find out a lot about what may or may not work for *your* organization and board by looking at their successes and missteps.

Connecting with peers may also reveal valuable context: the challenges they're encountering, the trends they're seeing, the knowledge they're gathering, and so on. Don't be shy about reaching out to people serving on other boards to compare notes and pick up helpful intel. In a similar vein, don't be shy about sharing your knowledge!

Adapting best practices (for you)

Few phrases are as overused or as misleading as "best practices." It implies that the perfect formula for success, a common recipe any board can follow to become more effective, exists somewhere. It's an appealing but flawed idea.

The best boards don't just copy and paste. They know themselves deeply and adapt their practices to fit their unique values, size, situation, and aspirations. What follows in this chapter is an overview of commonly held responsibilities and widely used practices to fulfill these duties. Treat this information as a starting point, not a checklist.

Getting to Work: Core Board Responsibilities

Now that you have a clearer sense of your values, your context, and what your organization may need from its board, you should start to get a better understanding of the responsibilities that show up most consistently across a healthy, high-functioning nonprofit board.

Setting and safeguarding the mission

The first and most important responsibility your board will ever have is to set and safeguard your organization's mission. This starts with ensuring that the mission is clearly written and understood by every member of the board and staff. From there, it should be used as a filter for significant decisions, including strategic planning and budgeting. You should regularly check in on whether your programs and services are aligned with your mission by asking thoughtful questions that keep you on track throughout the year.

It's also worth remembering that missions aren't meant to be set in stone. As your organization, and the world, evolves, so will your mission. When (not if) the time comes to revisit your mission, make sure you're bringing the right voices into the conversation. Consult your community, your partners, and your staff. Here are a few things you can do to keep the mission front and center:

- **Build in regular reviews of the plan.** Boards often get distracted by operational and financial oversight, and mission drifts can occur gradually without anyone noticing. A scheduled, structured review ensures mission alignment is intact and not just assumed. Whether it's the responsibility of a committee or part of your board's annual calendar, you should build in a review.
- **Visualize your spending.** Your board needs more than just financial data; it needs insight into the organization's impact. Visual models, such as a graphs, charts, and summary tables can highlight trends, patterns, information and stories alongside numbers, helping move the board from "Are we financially healthy?" to "Are we effectively serving our community and ensuring our costs are serving the mission?"
- **Share mission moments in board meetings.** Start your board meetings with a client story, a staff spotlight, a program highlight — something that reconnects your board directors to the *why* of the organization. It's easy to implement and ensures the mission is top of mind before you jump into governance activity.
- **Leverage strategic planning to ask hard questions.** One of the best times to reflect on your organization is during strategic planning. Make sure to ask, "Are we still the right organization to be doing this work? Is our theory of change still valid?"

Hiring, supporting, and evaluating an executive leader

Many nonprofit organizations start with no staff, and in those early days, the board often wears both hats of governance and management. But, as your organization grows in revenue and complexity, it's impossible to volunteer your way through operations. At some point, the board will look to hire a CEO or executive director. It's a practical necessity and the right thing to do for the long-term health of the organization.

Once that decision is made, the board takes on one of its most significant responsibilities: hiring, supporting, evaluating, and, if necessary, terminating an executive leader. That means owning the entire process, from writing a job description and setting compensation, to conducting performance evaluations (see the nearby sidebar "Looking at the board's hiring role, start to finish"). Next to setting and safeguarding the organization's mission, hiring a qualified and competent leader is the second most important responsibility your board can carry out.

And the stakes are high. The board-executive relationship is one of the most influential factors in the long-term success of your organization . . . and one of the most common sources of struggle. Some boards don't fully understand how to effectively support their leader. Others overstep. And many more shy away from hard conversations. If these dysfunctions are left unaddressed, they'll put your mission at risk.

TIP

For more about building and maintaining a strong relationship with your executive leadership, flip to Chapter 19.

Setting and monitoring the strategic direction

Through strategic planning, your organization gets clarity on where it's going, why it matters, and how it will get there. When your board creates a thoughtful, forward-looking plan, you're fulfilling your legal duty of care, ensuring your organization's resources are being used wisely in service of the mission.

A board's role in the strategic planning process includes ensuring that planning actually happens, participating when invited, and approving the final plan. From there, the board's role will shift to monitoring the plan against identified metrics and deadlines, and making budgeting decisions that are aligned with the strategic goals.

We recommend asking good questions, pressure-testing any assumptions presented, and ensuring that good research informs the process. Offer your perspective at the right time but also know that you won't always get your way, and that's okay. At the end of the day, the nonprofit's employees have to drive execution, and a plan they don't believe in won't get very far.

Also keep in mind that there's no single right way to plan or ideal horizon to set your sights on. Organizations come in all shapes, sizes, and missions, with boards and staff at varying levels of capacity and experience. What matters most is that strategic planning happens, and the people you serve have a meaningful voice in it. Jump to Chapter 12 for a deep dive on how to get your planning done.

Overseeing program performance

Your board has a legal obligation to stay informed about the organization's activities and whether it's doing what it promised. You fulfill that obligation through performance monitoring: tracking things like whether the organization reached an agreed-upon number of people, delivered services within a certain time frame, or achieved a particular social impact.

But this oversight is about more than legal compliance. Your donors, partners, and stakeholders have invested in your mission and deserve to know if their investment is making a difference. Your board needs to take performance monitoring seriously to build and sustain the trust and credibility that keeps your organization healthy over the long term.

TIP

Board directors need to actively seek out the right information and ask the right questions when monitoring the performance and impact of programming. You can do this well in many ways, including any combination of the following:

- **Require regular reporting from your CEO/management team.** Your executive leader should be providing regular performance reports in an agreed-upon format. These reports should go beyond the numbers and bring in metrics and storytelling that can help the board understand not just what happened but why it matters and what's coming next.
- **Use metrics that matter.** Say your nonprofit runs a workshop on how to eat healthier, and 100 people attend. If you only track attendance, it may seem like you're making a great impact! However, if the goal is to get people to *change their habits*, the number of seats you fill isn't the metric that measures your impact. If only 2 out of the 100 attendees changed their habits, the program may not be working. Boards need to ask for the metrics that reflect actual impact, not just activity.
- **Listen to what staff members have to say.** Hearing directly from the people doing the work can bring the mission to life in a way that data cannot. Anecdotal information from employees can keep the board grounded in reality and offer a real view into the organization's impact. Work with your executive leader to find appropriate opportunities to add staff presentations to your meetings throughout the year.

» **Challenge the status quo.** Don't continue a program simply because you've always done it. If the data doesn't support it, you need to ask hard questions and, if needed, make difficult decisions. You're there to uphold the mission, not tradition.

Ensuring legal and ethical integrity

Although it's not the most glamorous part of board service, ensuring the legal and ethical integrity of your organization is critical to sustaining the public trust needed for longevity. Rooted in all three of your legal duties (care, loyalty, and obedience), this responsibility shows up in big and small ways.

On the practical side, ensuring your nonprofit's integrity means staying on top of IRS filings and following your bylaws. But it also means setting the tone for how your organization operates. That may include creating a clear code of conduct, establishing policies that protect your staff and the services you provide, and advancing a culture where transparency and integrity exist at all levels of your organization.

REMEMBER

True transparency is more than just making information available; it's about ensuring people *actually understand* the information you share. Making your IRS Form 990s (see Chapter 15) easily accessible on your website is a good start, but consider going a step further. Many boards release an annual report summarizing their financials, metrics, and impact stories in a clear, accessible format. When done well and consistently, this can seriously help build trust with your donors and the community you serve.

TIP

See Chapter 16 for more information about legal requirements your organization needs to uphold, and Chapter 3 for a refresher on your legal and ethical duties as a board and as a board director.

Securing resources for the organization

Without consistent and reliable funding, your nonprofit cannot fulfill its mission. Thus, ensuring the organization is well resourced and that those resources are being spent wisely are core responsibilities of the board. There are two sides to this.

The first is financial oversight, including keeping an eye on the budget, performing audits, setting financial policy, and managing financial performance to ensure money is being spent in the best interest of the organization. You can read more about how to effectively govern nonprofit finances in Chapter 15.

The second is fundraising. Boards play a central role in helping secure the funds that keep the lights on. Depending on your organization's scale and circumstances, including how long you've been operating, this may mean working alongside staff to secure grants, showing up to fundraising events, personally asking for donations, or growing relationships with donors and the community. For more on the board's role in fundraising, see Chapter 13.

Enhancing the organization's public reputation

Your organization's reputation in the community is one of the most valuable assets you have. A good reputation will encourage more people to participate in your programs and attract donors and volunteers to your mission. A bad one draws public scrutiny, drives turnover, and is likely to lead to a decline in donations.

- **As a board,** you must regularly monitor public opinion. Build and maintain relationships with coalition partners and peer organizations and their boards, follow media coverage both locally and nationally as it pertains to your nonprofit area, and encourage management to collect and report on feedback from the communities you serve. Additionally, make sure the board discusses how it would handle a major incident and put in place a written policy addressing the issue.
- **As an individual board director** and key ambassador of the mission, you can do many things to uplift the reputation of your organization. First, understand the mission, inside and out. If you can't articulate what your nonprofit does and why, you can't help it grow. From there, confidently share its story with people in your personal community, and talk about both why you give and why you serve on the board. You also should leverage your network by making introductions and invitations to friends and business colleagues to participate in events.

Anticipating risk and preparing for the unexpected

No organization is immune to risk. Financial shortfalls, public criticism, and natural disasters are just a few of the realities that nonprofits, like their for-profit counterparts, face every day. *Risk management* is the practice of identifying, assessing, planning for, and managing those threats and hopefully reducing the chance of your organization being knocked off course. And lots of things can go wrong, including:

- Governance mistakes, such as unchecked conflicts of interest; board mismanagement, errors, or omissions; or poor decision-making
- Financial challenges due to inadequate funding, mismanagement, poor performance, or economic downturns
- Fraud and theft, from within the organization or by outside actors
- Legal and compliance failures, including failing to file required reports, lacking necessary registrations, or violating regulations
- Reputational damage due to negative press or controversy
- Cybersecurity attacks or data breaches that expose sensitive data
- Natural disasters like fires, floods, or pandemics

REMEMBER

Day-to-day risk management is the responsibility of executive leadership and staff. Meanwhile, the board needs to ensure that a risk-management plan exists, is being implemented, and undergoes regular reviews and updates. Part of that work also means having an honest conversation as a board about the organization's *overall* risk tolerance: How much uncertainty are you willing to accept in pursuit of your mission? There's no universal right answer, but the following questions are worth pondering:

- Will you budget for grants that haven't been secured yet? And if so, at what threshold?
- How many months of operating reserves do you want the organization to maintain?
- How dependent are you willing to be on a single source of revenue/donor/funder?
- Which social issues are you willing to take a public stance on?
- If a program isn't performing, when do you make the cut, and who makes the call?

TIP

If you're just beginning your journey, here's the most important thing to hold on to: people first, always. Before worrying about protecting the organization's assets or property, make sure you plan to look after the health, safety, and well-being of the people you employ and the people you serve. We jump into risk management principles and best practices in Chapter 17.

Setting DEI policy

You cannot fully understand or serve a community without having diverse perspectives at the table. For this reason, the responsibility of setting policy around diversity, equity, and inclusion (DEI) has moved from being a nice gesture to becoming a common expectation of effective governance. Boards that take this duty seriously understand the critical role they play in setting the tone for the organization, and accept the reality that building a diverse team is critical for attracting and retaining the best talent and achieving better outcomes for the people they serve.

TIP

Boards should think about DEI on two levels: within the boardroom itself and across the organization as a whole.

Board diversity and inclusion

Your board should be representative of the communities your organization serves. Beyond mere representation, you should strive to foster a culture where information is accessible and board directors feel welcome to participate fully in any discussion. Board directors should also be educated on DEI principles so they can govern through an equity lens.

Organizational diversity and inclusion

At the organizational level, the board should work in partnership with executive leadership to set and oversee DEI efforts across staff and programs. This means taking a hard look at human resources, technology, facilities, and culture, and asking questions about whether any barriers are preventing people from fully participating in or being served by your programs.

REMEMBER

It's not the board's job to manage DEI efforts on the ground. That responsibility belongs to your organization's executive and staff. Your job is to set the expectation that this work matters, ensure there are resources to support it, and hold leadership accountable for making progress over time.

TIP

Before making any changes, it's critical to understand where your organization currently is. A climate survey can surface the experiences of staff, fellow board directors, and community stakeholders, and help identify gaps. We also highly recommend auditing your policies and benefits, looking at whether your parental leave policies are gender-neutral, whether you offer paid-time-off options for various religious holidays, whether accessibility accommodations are in place, and so on. These two steps together can give you a clear baseline. Once you know your gaps, you can plan for change and approve targeted investments and improvements across the organization, such as the following:

- Updating benefits and policies to better reflect the needs of your staff
- Investing in education on recognizing unconscious bias or building cultural competency
- Improving employment policies by softening dress codes, strengthening anti-harassment and anti-discrimination efforts, and offering other accommodations
- Addressing the physical and digital accessibility of your workplace

REMEMBER

Building a diverse and inclusive organization takes time and intention. Boards that approach this work with humility, listening to the people most affected by their work and committing to continuous improvement, will simply be better at serving their communities than those that don't.

Building and managing a competent board

This final responsibility is the most foundational of all, because without a competent, engaged, and well-structured board, none of the other responsibilities covered in this chapter can be effectively fulfilled. Building and growing your board isn't a one-time task; it's an ongoing commitment to ensure that the right people are at the table, that they're educated and prepared to govern well, and that there's continuous renewal. Everything depends on this.

IN THIS CHAPTER

» Defining board officers' roles and responsibilities

» Working together as a team to lead the board

» Understanding what goes into board elections

» Finding ways to flex your leadership muscles

Chapter 5
Designing Effective Board Leadership

Every team needs leaders: people who step up to drive strategy and execute work that champions a positive, productive culture. They connect people to their strengths while holding others accountable. Without good leadership, teams can fall quickly into dysfunction and go unchecked; meetings drift, momentum is lost, and work loses steam.

A board is no different. Nonprofits are busy, complex businesses, and boards are responsible for a serious workload: setting mission and direction, hiring and assessing management, overseeing finances, monitoring mission impact, being accountable to the community, and more (as we explain in Chapter 4). Board officer leadership is what keeps the board team focused and functional.

In this chapter, we cover everything you need to know about building strong board leadership, including how board officers get elected and work together, as well as these key positions' responsibilities.

TIP

Chapter 3 has details on the legal obligations of a board director, so if you're a current or aspiring officer, we suggest you start there. (Honestly, we think every director should start there.)

Getting an Overview of Officer Roles

Strong nonprofit leadership depends on clear roles, shared accountability, and disciplined governance. Officers provide the structure that keeps board work focused, efficient, and aligned with the organization's mission. *Officers* are elected leaders responsible for ensuring the board is well managed and the organization governed effectively. They keep meetings organized, advance an annual work plan, partner with the executive on strategy, and ensure the right issues get the attention they need. Most states require at least three officer positions, though most boards expand to include the following roles:

- **President:** Partners with the executive to lead the organization, drive the work of the board, and facilitate meetings
- **Vice president:** Supports the president in carrying out their duties, steps in to lead meetings or functions in the president's absence, and assists with key strategic initiatives
- **Secretary:** Maintains accurate records of the board; prepares and shares agendas, minutes, and materials for meetings; and makes sure the organization is meeting its filing requirements
- **Treasurer:** Oversees the financial health of the organization by supporting the delivery of budgets, preparing reports for the board, and coordinating audits or reviews

Though many organizations use this four-person slate, others operate with just the core three positions (president, secretary, and treasurer). You can also choose to have two vice presidents or co-presidents, or to combine the treasurer and secretary roles into one. The right structure depends on your needs. Flip to your bylaws to see what your organization requires.

REMEMBER

When you join a board, you become a *director*. Everyone on the board holds that title. Officers are directors who have taken on an additional elected role to help with leading and managing the work of the board. So although all officers are directors, not all directors are officers. That said, holding that extra title doesn't make you more important. In decision-making, all directors are equal.

Looking at Key Responsibilities of the Board Leadership Team

Think of the officers of the board the way you would a C-suite in a business. This team (often referred to as the *executive committee*) keeps a high-level eye on organizational goals, setting and overseeing the board's direction and work. Bylaws typically grant this group expanded authority to act on behalf of the board between regular meetings and in the case of an urgent situation. Unlike regular directors, who don't have power to act on their own, officers have additional, limited authority to sign contracts, move money, hire staff, or bind the organization to certain decisions. When you think about what the officer team is really doing, it reflects the three core fiduciary duties every director is responsible for: the duties of care, loyalty, and obedience. The president holds the strategic vision, the treasurer looks over the financial integrity, and the secretary tends to legal compliance. Together, they make sure leadership is present and paying attention to every pillar of good governance and are responsible for the following:

- **Setting direction for the board:** Drawing up the annual workplan, monitoring committee work, and supporting work if things begin to stall out or fall short of target
- **Leading the meeting and agenda process:** Making sure the right issues get in front of the full board and that meeting time is used for the highest and best purposes
- **Partnering with the executive as the board's primary point of contact:** Staying informed on what's happening in the organization and supporting performance management more directly by coordinating any formal board-level action
- **Speaking on behalf of the board in public:** Representing the organization to stakeholders, donors, partners, or the media
- **Acting when the full board can't convene:** Making decisions, especially in time-sensitive situations between meetings, and then communicating those decisions back to the whole board
- **Serving as the first stop for grievances and ethical concerns:** Ensuring complaints or conflicts of interest are handled confidentially and with integrity
- **Addressing dysfunction when it arises:** Dealing interpersonal issues between directors or a breakdown in culture

REMEMBER

As always, check your bylaws to get more information about the responsibilities and authority granted to your board officers. The bylaws should be able to provide clarity about what both officers as a whole and individual positions are responsible for.

Electing Officers for Your Board

Not everyone who is a great board director is ready to be an officer. These positions call for a higher level of engagement and responsibility and are best suited for those who are familiar with the organization, have solid governance and technical expertise, and demonstrate a willingness to learn. Valuing collaboration and humility, with the self-awareness to know how to lead without dominating, is equally important.

REMEMBER

Above all, officers need time. These positions require a major commitment beyond the boardroom, including time to meet with the executive, show up in the community, and field concerns from fellow directors. Officers also get the late night calls when things go sideways. So before you raise your hand (which we believe you should aspire to do!), be honest about your capacity.

This section takes you through everything you need to know about the election process, including who gets a vote, why establishing term limits is important, and how to manage succession so transitions don't derail your board.

Examining the election process

Every organization has a different approach to electing officers, but they all follow the same democratic principle: Officers are elected by a vote. Who gets to vote, however, is up to your governance structure. No federal or state requirements cover this process, so look to your bylaws for the rules. When you do, here's what you're likely to find:

- **Who votes:** In board-driven organizations, directors elect officers. In member-driven organizations, the membership votes. ***Note:*** Members aren't donors or followers but individuals who formally joined the organization according to the terms laid out in your bylaws. They often pay dues or have to meet some sort of eligibility criteria. Think alumni or trade associations, credit unions, and co-ops.
- **How people cast votes:** Voting may happen at an annual meeting, by mail-in or paper ballot, or online. Your bylaws just have to permit the method you

choose. One thing to consider is whether your process will be anonymous. Secret ballots can encourage participants to be honest about what they want, especially on a smaller board where everyone knows each other.

- **When elections take place:** Elections occur one of two ways: automatically on a set schedule (annually or biannually) or when an officer position is vacated.

REMEMBER

Your bylaws should note any eligibility requirements to be a board officer, such as minimum tenure on the board, experience as committee chair, or specific technical experience. You also want to confirm the quorum required for a valid election and whether any limits to the number of terms someone can serve apply. (Head to the following section for more on term limits.)

TIP

Keep it as simple as your situation allows. The complexity of the election process depends on your governance structure and size. A 40-person board needs a development pipeline and nominating process. A board of five may just raise hands at the last meeting of the year. In member-driven organizations with thousands of eligible voters, organizations need something more sophisticated altogether.

Tackling term limits and timing considerations

In Chapter 8, we talk about the importance of term limits for board service. Well, the same goes for officer positions. Being an officer is a tall task. It requires more time, energy, and responsibility than just being a director. Without rotation, the board faces serious risks: burnout, consolidation of knowledge into a few key people, having one person dominate the room for too long, and others. (We cover the distinction between director and officer in the earlier section "Getting an Overview of Officer Roles.")

Term limits force the entire board to share the load of leadership. They protect the longevity of everyone involved and are more likely to lead to a healthier, more productive board culture. Fresh perspectives in leadership can keep the group nimble and innovative.

TIP

Before electing directors to officer positions, check where each candidate is in their board term. Doing so helps in a couple of ways:

- If someone is in their final year on the board, electing them to an officer position creates risk and makes it far more difficult for whoever follows. You want runway for them to serve a full term while also having the ability to overlap with the next officer and transition responsibilities. The goal is continuity!

- We also caution against electing directors who are in their first year of service. They're still learning about the organization and how the board operates, and taking on an officer role too soon can be overwhelming to them and risky to the board.

Setting the stage for succession management

A board president reaches the end of their term, and no one wants to raise their hand and step up. The treasurer resigns, and no one has the financial expertise needed to backfill. Situations like these are more common than you'd expect. They're risky moments in the life cycle of the board, but they're unnecessary ones. The reality is that the succession of board officers is far more predictable than that of the executive position. Officer terms end on a known schedule, and vacancies rarely sneak up on you. And yet most boards still wait until their hand is forced.

Given the importance of these positions, the board has a vital responsibility to make sure they have a plan for turnover at the top — and doing so is easier than you may think:

- Set term limits to ensure turnover remains predictable.
- Document each officer's role by maintaining up-to-date job descriptions.
- Keep a running list of directors who've expressed interest so you're never starting from zero.
- Approach candidates directly and well in advance of the transition.
- Leverage committee chairs as a pathway for development. They're already leading on the board and are perfectly positioned to continue to grow.
- Design transitions so outgoing and incoming officers have the opportunity to overlap and transfer knowledge.
- Share stories to inspire and motivate others, and make sure people understand officer leadership to be achievable and meaningful.

Taking a Closer Look at the Officer Roles

Serving as an officer deepens your understanding of the organization in ways that make you a better director. Although officers have a collective responsibility to the board, each individual position has its own set of duties. The following sections outline some best practices and norms for those who raise their hands and step up into officer roles.

Perusing the board president's role

The *board president* (sometimes also referred to as the *chairperson* or *chair*) is the leader of the board. This position is established as state law requires and comes with significant governance responsibility. The president provides strategic leadership, fosters a collaborative partnership with the executive, and directs the board's business. Specifically, duties of the role include the following:

- **Set the agenda and facilitate meetings:** Shape board meetings so they're strategic, productive, interactive, and focused on the things that actually matter. Work collaboratively with the executive so that discussions remain on topic and the conversation stays focused on governance rather than operational details. (Flip to Chapter 10 for details on how to run a great meeting.)
- **Monitor board performance and accountability:** Lead the development of the annual workplan (as we explain in Chapter 9), assign work to committees, and make sure committee work is driving results. Regularly meet with committee chairs to support their leadership, and make sure the annual assessment of the board occurs (Chapter 18).
- **Serve as the board spokesperson:** In collaboration with your executive committee, provide unified and transparent messaging when asked to speak on behalf of the board and organization, particularly in times of change or crisis.
- **Navigate difficult board dynamics:** Mediate (inevitable) conflict, ensure respect among directors, and uphold the integrity of discussions. Address any disruptive behaviors swiftly and privately.
- **Serve as a board signatory:** When necessary, sign documents or contracts as required or authorized by board action.
- **Support engagement:** Serve as the primary contact for all directors on matters of the board. Make sure people are engaged and active in committee work and strategic projects.

REMEMBER

This role demands an exceptional level of personal commitment and the highest level of personal integrity. If you've been elected to this position, your fellow directors have placed their confidence in your ability to guide, mediate, and advance the organization's goals. Here are some key ways you can guarantee your success as a board president:

- **Meet with your executive before *every* board meeting.** No exceptions. You never want surprises in the boardroom, and the best way prevent them is to quickly check in before a meeting.
- **Check in with new or quiet directors before meetings.** A quick word of encouragement or an invitation can go a long way to helping someone find their voice as the table. For example, "I'd love to hear your take on agenda item four!"
- **Actually run meetings.** Prepare agendas thoughtfully, think through facilitation logistics, start and end things on time, and keep discussion moving along.
- **Have a plan for how to deal with directors who talk too much.** Having a few neutral phrases in your pocket can make diffusing these situations easier and keep the dialogue moving forward. Try something like "That's helpful context. Let's hear from others." or "We only have ten more minutes, and I want to make sure everyone can be heard."
- **Never forget that directors are your peers.** Don't let the title of president go to your head. You run the meetings, but you don't own all the decisions or have authority to give orders. The best presidents lead through the soft influence they build by cultivating real relationships with the people they serve alongside.
- **Keep the board focused on the organization's strategic goals.** The board can easily end up in a reactive mindset over small things. When short-term issues emerge, pause and ask, "How does this connect to where we said we want to go?"
- **Plan for your last day on your first day.** Take time to write down what you want to accomplish during your tenure and share this information with your executive committee and executive leader. More importantly, start looking for your successor.
- **Take a break.** When you're on vacation, be truly offline. Leverage your VP and executive committee to share the load.
- **Ask for help.** You aren't expected to have all the answers or all the time. When things get hard or you're pressed for time, remember that you're on a team and ask for the help you need.

- **Have fun!** Okay, being board president can be a heck of a lot of work, but it's also the single most rewarding role you can fill on the board. You get to be close to the action, influence the direction of the organization, take on interesting challenges, meet new people, and really make a difference.

TIP

Chapters 9 and 10 show you how to organize the board's work and run effective meetings. Chapter 18 gives you tools to monitor board performance, and Chapter 19 lays out everything you need to know about building a relationship with your executive partner. Plus, check out our online appendix for an onboarding checklist!

Viewing the board vice president's duties

Many organizations choose to establish a vice president position, recognizing the benefits to having a clear line of succession and a method for developing board leadership. The vice president should take an active role in board leadership, providing support to the president in leading the board while also taking the point position on a variety of strategic initiatives. The vice president's responsibilities include these:

- **Support and cover the president:** If the president is absent or unable to serve, step up to preside over meetings, sign documents, engage with the executive, and serve as spokesperson.
- **Prepare for the presidency:** Strengthen your knowledge of board policies and procedures, committee work, the strategic plan, financials, and other organizational initiatives. Shadow the president in key functions, from meeting with the executive to dealing with interpersonal issues.
- **Take lead on strategic board projects:** This work may include things like leading a specific committee, overseeing a governance improvement initiative, representing the board publicly at community events, supporting board recruitment or engagement activities, or assisting with evaluation and education.
- **Support board engagement goals:** Develop your own personal relationships with board directors. Help identify gaps in participation and culture. Model collaborative leadership, healthy dialogue, and good behaviors.

TIP

If you step into the vice president role, you need to bring the same level of commitment and integrity expected of the president as well as a readiness to step up when called on. Familiarize yourself with everything expected of the president; we lay those out in the preceding section. If any of them makes you uncomfortable, use that to develop a plan for your own growth.

Talking about the board treasurer's position

The treasurer is the board's lead financial steward and the director who's responsible for ensuring the organization's money is being managed compliantly. To be clear: This individual is neither your CFO nor your bookkeeper. Rather, they're there to provide oversight on behalf of the full board and to serve as liaison to any finance staff or vendors.

WARNING

This officer position carries a significant fiduciary duty. Funders and regulators look closely at an organization's financials, and the treasurer's diligence (or lack thereof) can directly affect public trust.

Here are some of a treasurer's key responsibilities:

- **Support long-term financial health:** Offer a financial perspective on any strategic or operational decisions and help the board understand how new programs, investments, or changes to the organization affect long-term sustainability. Monitor reserve levels and risk exposure and bring forward recommendations for action on any trends that cause concern.
- **Lead the finance committee:** Set the agenda, schedule and facilitate meetings, and work alongside staff to accomplish the board's and organization's goals.
- **Take on financial reporting and transparency:** Review and interpret any financial reports, ensuring accuracy and compliance with generally accepted accounting principles. Help tell the story of the numbers, turning complex data into accessible summaries that any director can follow. Make sure tax returns are filed and records are being properly maintained.
- **Oversee the budgeting process:** Collaborate with any executive management, financial staff, or accounting partners. Review the budget against actual performance on a regular basis and flag concerns for the board.
- **Serve as the board's primary contact for external relationships:** Those include finance staff, accountants, auditors, and consultants delivering financial services.
- **Monitor internal controls:** Help develop and maintain a financial controls handbook that documents procedures and accountability mechanisms that protect the organization.
- **Serve as an authorized signatory:** Financial accounts may require a signatory.

REMEMBER

The treasurer position can look dramatically different depending on an organization's scale. In a small nonprofit with no staff, the treasurer may serve in more of a day-to-day function. In a larger organization, the role shifts to partnership with the chief executive to ensure sound financial management.

Eyeing technical qualifications

Unlike the other officer positions in the preceding sections, the treasurer position calls for technical expertise. All directors should have at least a basic level of financial literacy, but the treasurer needs to know how to read and interpret financial statements, how to ask auditors and financial leaders good questions, and how to read between the numbers to sniff out problems.

TIP

When recruiting for your board, don't just look for one finance pro to fill the seat of treasurer. Build depth on your bench. Seek out directors who have managed budgets at a significant level in the course of their careers and who know how to ask informed questions even if finance isn't their primary domain of expertise. As we discuss in Chapter 15, nonprofit finance is quirky (fund accounting, restricted gifts, compliance requirements, and so on), so the more people you have on your board who are comfortable with the numbers, the better.

Becoming a great board treasurer

Here are some key ways you can ensure your success as a board treasurer:

- **Have your predecessor give you a deep-dive of the organization's financial story before you take over responsibility for the role.** Walk through a few years of financials, major investments on the horizon, and anything that's currently keeping the outgoing treasurer up at night.
- **Establish a strong relationship with the chief executive leader and financial staff.** They're the only ones who can really help you get to the truth of the numbers.
- **Build and use a simple one-page financial dashboard for board meetings.** Most directors won't read through a 12-page financial report (and won't understand what they're looking at if they do). Instead, pick out five to eight numbers that matter and explain those. Work with financial staff on this task if the organization has it.
- **Try to avoid getting pulled into the organization's day-to-day financial operations.** When you get involved in cutting checks and reconciling the books, maintaining independence and oversight is harder.
- **Don't let the board off the hook.** If people aren't asking questions or aren't engaging with your reports, you need to figure out why. Are they disengaged?

Do they not understand what they're looking at? Are they just afraid to ask a "dumb" question? Whatever it is, get to the bottom of it and correct it quickly.

- **Find and train a successor early and advocate for the expertise you need on the board.** Being the only person on the board who understands the money creates an enormous risk if something happens to you.

TIP

If you're taking up the helm as treasurer, you may find a few chapters in particular very useful:

- Chapter 11 has a section about the finance committee and tips for how to make the most out of that group.
- Chapter 15 is a high-level resource that can help you check where you may have gaps in knowledge about nonprofit finance.
- Chapter 17 dives into all the risks, including financial, that a nonprofit may face.

Beyond this book, we also recommend BDO's catalog of nonprofit financial management trainings at `bdocnap.matrixlms.com/visitor_class_catalog`. If you want to get into the weeds, you also can pick a copy of *Nonprofit Bookkeeping & Accounting For Dummies* by Marie Loughran (Wiley).

Seeing what the board secretary's role entails

The board secretary is more than just your minute-taker. They're your recordkeeper, logistic manager, wordsmith, and resident bylaws expert all rolled into one. When operating at the highest possible level, the board secretary serves as a governance expert, and directors should look to them for leadership when revising bylaws and interpreting policy. The secretary may even chair the governance committee and, as the steward of institutional knowledge, guide onboarding for new directors.

Most state laws require boards to appoint a secretary. Like all other officer positions, you can find their specific responsibilities defined in your bylaws. Common duties include the following:

- **Take meeting minutes:** Create a written record of all board meetings, decisions and votes, rationale behind the actions, and attendance. Proofread and distribute the minutes to all attendees in a timely matter.
- **Coordinate logistics for board meetings:** That includes scheduling, sending reminders, confirming attendance and quorum, and distributing packets in advance.

» **Manage records and documents:** Ensure board records and governing documents are properly stored and easy to access, including bylaws, policies, minutes, budgets, strategic plans, executive evaluations, committee charters, and more.

» **Manage bylaws and compliance:** Have a solid working knowledge of the bylaws and governance policies and field questions as they arise. Make sure the board operates compliantly at all times.

» **Track meeting attendance and board terms:** Maintain a current roster of all directors. Support the board in planning for recruitment and succession.

REMEMBER

Board secretary may not be the most glamorous or visible position, but without a strong secretary your board will struggle. Records will go missing. Decisions will get disputed. Compliance deadlines will be missed. Important history will be forgotten.

As always, this role can look quite different depending on the size and staffing of your organization. In a large nonprofit, a staff member may be hired to support logistics like assembling packets or even recording minutes. Yet the secretary is still responsible for reviewing and ensuring the accuracy of those materials.

REMEMBER

The secretary should attend every board meeting but not every committee meeting. We recommend the secretary work with each committee to designate a notetaker, provide training on how to take good minutes, create templates to ensure consistency across collected documentation, and help committee notetakers refine their reports ahead of full meetings.

TIP

As you build your knowledge based to better support the board, we have several chapters we think can make a big difference to you:

» In Chapter 8, we get into the nuts and bolts of how bylaws are written. Grab a copy of your organization's bylaws before you dig in.

» In Chapter 10, we've included a whole section on how to take minutes that both protect your board and are useful to fellow directors.

» In Chapter 16, you can familiarize yourself with the types of board polices you'll be expected to monitor.

Modeling a Culture of Leadership

If you're on a board, you should be ready to lead. That means being open to serving in an officer role at some point during your tenure. Board service is fundamentally about leadership, and if the idea of stepping into that responsibility feels far off or unappealing, you may want to consider whether now is the right time to be serving.

That said, leadership is going to look different depending on where you are in your term. In your first year, you're finding your feet and focusing on learning the organization's history and story and how the board works together. As you move into the middle years, look for opportunities to step up: Lead a board project, chair a committee, or mentor a new director. Toward the end of your term, you should be actively engaged and possibly even considering taking on an officer role, depending on your capacity and expertise.

Here's a menu of methods for building your leadership muscle, from easiest to most involved:

- Attend workshops and trainings on nonprofit board leadership and governance.
- Serve as a board buddy/mentor to new board directors.
- Participate in a book club focused on nonprofit topics (or organize one if it doesn't exist).
- Act as an ambassador by attending the organization's programs and events and educating donors and supporters on the board's work.
- Speak at a gala or fundraising event about your experience on the board, highlighting the board's accomplishments and directors' work together.
- Lead an initiative or project for the board, such as revising bylaws or facilitating strategic planning.
- Serve on a committee to help shape board policy and fulfill the operating responsibilities of the board.
- Chair a committee.
- Shadow a board officer and assist them with some of their common responsibilities.

TIP

Assessing and identifying leadership potential starts as early as the recruitment process. When bringing on new directors, ask openly about their interest in future leadership and revisit that conversation regularly. Your board evaluation process (the one we discuss in Chapter 18) can be an excellent way of getting people to reflect and grow in the right direction.

IN THIS CHAPTER

- » **Considering what it takes to recruit a diverse and effective board**
- » **Navigating the three stages of a recruitment cycle**
- » **Creating an onboarding experience that helps new directors thrive**

Chapter 6
Recruiting and Onboarding Board Directors

You don't build a great board by accident. It takes careful planning, ongoing outreach, and an organization-wide commitment to setting new directors up for success as soon as they arrive at their first board meeting.

A question we often get from nonprofit boards is, *How do we find good directors?* For a long time, many boards relied almost exclusively on people in their personal networks to fill seats: friends, work colleagues, neighbors, family members. But these this approach tends to produce boards that look and think a lot alike, making it harder to represent the diverse, dynamic groups your organization serves and, frankly, likely needs to survive.

In this chapter, we walk you through the full cycle of board recruitment, from figuring out who will be the right fit and running a search, to onboarding new directors in a way that prepares them for long-term success. We also make the case for adding an annual cohort of fresh recruits rather than bringing in new members throughout the year. Read on to find out how to convince great people to join you in your boardroom.

Recruiting an Effective Board

Anyone who has ever been part of a board knows that the difference between getting things done and spinning your wheels comes down to the people in the room. A board with engaged directors who lean in to the work together can help a nonprofit fulfill its mission and have a greater impact in its community, whereas a board with the wrong mix of directors can make the hard work of governance a whole lot harder. Recruiting new directors who can do the work is one of the most consequential things you'll do during your tenure on the board.

But boards require directors to go above and beyond having a passion for the mission and making an annual donation. True governance requires a high level of cultural competency. board directors must focus an inclusive eye on ensuring the organization is creating more opportunities for diverse groups of people to give, become involved, attend programs, and Be accountable to keeping their nonprofit and its community sustainable and thriving.

When we look at what today's boards need, here are some of the things that stand head and shoulders above the rest:

- **Diverse perspectives:** Having a broad range of professional and personal experiences in the room improves the overall quality of your decision-making . . . especially when directors' experiences directly connect back to your organization's strategic priorities. You're more likely to avoid blind spots, have more robust discussions, and better serve your community's needs.
- **Sound financial and business judgment:** The board is responsible for overseeing the organization's fiscal health and strategic direction (more on that in Chapter 4). Having directors who are familiar and comfortable with the operational and financial demands that come with running a business will make your board better at evaluating risk and ensuring long-term sustainability.
- **Comfort with ambiguity:** Today's nonprofit boards must hold steady through constant change and be able to adapt to shifting economic, political, and social conditions. The best board directors are comfortable in the face of uncertainty and have the ability to plan for the future but will support a pivot if the moment calls for it.
- **Candor and the courage to speak up:** Having the willingness to raise your hand, ask questions, and dissent is a part of your duty. If something doesn't add up in the boardroom, you need directors who will ask hard questions or voice concerns, even if it causes discomfort.

» **Collaborative leadership:** Great board directors check their ego at the door and work with the organization's staff as a team, recognizing that good governance requires shared effort. You want to find people who listen, build on others' ideas, and are willing to partner with both fellow board directors and staff to move the mission forward.

» **Curiosity and a willingness to learn:** A good board director has the curiosity to learn more about how their nonprofit (and the nonprofit sector) works. directors don't need to master nonprofit management principles before their first board meeting, but they must be ready and willing to figure out the quirks of the organization and how to best fulfill their governance functions.

TIP

Don't get us wrong: You need people on your board who care deeply, have the time to show up and do the work, and are willing to donate to the cause. But you should also be looking for directors who can embrace community-centric values and governance practices. When you're recruiting, ask potential board directors about their values and how they align with the organization's mission.

MAKING THE CASE FOR A COHORT RECRUITMENT MODEL

Many boards recruit directors year-round, filling a seat here and there as they find someone who's interested in their organization. However, recruitment must be more than just filling seats in the boardroom. You need to be strategic, taking into consideration the organization's strengths and weaknesses as well as the challenges ahead, with an eye on candidates who have a steady hand for governance and can provide diverse subject-matter expertise.

Boards that want to be intentional about recruiting new directors have adopted cohort-style recruitment, seeking out and onboarding a *group* of new directors once a year. Candidates move through the same application, interview, and orientation process on a shared timeline and join the board together. This approach offers the following advantages:

- **Strategic recruitment:** Recruiting a cohort encourages you to assess what the board needs before seeking out new directors. Do you need a legal expert to help revamp your bylaws? Do you need someone familiar with the local real estate market because you're thinking of building a new facility? You can survey your current board to identify gaps in skills, expertise, and diversity, and intentionally recruit new directors to fill them.

(continued)

(continued)

- **Stronger relationships:** When directors join the board as a cohort, they go through the experience of being newbies together. Just like an incoming class of college freshmen, they create a community in which they feel safe to ask questions, admit uncertainty, and figure things out alongside one another.
- **Improved onboarding:** IA cohort model gives you the opportunity to design a structured onboarding program that can be used to refresh and update the full board on policies and procedures each year.
- **Improved succession planning:** An annual cohort creates a natural rhythm for board renewal. When directors join and rotate off the board in groups, it becomes easier to anticipate and manage vacancies.
- **Energy management:** Recruiting is time-intensive. Shifting to a cohort model allows the board to focus its energy on an intense recruiting effort rather than dealing with vacancies as a constant background task. After making a big recruiting push together, the board can refocus on its other business for the rest of the year.

The shift to a cohort model requires work, and it won't suit every organization. But for boards looking to streamline the process and manage their energy, it pays dividends by promoting overall cohesion, capability, and continuity.

Stage 1: Assessing Your Board's Needs and Preparing to Recruit

Hold your horses! Before you run off to recruit new directors, you need to know what (and whom) you're looking for. This phase is all about taking stock of your current needs and identifying skill, expertise, and diversity gaps. You may need to refresh yourselves on the organization's long-term strategic priorities before preparing the materials and messaging you'll use to run an effective search. This helps ensure that board directors are ready to actively participate in the process.

Compiling your wish list

Before you put out a call for new directors, you need to identify your board director wish list. This involves three key activities, which are covered in the following sections. Your wish list outlines the skills and expertise you'll prioritize in your recruitment effort. You can use it to draft your job posting and help focus your search for candidates.

Creating and updating your board matrix

Your *board matrix* is a strategic tool that maps information such as the professional skills, company affiliations, and expertise of your current directors. Your matrix also collects demographic data, including age, gender, race, physical ability, and other identity markers. It's important to clearly present this data so you can assess the diversity of your board and fill any gaps. For example, if you're the director of a nonprofit that predominantly serves the female-identifying community, but your board is 80 percent male-identifying, you may need to recruit more female-identifying members.

Reviewing your strategic goals

What initiatives are you trying to achieve over the next three to five years? Does your board have the talent it needs to successfully tackle them? Reviewing your strategic plan and goals will help you determine which skills would be most valuable in the boardroom.

For example, an organization with a large facility needing capital improvements would benefit from having folks who work in real estate investment or engineering. Or, if your organization is planning to expand or add a new program, you may want to find directors with experience in launching or running similar programs or those who have expertise in change management.

Consulting with your executive leader

Your executive leader will have valuable insight into the day-to-day functions of the organization and can identify gaps that may not be obvious from your altitude as a director. Solicit input on the types of directors they hope to have. For example, if the executive director is overseeing all the fundraising activities, they may want directors who have experience with fundraising to help them solicit donations and grants from individuals and institutions.

Preparing your materials

Your board's recruitment process will require a little bit of paperwork. You need information about the organization, its strategic goals, the role of the board, and your expectations of individual ready to go before you launch the search. If this is your first time doing board recruitment, this step will be more work up front, but it will lay a foundation for future recruitment, reducing the workload and allowing you to update your materials each year.

Writing a job description

After compiling your wish list, you'll develop a board director job description. Even though board service is a *volunteer* job, it's still a job. A well-written job description supports good governance by clearly outlining the board's expectations around the role and its responsibilities. It also gives interested candidates an idea of what board service will entail.

You should highlight the specific skills you're looking for, including areas of expertise, professional background, community ties, or other desirable qualities. This will help interested candidates identify the ways they can contribute to the organization. As your board and the nonprofit evolve over the years, the responsibilities and qualifications of board directors will also evolve, and your job description will need to be updated.

Creating an application

Once you have your job description, you must decide what information you need to collect to assess candidates. Many boards request a résumé and cover letter, but you may also consider asking a few screening questions. You also need an easy way for people to submit their application materials. While you certainly can have candidates email their materials, using an online form connected to your board's shared files streamlines the process. This approach keeps applications better organized, ensures that everyone submits the same information, and improves the candidate experience.

Plus, you can give everyone who will be evaluating the candidates easy access to the applications. You can find many free options for creating your online form, including Google Forms (`https://workspace.google.com/products/forms/`), Microsoft Forms (`https://forms.office.com`), and Jotform (`https://www.jotform.com`), to name just a few.

Building your landing page

Finally, your organization needs a web page or public posting about the board and its search for new directors. This page or posting on your nonprofit's website should provide information about who is on your board, a copy of the job description, details about the application process and timeline, and a link to the application itself. This improves transparency and helps bring credibility and polish to the process.

TIP

Include an email address on the landing page in case candidates have trouble accessing the application or have questions about the process. We recommend providing the nonprofit's general email or the email address for the board liaison or executive director, or creating an email address specifically for the board.

Other housekeeping tasks

There are a few more things that can enhance the overall candidate experience and reduce your workload further down the line, including:

- » Create an overview of the organization's key programs and initiatives (or make a copy of the board's annual report). Candidates need to know what you do, how often you do it, and its impact.
- » Update your board contract.
- » Create or update an organizational prospectus, which can serve as a PR document that provides deeper insight into the organization's work, financial performance, and impact data.
- » Put together a resource packet, including recent annual reports, IRS Form 990s (which contain your nonprofit's financial data), a summary of your strategic plan, and other information of interest to candidates.
- » Ready key governance documents such as the conflict of interest disclosure and your board code of conduct (see Chapter 16).
- » Get a copy of your directors and officers (D&O) insurance policy.

REMEMBER

Transparency goes a long way in sustaining public trust and inspiring the confidence someone needs to say *yes* to joining your board. While not strictly necessary, having these additional materials on hand can enhance the candidates' overall experience and help them make a well-informed decision about whether to apply for a position on your board.

Involving your entire board

After the paperwork is done, the entire board needs to be brought up to speed on what the recruitment process will look like and how they are expected to participate. A well-prepared board understands the timeline, respects the process and those responsible for leading it, and engages their larger networks to support the search. Recruitment is a team effort.

Managing recruitment via committee

Because board recruitment can be a time-intensive endeavor, it is best managed as a committee project. This shifts the burden of sourcing, interviewing, and onboarding new directors to a dedicated group who can focus their energy on ensuring the whole process is thoughtful and well designed.

Small organizations may choose to set up a task force to handle this project, whereas large organizations may have a nominating committee dedicated solely to board recruitment. For most, though, the governance committee can handle this responsibility (see Chapter 11 to find out more about this).

REMEMBER

While an individual committee should take the lead on identifying and vetting candidates, the full board must remain involved in the final selection. You should not, and likely cannot, delegate the authority to add or remove board directors to a small subsection of the board (see Chapter 8 for more about following your bylaws).

Creating talking points for directors

Your current board is critical to recruiting new directors and can be your most effective advocates and talent scouts . . . that is, if you give them the tools they need to succeed. board directors must feel confident talking about what they're inviting people into, and even long-standing directors can use a little help.

TIP

We recommend creating a cheat sheet, just for internal reference, to serve as a go-to resource for directors who talk about board service with prospective candidates. This should be no more than one or two pages long and cover things like

- The organization's mission statement and a few bullet points about your current strategic plan or what's on the three- to five-year horizon
- Some impact statistics from the prior year (total budget, number of people served, and the like) to provide an overview of the organization
- The basic details of board service (number of meetings per year, monthly time commitment, giving expectations, and so on)
- An outline of the application steps, including the overall timeline from recruitment to onboarding
- A clear point of contact or link to a landing page, so people know how to apply if they're interested

Finding your story

Board directors should be ready to tell the story of why they serve, whether they share an anecdote from their personal experience or a testimonial reflecting the organization's impact. This isn't something a committee or fellow board director can prepare for them. Instead, encourage board directors to take a little time to reflect, write some notes down, and practice telling their story to someone. Having board directors pair up and share their stories with one another may even make for a great breakout session at your next board meeting.

Stage 2: Actively Recruiting New Directors

With preparation complete, it's time to launch your search for new directors! This phase covers everything from spreading the word across an array of platforms and mobilizing your personal network, to hosting informational opportunities, reviewing applications, conducting interviews, and ultimately bringing a slate of candidates to a vote before the board.

Spreading the word

The most important step in recruiting is to make sure people know the opportunity exists. Once you've announced that you're looking for board directors, you can boost the signal in several ways, including:

- Post the opening through your organization's communication channels, including your website, social media platforms, and newsletter.
- Share the information on popular online platforms such as LinkedIn (`https://www.linkedin.com/`) and Idealist (`https://www.idealist.org/en`).
- Reach out to the local chamber of commerce, your community partners, and your state nonprofit association.
- Contact past board directors for recommendations.
- Reach out to people who serve on boards with a similar mission to see if they know anyone who may be a good fit.

Mobilizing individual directors

Getting the word out doesn't stop there. Individual board directors can make it easier for the right people to find your organization by sharing and amplifying the opportunity in both their real and their digital life. In fact, personal outreach is the single most effective recruitment tool available.

Unfortunately, we've found that many board directors hesitate in this regard, usually thinking they don't know anyone or aren't very good at doing personal outreach. Here's the thing: You probably know more people than you think — current colleagues, former coworkers, people you volunteer with, folks you've met through professional networking, and so on.

You may be overthinking what outreach involves. Here are just a few things you can do to get the word out:

- Post the opportunity on social media (ask staff for sample language if you need it) and tag two or three people.
- Reshare one or two of the organization's posts and add a sentence about why you serve on the board.
- Drop the opportunity in two or three relevant online spaces, such as your alumni networks and newsletters, LinkedIn groups, professional associations you're affiliated with, or other community organizations you volunteer for.
- Attend a local community event, panel, or professional gathering with recruitment in mind and talk about your organization and the opportunity to serve on the board.
- Send a text or direct message ("Thought of you when I saw this. Do you know anyone who might be a good fit?") to one or two people, along with the link to the announcement or application. You don't have to know the right candidate yourself; sometimes the best possibilities are one connection removed.

REMEMBER

Even if your reach is small, even if none of your leads become candidates, every bit of outreach expands the visibility of your organization and improves its chances of finding the right folks.

Reviewing applications

Once the word is out, applications will — hopefully — start coming in. As in any hiring process, it's important to follow a structured, objective approach when reviewing candidate materials. Use your job description to create the rubric for evaluating candidates against the gaps on your board. Some factors you may consider when reviewing résumés and cover letters include things like your personal connection or passion for the mission, relevant career or life experience that aligns with the organizations goals, previous board service, and other community connections or volunteer engagements.

Conducting interviews

Finally, the fun part! Conducting interviews with prospective board directors is similar to interviewing applicants for a regular job. It's an opportunity to get to know the candidates beyond their résumé and hear their story, as well as clarify their expectations about board work and assess how they'll fit into your organization. Before you jump in, though, your board needs to be aligned on the following things:

» **How many rounds of interviews will there be?** More interviews require more time, energy, and coordination while offering diminishing returns. For that reason, we recommend no more than two or three rounds.

» **Who will participate in each round?** Ideally, you'll have the same group of individuals running interviews so they can assess candidates consistently. Typically, the board president and directors of the governance committee are involved. If your nonprofit has a CEO/executive director, you can ask them to participate as well.

» **What will you ask candidates?** Using a standard set of questions across all interviews allows you to easily compare and contrast candidates' answers and make the right pick. You can find some specific questions in the next section, "Asking good questions."

» **Where will you conduct interviews?** Whether interviews occur online, at a coffee shop, in your organization's offices, or some other place, make sure all the details are thoughtfully coordinated and communicated. Take into consideration whether you plan to discuss any sensitive information about the organization that may not be appropriate for a public space.

» **Who will coordinate scheduling?** It seems like a minor point, but wrangling multiple calendars to find a time that works for board directors and candidates can be quite time-consuming. It's best to assign a single person to oversee this bit of administrative work.

Asking good questions

As you prepare the questions you're going to ask candidates, think about what will deepen your understanding of their qualifications and potential fit. This section isn't about what the right answers to your questions are; rather, it's meant as a guide for deciding on the right questions to ask. Here are some topics you may explore to better assess each candidate's suitability for the mission, skills and abilities, willingness to commit time and energy, and governance knowledge:

» **Connection to the mission:** What drew you to our organization, and what do you hope to get out of board service?

» **Background and expertise:** Walk us briefly through your career or life experience and tell us about what you consider to be your core areas of expertise, particularly any that you think would be valuable to our board right now.

- **Prior board experience:** What other boards have you served on, and what were the most important lessons you took from those experiences? If this is your first board role, what draws you to board service now, and how will you educate yourself about your role on the board?
- **Governance philosophy:** How would you define good governance, and what role do you think a board should play when working with the organization's staff?
- **Time and availability:** Our board directors typically commit [X] hours per month to their service. Realistically, how much time can you give, and do you have any current commitments or limitations we should know about?
- **Willingness to fundraise:** Are you willing to take an active role in fundraising, including making introductions to potential donors in your network and helping cultivate relationships?
- **Strategic thinking:** We're currently focused on [XYZ priorities]. Where do you see opportunities for us to build relationships or partnerships?
- **Handling adversity:** Tell us about a difficult issue a board you've served on has faced or, if you haven't served, a tough team or organizational decision you helped navigate. What was your role, and how did you handle disagreement?

TIP

You should tailor your approach to the unique needs of your organization and the culture of your board. Be prepared to listen to your candidates' answers, ask follow-ups where needed, and gently guide the conversation toward the information that will help you make a good decision.

Answering questions

It's important to remember that interviews are a two-way street. Not only are you trying to find the right fit for your board, but your candidates are also trying to determine if your board is a good fit for them. If you want to attract the best talent, you need to create space for your candidates to ask questions and then provide thorough and candid answers. Here are some questions you should be prepared to answer:

- What are the long-term goals or strategic priorities of the organization?
- What are the biggest challenges or risks facing the organization?

» What is the organization's financial situation? What are your major lines of revenue and your biggest expenses? Are you running a surplus or a deficit? Do you have operating reserves or an endowment?

» What is the relationship between the board and the executive like?

» How would you describe the role of the board? Is the board more hands on and involved in the daily operations, or more strategic?

» What does a typical year look like for a board director? What are the expectations with regard to time and participation? Are meetings in person, virtual, or a combination?

» Is there a giving requirement?

» What do you expect my unique contribution to be? Was there something specific about my application that stood out or seemed valuable to the board?

» How big is the board, and who else serves on it?

» Do you have D&O insurance?

» If I joined, what would my first six months look like?

REMEMBER

The questions a candidate asks can tell you a lot. Someone who asks about financials, strategy, and culture is thinking like a fiduciary. Someone who asks only about events and perks may be looking for prestige and a line to add to their résumé. Pay attention to what people are curious about. And always be honest with your answers. Don't be afraid to say, "I don't know," refer to your board leadership with the question and then follow up with an answer.

Involving the executive leader

Your CEO/executive director is a key partner in the recruitment process, because they are the person who's most familiar with the day-to-day needs of the organization. However, they should *not* vote on who joins the board. One of the board's primary responsibilities is to oversee the chief executive, and if they help choose their own boss, it creates a structural conflict of interest. Barring them from voting protects the independence of the board and keeps the line between management and governance clearer.

The most appropriate ways to engage your executive leader in the recruiting process include gathering their input on visible skill gaps on the board, asking them to seek recommendations on potential candidates from the community, having them participate in interviews and share their impressions on candidate chemistry and fit.

Opportunities to engage candidates

Beyond applications and interviews, you can engage prospective board directors in other ways, both during the recruitment cycle and over the course of the entire year. You may invite candidates to take part in some of these activities:

- » Review the prospectus and other materials about the organization (such as the packets you assembled during Stage 1 of the recruiting process).
- » Participate in volunteer experiences at a program site or on a service day.
- » Make a site visit or take a program tour.
- » Informally have coffee with a board director.
- » Attend your annual fundraiser.
- » Support a committee with specific project work.
- » Sit in and observe a public board meeting.

These opportunities can provide added insight into what board service looks like and deepen the personal connection someone has with your organization. They're also a chance to get to know a candidate better in a less formal setting.

Voting on the candidates

The final step of the recruiting stage is getting the whole board to vote on new directors. Your bylaws will outline the specific procedures and minimum number of votes required to approve someone, so make sure to check whether you need to follow a certain process. Otherwise, carve out time in a board meeting or hold a special session to review the profiles of your chosen slate of candidates.

The committee or board director leading the recruitment should share information about candidates' backgrounds, highlights from any interviews, and make their final recommendation. Once the vote happens, you can share the good news and begin onboarding your new class of board directors.

Stage 3: Onboarding and Integrating New Directors

The recruitment process doesn't end when a candidate says *yes*. This final phase, which involves onboarding and integration, focuses on setting new board directors up for long-term success. By offering a structured experience, you can guide them through their first year, rapidly deepen their understanding of the organization and board culture, and help them build real relationships with fellow board directors. Done well, and your new cohort will feel confident and ready to contribute within just a few months. Done poorly, and you may find yourself dealing with dysfunction or, worse, with another board seat to fill.

Onboarding for retention

Onboarding is where retention begins. It's more than just handing out a packet of materials or having a pep talk over coffee. It should be a carefully designed series of educational and social experiences that new directors participate in over the course of a year, each one bringing them closer and deeper into the organization.

Signing the paperwork

Just like new employees, new board directors have paperwork to sign at the beginning of their commitment, including a board contract, code of conduct, conflict of interest disclosure, confidentiality agreement, and a board policy or procedure acknowledgement form. Collect and file these forms in a secure location, alongside all your other board records.

Breaking the ice

Before you dive into the work of the board, create an opportunity for social connection. A welcome dinner or social activity can bring new board directors together with existing directors in a relaxed setting. This is a chance to break the ice, build personal connections, and create a sense of community that will be critical to having candid and difficult conversations down the road.

REMEMBER

One of the most common reasons people sign up for board service is to expand their social or professional network and meet new people. Take a proactive approach to socializing with new board directors. Organize these get-togethers to coincide with events and programs your nonprofit sponsors.

For example, if you're on the board of an arts nonprofit, host a meetup at a nearby restaurant to welcome new board directors before they attend the show. The combination of gathering as a community and then seeing the mission in action will remind everyone why they're serving on the board.

Pairing new directors with a buddy

Pair each new board director with an existing director who can act as a resource and guide. Having a board buddy can help new directors feel more comfortable asking questions, ease their introductions to staff and programming, and provide a sounding board when they're navigating board business early on.

Encourage board directors to check in regularly with their buddy, ideally twice a year or before/after a board meeting. Grabbing a coffee together or signing up to volunteer side by side is an easy way for buddies to connect. This mentorship also helps new board directors feel empowered to fulfill their goals for serving on the board. The more supported a new director is, the more likely they will be to get involved and make an impact, paving the way for potential new leaders on the board.

Conducting orientation sessions

Every board director needs to understand their legal duties, their governance responsibilities, and the organization's work if they are going to serve effectively. Your board can provide orientation opportunities through one-day educational retreats, book or reading assignments (for example, from this book!), mini lessons on the organizations finances, programs, and operations, and hands-on volunteer assignments.

Allowing committee drop-ins

Sometimes it's obvious where a board director will contribute (such as an accountant hopping onto the finance committee), but just as often, it's not. Invite new directors to sit in on various committee meetings during their first 90 days, before committing to joining one.

This gives them a low-pressure opportunity to observe the board's work and identify where their skills and interests are the best fit. It's also another fantastic opportunity to deepen their overall understanding of the organization's mission and the board's governance role.

Encouraging program experiences

What's more compelling than experiencing your organization's mission and programs firsthand? But trying to figure out where to jump into the annual calendar of activities and experiences can be overwhelming. Point out several opportunities in the first few months where new directors can deepen their personal connection to the mission. This may include attending or volunteering for a program or community event, meeting with a program beneficiary or hearing a firsthand impact story, shadowing a staff director for a day, or touring key community sites or facilities.

Accessing technology

Ensure new board directors have all the tools they need to participate fully from day one, including access to your board's online portal, shared drives, email, and any other digital platforms you use. Create a simple technology checklist and a data/tech policy to ensure that nothing falls through the cracks. Offer a hands-on tutorial on how to find information and navigate platforms and programs. Don't assume that people can figure out your tech stack.

TIP

If you're on the board of a large nonprofit with many employees, your organization likely has training materials you can rely on, and the staff are already positioned to provide both tech orientation and support.

Other touchpoints and onboarding ideas

We've covered only a few ways to create a welcoming and effective onboarding experience. Here are some additional ideas you may want to explore:

- Offer new directors a handwritten welcome note from the board president and/or the executive director.
- Feature profiles of new directors in a newsletter or on social media.
- Hand out a small packet of quick-reference materials, including a cheat sheet on board norms and mission details, a glossary of organization-specific acronyms, and an org chart.
- Provide a first meeting survival guide that shares where to park, how long meetings run, if food is provided, how the agenda is created, if phones are allowed, and so on.
- Schedule a three-month check-in to ask new directors what they want more information about or what they wish they knew sooner.
- Celebrate their first full year with a small acknowledgment like a note from the board president or a shoutout at the final board meeting of the year.

Thinking of Recruiting as a Year-Long Activity

Recruiting new directors requires a lot of energy, and it's a year-round responsibility, with strong boards weaving recruitment opportunities into the rhythm of their annual calendar. Every month, your board will likely engage in different tasks that support recruiting success, whether you're engaging in outreach, vetting candidates, onboarding new directors, or developing the organizational knowledge, governance skills, and interpersonal connections of current directors. Table 6-1 shows an example of a board recruitment calendar.

TABLE 6-1 Recruitment Calendar

Month	Activity
January	Create and complete a board demographics and skills survey. Update the board job description and recruitment materials.
February	Provide information during board meetings on the recruitment outlook and how to participate.
March	Launch your recruitment effort, sharing your search broadly online and through personal networks.
April	Host a town hall for interested candidates.
May	Review applications and conduct interviews.
June	Present a slate of candidates to the board for a vote. Notify all approved candidates and begin the onboarding paperwork.
July	Prepare onboarding materials and presentations.
August	Begin onboarding and host a welcome dinner.
September through December	Encourage new board directors to sit in on different committees and determine where they would like to support the board's work.

Even when you aren't actively soliciting applications, your board should always be seeking to build genuine relationships with prospective directors. Every community event, professional gathering, donor conversation, or volunteer interaction is an opportunity to identify someone who may one day serve on the board. Encourage every board director to keep a running list of people they would like to see more involved and have them nurture those relationships long before a real ask is on the table.

IN THIS CHAPTER

» **Understanding what motivates people to join a nonprofit board**

» **Looking at the various levels of member engagement**

» **Identifying creative ways to engage your board throughout the year**

Chapter 7

Energizing and Engaging Your Board

You've built your board! You've recruited passionate and skillful people who care about your mission, who are ready and raring to go — so now what? Having the right people in the room is only half the battle; the other half is keeping them engaged, energized, and pointed in the right direction. *Board engagement* is the ongoing and intentional practice of keeping directors informed, involved, and invested in the organization's mission and work. It's not a single event or a once-a-year retreat but rather the culture you consistently create meeting by meeting and conversation by conversation that powers the whole thing.

In this chapter, we cover all the different ways you can get your board to show up and lean into the work of the board, from facilitating retreats to assigning board buddies to volunteerism and more!

Breaking Down Motivations for Board Service

Everyone joins a board for different reasons. Understanding personal motivation is an important part of identifying and offering opportunities for engagement and unlocking people's best contributions. Here are several reasons people are motivated to join a board:

- **Passion for a cause:** The vast majority of directors join a board because they care about the cause, whether that's animal welfare, education equity, the arts, or community health. These convictions drive a desire to serve and create directors who are lifelong champions of the work.
- **Personal connection to the mission:** Sometimes passion runs even deeper. A former ballet dancer joins the board of their local dance nonprofit. A parent who has a child with disabilities becomes an advocate for accessible recreation. Directors driven by both passion and a personal connection can be the loudest and most provocative ambassadors for your mission.
- **Professional connection to the mission:** For others, the connection is rooted in career and expertise, such as when a lawyer joins a social justice advocacy organization, an architect lends their skills to a historic community theatre, or a doctor serves a health clinic. Directors connected to the mission through their profession bring valuable knowledge that strengthens the board.
- **Networking:** Board service introduces you to people with different perspectives and backgrounds, all united behind a common cause. It can be a great way to connect with people who have shared values.
- **Recognition and status:** Being asked to serve on a board is an honor and signals to others that people trust and respect your judgement. For some, that sense of distinction is a key motivator.
- **Growth:** Board service stretches you. It asks you to build skills you didn't have or even know you needed, such as strategic thinking, financial literacy, conflict navigation, and public speaking. Some directors seek out service for exactly this reason.

REMEMBER

People are complex, and their motivations for board service are, too. Beyond the reasons listed here, directors are also motivated by legacy, faith and family, a connection to the leader or staff, or even just curiosity. None of these motivations is better than another. Whatever the reason, the more you know about why someone shows up, the easier getting them to stay is.

Navigating the Engagement Spectrum

Board engagement is a spectrum. At one end are directors who actively cause dysfunction, undermine leadership, create division, neglect their duties, and indulge in bad behaviors. In the middle are directors who show up but don't really contribute. This passive mix ranges from those who barely show up and rubber stamp decisions to those who attend reliably but hold back from taking initiative.

At the other end are active, engaged directors: prepared, passionate, and showing up above and beyond at times to advocate, fundraise, and champion the mission. Most boards have a mix of all three, and the goal of any board is to move as many people as possible out of dysfunction and into being champions.

Table 7-1 shows different levels of engagement that a director may show during their time on the board, from disengagement to passive participation to being a loud and passionate champion. Higher engagement drives critical thinking and innovation, where directors are more likely to feel comfortable sharing opinions, engaging in debate, and offering up resources.

TABLE 7-1 Stages of Board Director Engagement

	Stage 1 Detractor	Stage 2 Passenger and Observer	Stage 3 Engaged Listener	Stage 4 Active Contributor	Stage 5 Champion and Strategic Partner
Director behaviors	Poor attendance Undermines leadership Creates division Leaks confidential info Micromanages staff Acts in self-interest Blocks decision	Mixed attendance Minimal preparation Never speaks up or asks questions Votes with majority No follow-through Disengaged between meetings	Solid attendance Occasionally raises good questions Listens actively Follows important issues and reports Limited initiative	Shows up prepared and ready to participate Leads committees Builds personal relationships with others on the board Raises hand for projects Gives candid feedback Use own network to help organization Mentors peers Holds self-accountable Shows up to events outside the boardroom	Advocates publicly for the mission Gives, fundraises, and connects donors Develops future board leaders Coaches new directors Recruits new board directors Speaks publicly on behalf of the board Never stops falling in love with the mission

REMEMBER

The way directors show up year-to-year will shift. Use Table 7-1 as a tool for identifying patterns in behaviors and to figure out how someone may need more support. If someone who was once highly engaged suddenly begins showing signs of disengagement, you may want to check in with them. On the other hand, if a director consistently is falling into patterns of dysfunction, coaching and mentorship is part of helping them grow.

REMEMBER

Building board engagement calls for a combination of aspiration and action. Directors need to be pointed toward a standard of behavior, and that standard needs to be written down and understood. They also need to be given clear opportunities and stepping stones to get them where you want them to be.

An engagement matrix, such as the one shown in Figure 7-1, is a map that shows events, meetings, and opportunities that directors can participate in throughout the year, with an explanation of what you expect in terms of participation. You can take it a step farther and use it to track participation by different directors in initiatives as well. In the remaining sections of the chapter, we look at each of the eight areas of the engagement matrix in more detail.

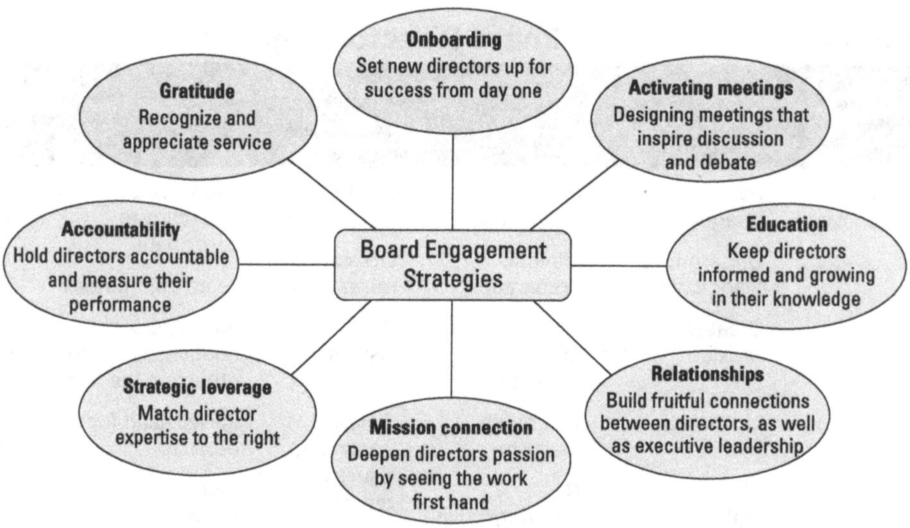

FIGURE 7-1: Engagement matrix.

Prioritizing Onboarding

In Chapter 6, we dive into how to effectively run an onboarding process to set your new directors up for long-term success. Here we provide an additional layer of context, with a focus on how reinforcing your engagement culture begins before someone ever steps foot on the board.

Providing quality written materials

Few directors receive training before joining a board, which means your written resources and educational materials are a defining aspect of understanding what good service looks like. When directors have clear documents in hand from day one, they can spend less time figuring things out and more time engaged with the work at hand. Here are the documents that most influence board behaviors:

- **Code of conduct:** A written *code of conduct* sets the tone for how you expect directors to show up in the boardroom. It outlines values and behavioral expectations and covers things like confidentiality, social media conduct, and the house rules of the boardroom. Chapter 16 can help you write one.
- **Job description:** Board membership may be a volunteer job, but it's still a job. A written job description should cover the fiduciary duties, time commitment, responsibilities, and minimum requirements of board service. Check the online appendix for a sample.
- **Board agreement:** The *board agreement* is a commitment letter that outlines the service term and expectations around attendance, financial giving (if any), and committee participation. It also should explain what happens if members don't meet these expectations. ***Remember:*** You can't hold anyone accountable unless they know what they're accountable for.
- **Orientation handbook:** The handbook is simply a booklet with organizational history, the current strategic plan, a financial overview, a glossary of common terms, and anything else you think a director may want to reference when figuring out how the board operates.
- **Meeting calendar:** The calendar provides a clear outline of all the critical dates for meetings, events, fundraising activities, and anything else that may require board participation.
- **Samples of your board evaluation tool:** Allow directors to see how the board evaluates itself to reinforce engagement expectations.

Setting expectations in recruitment

Culture lives in every moment of the board life cycle, including the time before someone even joins. During recruitment, directors running the process should orient candidates into the organization's programs, offer them opportunities to interact with current directors, and invite them to upcoming events. Those directors should be candid about their board service and the demands that come with it. Never sugarcoat the organizational context or the requirements for engagement. Doing so only leads to frustration later down the line.

Welcoming people with style

The way you welcome someone communicates what kind of board you are. Is it warm or transactional? Energized or going through the motions? Do you do something to mark the occasion (both when people arrive and leave the board), or do you carry on like nothing has happened? After the recruitment process, onboarding is a new director's first real data point on the group, and it says a lot about how you care for one another. So make it count!

REMEMBER

Board meetings don't end up being good times for socializing unless you thoughtfully build in time before and after to connect. Consider also adding in an opportunity for dinner or a mocktail, and go out of your way to say hello first.

TIP

Every year, host a board-wide orientation session for new members and invite the entire board to attend. Getting caught up in board work is easy, and setting aside time for directors to refresh themselves on the organization's work and their own fiduciary responsibilities can be grounding.

Intentionally invite new directors to assist with a task or decision early in their tenure and help make the connection between the need of the board and their expertise. This move makes them feel useful and valuable early on and starts to excite them about engaging.

Activating Your Meetings

In and around the moments you come together to meet and discuss the business of the board is where engagement really lives and dies. For most directors, board and committee meetings are their primary form of engagement, which means the stakes are high. To make the most of this method of engagement, you need to plan ahead, communicate consistently, design interactive meetings, and carve out time for the bigger, juicer conversations.

Planning

Start by setting your annual calendar as far in advance as possible. People have busy lives, and you can't expect them to show up with little to no notice to plan around it. This scheduling goes beyond board meetings and includes fundraising events, advocacy opportunities, volunteer days, and any other touchpoints where you want the board to show up. Make the plan stronger by including a note on what you expect from directors at each of these types of functions. Is it just their presence, or do you want them to participate in some way? The more they know, the more likely they'll show. For more on planning an annual board calendar, see Chapter 9.

Using breakout groups and discussion

One of our favorite ways to encourage engagement in the boardroom is by building in time for discussion. Share questions in advance so directors can come prepared, go around the table requesting input, or use breakout groups to deep-dive into a specific topic. Distribute any necessary reports or briefings before the meeting with enough time for people to read and process them. Chapter 10 gets into the nitty-gritty of how to run a great board meeting.

Retreating (the good kind!)

Retreats are day-long events where the board and executive leaders gather for a structured, focused deep-dive into specific strategic priorities or governance work. These sessions are well suited for the big, hairy problems that need more time and breathing room than a standard board meeting can provide, as well as for educational activities and team building. Retreats can be very inspiring and provide the perfect forum for strengthening the function and clarity of the board.

WARNING

Some boards turn to retreats hoping that a single day can solve the problem of disengagement or dysfunction. But a single retreat *cannot* fix deeper issues. Instead of getting together and hoping that you can talk it out, flip to Chapter 18 and run a board assessment.

Communicating between meetings

Communication is a keystone of board culture. The frequency, transparency, and quality of conversations directly influence the sense of trust and inclusion that exists on your board. Even if your board meets as frequently as once a month, a lot is going to happen in between meetings that needs to be communicated. Depending on your practices, that communication will make you stronger or drive dysfunction. Here are a few quick tips:

- **Standardize information flow.** Set the expectation that general board-wide communication comes from board president or executive leadership.
- **Recap board meetings.** Within 48 to 72 hours after every board and committee meeting, the president or committee chair should follow up in writing with a recap of any action items and asks of attendees and a copy of minutes.
- **Understand urgent versus important.** Not every piece of information needs to be shared right away. Teach your board the difference between *important* information (that can wait until the next meeting) and *urgent* information (that needs to be shared up or out sooner rather than later).

» **Limit information overload.** Everyone responsible for delivering reports to the board needs to become exceptional at creating *executive briefs* (one-to-two-page documents that synthesize and summarize complex initiatives into something accessible and digestible). As your board takes on more and more projects, this approach is key to managing information overload.

» **Avoid gossip.** The board gets access to sensitive information about the organization, staff, and other directors and donors. Set expectations early that what's shared in the boardroom stays there and that concerns need to be raised directly through the right channels, not in the backrooms.

WARNING

Reply all is almost never necessary when participating in general communications. Make BCC your friend for general announcements and generic updates, and if your email is running longer than two or three paragraphs, consider saving it for a meeting. Your other directors will thank you.

Investigating an online board portal

Many nonprofits use a mix of email and cloud-based file storage tools to manage their data, and this setup works perfectly fine. New tools that boards can use are now emerging. These *board portals* are online platforms that serve as an online hub for communication, document sharing, and general activity. If your budget allows, consider exploring and investing in a dedicated tool.

WARNING

Before committing to any tool, do your due diligence: Check the bylaws about anything pertaining to communications, survey the board about their concerns, and confirm you have the capacity to manage the setup or transition. Some vendors offer discounts or free software to nonprofits, too.

Educating the Board

For directors to feel like they can confidently engage with the work of your organization, the board needs to educate itself. This education can be as simple as sharing an article and as robust as paying for everyone to attend a certification program. Though the sky is the limit, a few things you can do include asking staff to present on subject matter specific topics, organizing a workshop with a consultant or trainer (like us!), hosting guest speakers from the community, attending networking events in your sector, taking an online course, or sharing and discussing relevant articles and books.

TIP

Investing in capacity building for the board is an investment in the organization and mission. The more knowledgeable your board, the better members can show up and do their duty. Budget enough to hire or pay for professional services to up level your team.

Creating Impactful Relationships

The relationships you have with your peers on the board can make or break everything else that goes on. People simply do better work alongside people they know and like. That means you allot time for one-on-ones with executive leaders, opportunities for directors to connect with one another, and social activities and outings and address conflict quickly when it rears its ugly head.

Establishing executive one-on-ones

REMEMBER

We can't understate the value of building a personal relationship with your executive leader. A strong personal connection fosters deeper trust, leads to more candid conversations, and makes navigating challenges easier when they arise. Start by taking your executive leader out for coffee or lunch (and pick up the tab!) and use the opportunity both to learn more about who they are personally and to share more about your connection to the work.

Taking advantage of the board buddy system

In Chapter 6, we introduce the board buddy system to help new directors get up to speed with board business faster. Pairing seasoned directors with new ones benefits both parties: It creates the opportunity for direct, personal connection, can reenergize longtime directors, opens up a channel for questions, and perhaps leads to a fresh perspective on what service means and why it matters. To make the most of your board buddy system, remember the following:

- **Identify the directors who are ready and able to mentor.** Make the ask during a board meeting so you can explain the system.
- **Personally connect and introduce mentors with new directors.** You can do so by email or in person before or after a board meeting.
- **Direct mentors to set up a kick-off meeting covering a few key areas.** These include why the new director joined; a walk-through of the most recent board meeting; an overview of committees; and upcoming events and volunteer opportunities.

» **Have buddies meet regularly.** For the first year, have mentors check in with the new director at least once a quarter to continue informal education and build rapport.

» **Report to board leadership about questions new directors are asking and any positive or constructive feedback they're receiving.** This information helps the board get better in the future with their next class of directors.

Social events and informal gatherings

The boardroom isn't the only place your board should get together. Stepping outside and giving directors a chance to connect as people and get to know each other beyond their professional roles can be seriously valuable. These types of personal connections can lead to far more open, honest conversations. We're talking about grabbing a bite to eat before or a drink after a meeting, hosting a holiday party or celebration when someone joins or retires from the board, and all types of casual check-ins, coffee chats, and informal connection points.

WARNING

You need to strike a delicate balance between grounding directors in their professional duties and encouraging personal connection. When directors become too friendly with each other, they tend to divert to majority rule or groupthink instead of speaking up when something goes wrong, the same way anyone may avoid saying something awkward in front of their friends.

Addressing dysfunction

The quickest way to destroy the culture of your board is to allow dysfunction to go unchecked. Common culprits include directors who shut down conversation or bully the room; conflicts with the executive leader or micromanagement by the board; and bad behaviors like poor attendance or arriving unprepared. If you want people to be excited to show up to the boardroom and collaboratively work together, you need to have the hard conversations. Check out Chapter 23 for tips on how to navigate the ten most common dysfunctions we encounter on boards.

Fostering a Mission Connection

Help directors deepen their passion for the mission by finding opportunities for them to see the organization in action firsthand. These chances look very different depending on what your nonprofit does, but they may include site visits, volunteer opportunities, storytelling, and organized advocacy.

Surveying site visits and program tours

What better way to get energized around the mission than seeing the work in action? Site visits and program tours are low-lift, high-impact engagement opportunities that give directors a chance to connect with the organization. They're a chance to talk about the facilities and resources involved in program delivery, learn about the history of the organization, and maybe even interact with people doing the work day-to-day.

TIP

Visits and tours are more than a nice-to-do; they inform decision-making in the boardroom by grounding people's understanding in the reality of what making the mission happen takes. We recommend organizing a group, building it into onboarding, and keeping it human — make sure to leave room for conversation and questions.

Providing volunteer opportunities

Something is incredibly fulfilling about mission in motion while directly being a part of it, standing alongside and connecting with other volunteers and program attendees. Sort donations at a food bank. Usher for a performance. Staff a registration table at an event. Serve as a guide for a youth program. These experiences in the field are as important as those in the boardroom.

Reporting through storytelling and impact

Forgetting the human impact piece of the work is easy when you're caught up in governance process, financials, and committee reports. Remind directors regularly and vividly about why the work matters through storytelling and impact reporting. This tactic doesn't have to be elaborate, either. Consider doing things like opening board meetings with a mission story, writing impact reports that highlight both numbers and people, sharing photos or video from programs, or inviting staff to present about their work.

TIP

Start your next meeting with a *mission moment.* Invite a director or staff to share something they experienced, witnessed, or heard that brought the organization's mission to life. Tee someone up so they can come prepared and inspire those in the room. Hearing these personal stories before jumping into board business can ground every in *why* they're there.

Pushing for advocacy and ambassadorship

For fostering a sense of connection to the mission, advocacy and ambassadorship are the most personal engagement requests of all. You're asking directors to take the mission out into the world, into their everyday lives. Ask directors to share the story of why they serve on social media and with family and friends. Connect them to donors who share similar passions or backgrounds.

Invite directors to represent the board at community events alongside the executive leader. Request participation in educational conversations with local leaders and legislators. All these moments are places for the board to share why they're proud of their service. Plus, when you ask someone to put their name and voice behind something, they're more likely to stay invested. We talk more about advocacy and ambassadorship in Chapter 14.

Strategically Leveraging Expertise

We're pretty sure directors love nothing more than being valued for the expertise and perspectives they bring to the table. Finding creative and meaningful ways that take advantage of their professional and personal abilities is key to keeping people engaged.

Encouraging committee participation

As we discuss in Chapter 11, committees are the engines powering the board's work between meetings and one of the greatest sources of activity in board engagement. Every director should sit on a committee, and you should give careful thought to match individual expertise with committee needs. You can usually place directors with technical backgrounds where you can best leverage their skills right out of the gate (for example, putting a lawyer on the governance committee or an accountant on finance). Newer directors should rotate through committees (or sit in and observe committee meetings) before consulting with board leadership about where they'd be most effective.

REMEMBER

Make sure your director is excited about serving on a committee. Never force a director to serve on a committee that doesn't get them even more energized about serving on the board. That said, board leadership still needs to manage placement and expectations thoughtfully. Consider these examples:

- A director without any prior board experience or significant knowledge about the organization probably shouldn't start on the governance committee, where they may need to train other directors or draft bylaw updates.
- Someone new to fundraising can still be an exceptional networker and help fill tables at your gala or source auction items from community businesses.

» A director with a finance background can hop onto your finance committee and be successful with only a little bit of orientation.

Pinpointing people for special projects

From time to time, your organization will have board-level, strategic projects that need addressing. Maybe your facility needs an assessment, your brand needs a refresh, or you want to explore a merger with a local organization or update a governance policy. These are great opportunities to engage a director that has the right expertise. Just make sure the project has a defined scope, clear decision-making authority, and a timeline with deliverables.

Keeping People Accountable

When people are held to their commitments and understand how their contributions add to the organization's success, they're more likely to stay motivated to show up for the mission. You want to ensure the board is setting clear goals and expectations for service, calling for regular reflection, and driving group dialogue on how everyone can continue to grow together.

Implementing assessment

Considering assessment as a tool for board engagement may seem counterintuitive, but it's foundational! The assessment process is a chance for board directors to step back, reflect on their service and the board's work, and spend time exclusively thinking about how they can show up better for the mission. It also provides insight into gaps in knowledge, which can inform educational initiatives, and helps board leadership more effectively match opportunities on the board with the skills and expertise unique to each individual. We talk more about board assessment in Chapter 18.

Board fundraising expectations

As discussed in Chapter 13, giving is a vital part of a director's contribution to stewarding the organization's resources for long-term success. That said, giving looks different for everyone. Some directors may write a significant check; others may give a smaller amount, donate their professional services, or contribute in-kind support like supplies. What matters is that the gift is meaningful.

REMEMBER

Every board should strive for 100 percent giving participation from its members. This level of collective commitment shows that the board truly believes in the mission and is willing to step up to support its success.

Instituting an attendance policy

Good attendance is critical to good board service. You can't fulfill your duty of care, loyalty, and obedience (see Chapter 4 for more on these) if you don't know what's going on with the organization. If a director regularly misses meetings, they need to be removed from their position. We talk about this issue in Chapter 8, if you need guidance about attendance and removal.

Recognizing and Appreciating Service

The work of the board can be nonstop. Directors step up and give their time and expertise, their connections, and their own dollars — all voluntarily — on top of their already full lives. Saying thank you costs nothing and is arguably the single most important thing you can do to keep directors engaged.

Gratitude doesn't have to be grandiose to be meaningful, and you'll have many opportunities, big and small, to appreciate one another throughout the year. However, if you're looking for a special moment or just need a little push in the right direction, here are just a few ways to acknowledge directors:

- Handwritten thank-you notes from the executive or board president
- Personal phone calls to acknowledge specific contributions
- Birthday or board-anniversary acknowledgements
- Shoutouts in the organization's newsletters or blogs
- Acknowledgment at community gatherings, galas, and events
- Social media spotlights featuring individuals

TIP

If you're part of board leadership, thank directors publicly in meetings, especially when a director is finishing up their term. Thanking the board for their continued work as a group is also a good idea. Even just being a director is hard work, so thanking everyone for volunteering their time, insights, and passion for the cause fosters a positive, engaged culture.

3

Running Your Board

IN THIS PART . . .

Familiarize yourself with your bylaws with clarity and confidence.

Create and drive a board workplan that actually gets things done and moves the mission forward.

Get a crash course on facilitating board meetings, including taking minutes that can actually be useful.

Determine which board committees you need and how to effectively run them.

IN THIS CHAPTER

» Seeing bylaws as the foundation of good governance

» Breaking down what your bylaws should cover

» Putting together or changing the organization's bylaws

» Working with what's in (or not in) your bylaws

» Keeping your bylaws on the right side of common obstacles

Chapter 8
Living with Your Bylaws

Your organization's bylaws are one of its most significant documents. They serve as the rulebook that governs how your board operates and makes decisions. They dictate everything from how to legally call a meeting and conduct a binding vote to how many directors are needed in the room and what happens if the organization ever needs to dissolve.

WARNING

Every organization has bylaws, yet few directors take the time to read through and understand them. That's a big risk when one misstep can invalidate the board's work.

In this chapter, we examine the most common provisions you find in bylaws, share best practices for key clauses, and offer guidance on how to revise and maintain your bylaws over time. We also cover how bylaws address removing problematic board directors and running compliant board meetings, and what to do when your bylaws don't have the answer.

Understanding Why Bylaws Matter

Every board director in your organization should be able to answer three questions: Who's in charge and gets to make decisions? What's everyone responsible for? Who's protected when things go wrong? We call these questions the three *C's* — control, clarity, and coverage — and your bylaws hold the answers.

- **Control:** Bylaws outline the power structure of the board, answering questions like "Who's eligible to sit on the board, and for how long? Who can sign contracts or cut checks on the organization's behalf? How are decisions made?" And, in the case of conflict or dysfunction, bylaws also go through how to resolve it or remove a director.
- **Clarity:** Bylaws draw lines around who does what work. They define the roles of directors and officers, outline the scope of committee work, and authorize the hiring and scope of work for staff.
- **Coverage:** Most importantly, bylaws offer protection. They outline indemnification for board directors and officers and set key protections to ensure people can participate in governance without taking on unnecessary risk.

WARNING

Failure to follow your organization's bylaws opens your board up to real risk. Taking an action or calling a vote without following proper procedure can have severe consequences, including internal conflict and eroded trust, invalidated decisions, personal liability for directors, legal action, and loss of tax exempt status. The good news is that most of these risks are entirely avoidable when your board understands, follows, and maintains its own bylaws.

Cracking Open the Core Components of Good Bylaws

Although bylaws vary from organization to organization and state to state, some core pieces show up across most well-governed nonprofits, ranging from legally required provisions to widely recommended practices. The following sections look at these components in more detail.

Setting board size and adding/removing board directors

Three key clauses in your bylaws relate to the size of your board, how board directors are added, and how they get removed. Having these provisions be clear is critical so that transitions can go smoothly.

TIP

We recommend a board size of around 9 to 15 people for mid-size to larger organizations. Smaller nonprofits may opt to have a board with five to eight directors, fulfilling key officer roles (president, secretary, and treasurer) with additional advisory roles.

When adding new board directors, you need to define minimum eligibility requirements (age, location, and so on), the nomination process, and the vote threshold to approve new directors. This threshold is often the quorum of the board directors (which we cover in the later section "Quantifying a quorum").

Unfortunately, you may encounter a situation where a director needs to be removed from the board, whether that's because of a conflict of interest, continual disruption of meetings, or otherwise unethical or illegal misconduct. Your duty as a board is to take action to protect the organization and cycle these folks off. Your bylaws should outline the procedures and standards for removal, including the following:

- **Authority:** Who can call a vote to remove a director (it's usually board directors, but sometimes this privilege can be extended to a larger stakeholder group)
- **Grounds for removal:** Whether the removal has to be *for-cause* (such as breach of duty, missed meetings, and so on) or can be *at-will* (no reason required)
- **Administrative procedure:** The threshold for action on votes to remove a director (usually different from regular votes, including special meeting notice requirements, due process, and voting majority)

TIP

In many cases, you can take a variety of steps before jumping to removal, such as personal intervention or communication from the board president or a leave of absence (assuming your bylaws permit).

HELP! MY BYLAWS DON'T COVER HOW TO REMOVE A DIRECTOR

If your bylaws are silent on removal, check your state nonprofit corporation act, which acts as a sort of default rulebook. In many jurisdictions, directors can still be removed, with or without cause, by vote. You also can still request voluntary resignation.

Make sure to maintain a detailed written record, including reasons for removal, any associated evidence and dates of misbehavior, and related communications. Here are some sample criteria you can use that should exist in your board policies and procedures (not your bylaws) so as to give you flexibility in its interpretation and application:

- Violating the conflict-of-interest policy, including failure to disclose a conflict
- Failing to attend a minimum of 75 percent of board meetings in a one-year period
- Failing to attend three consecutive board meetings
- Attempting to use information obtained as a board director in such a way as to derive personal, financial, or other benefit
- Violating the confidentiality policy
- Verbally abusing board directors, staff, or community members
- Physically assaulting board directors, staff, or program participants at any time, in any place
- Actively working to subvert stated board policy or decisions
- Being accused or convicted of a felony
- Behaving improperly in a way that brings or risks bringing negative publicity to the organization
- Speaking against the organization, the board, or the CEO or staff in public
- Making or exhibiting racist or sexist comments or behavior

Specifying terms and term limits

A *term* is the length of time a director serves before they need to be reappointed or reelected. The most common term length is three years, though it can be as little as one year. A three-year term gives board directors time to get up to speed and engage meaningfully.

A *term limit* is the maximum number of terms a director can serve on the board. This restriction allows a rotation of fresh voices and serves as a protection against the consolidation of power into a few hands over time. The most common term structure is to have two three-year terms, for a total of six years of service.

WARNING

Some organizations forgo term limits to protect donor relationships and institutional knowledge. This thinking is flawed. Without term limits, boards get stuck. The same voices dominate the same conversations year after year. Friction grows between new and long-standing directors. Innovation collides with "how we've always done it" thinking. Burnout and disengagement become inevitable. You can steward key relationships and preserve organizational history in many other effective ways, but an indefinite board term isn't one of them. Thorough documentation, strong staff leadership, board alumni networks, and donor stewardship strategy can do all that work.

Establishing meeting norms

One of the more practical things your bylaws establish is the rules related to meetings, from how often they happen to how decisions get made. Here are the main kinds of stipulations the meeting bylaws usually cover:

- **Frequency:** The law generally requires nonprofit boards to meet a minimum of once per year, though most organizations consider having quarterly meetings best practice. Some busy boards even meet every other monthly or monthly! When you're considering meeting frequency, determining the right level of activity and necessary engagement is important.
- **Type:** Different types of meetings are usually categorized by purpose and urgency. Common types include the following:
  - **Regular meetings:** These are recurring, scheduled meetings used to oversee the general business of the organization, from approving budgets to making key decisions.
  - **Special meetings:** Special meetings occur outside the regular schedule and are usually meant to address urgent matters that can't wait until the next regular meeting.
  - **Committee meetings:** These meetings bring together smaller groups to work on projects (finance, governance, fundraising, and so on).

REMEMBER

Depending on your organization, your bylaws may also require additional meetings, whether to report to the director, host elections, or maintain public accountability.

» **Notice:** Your bylaws set the standard for informing directors of upcoming meetings — a regulation people often overlook. A notification is only *valid* if it's delivered through one of the methods your bylaws specify, such as email or mail, and within a certain timeline (for example, 48 hours before meeting). A valid notice includes when and where the meeting is being held and sometimes the agenda. Notice rules ensure transparency, prevent misuse of power, and allow directors adequately to prepare.

» **Format:** Interestingly, your bylaws may also outline the format by which you can hold meetings. In-person meetings have traditionally been the standard, but many organizations now explicitly allow meetings by phone or video conference as well.

WARNING

Failing to provide adequate notice or holding meetings in a format not permitted by your bylaws can invalidate the meeting and any decisions made during it. All this to say, before you book your next board meeting, double check your bylaws!

Quantifying a quorum

To legally hold a meeting and make decisions, your board must have a *quorum*, the minimum number of directors with authority to vote that must be in the room to have an official meeting. State laws often default to a simple majority (51 percent), but your bylaws ultimately dictate what you use, whether as a number or a percentage. A quorum ensures that a small number of board directors can't act on behalf of the organization, with some boards going as far as setting quorum at 100 percent to guarantee full representation.

WARNING

Without a quorum, any decisions made in the meeting are invalid. If your board regularly struggles to reach quorum, it's time to act. Occasional absences are normal, but you need to address chronic absence through direct communication and possibly removal. Some boards lower their quorum threshold to compensate, but doing so risks major decisions being made by an unrepresentative minority.

Making decisions

Generally speaking, one director equals one vote, though not everyone who attends a board meeting has a right to vote. Multiple clauses in your bylaws may affect how you go about casting a vote and making a valid decision, including meeting notice and quorum requirements (which we discuss in the preceding sections), conflict-of-interest disclosure, and voting methods. Before you make a decision as a board, check the bylaws to make sure you're legally casting your vote. A few things to consider include the following:

» **Voting electronically:** If you're with an older organization, your bylaws may not have been updated to specifically include voting by email; even if they have, you still may be looking strict requirements for approval.

» **Voting by proxy:** Most bylaws typically don't allow *proxy* votes, meaning directors can't have someone else show up to the board meeting and vote in their place.

Electing officers and running elections

Every board needs officers to lead its work and keep the organization running smoothly. Although state laws vary, most nonprofit organizations are required to have a president/chair, secretary, and treasurer at minimum. Many boards also add a Vice President, to provide stability and a path for succession. In some states, one person can hold more than one role, but generally best practice is to have seperate people in each position for checks and balances.

Your bylaws outline which officer roles your board has, what each role is responsible for, and how those positions are filled and vacated. This information also needs to include the election process, term lengths, and procedures for removing an officer if needed. You can read more about all things officers in Chapter 5.

Standing up committees and task forces

Committees and task forces are the engines of the board, advancing work on major projects in-between meetings and diving deeper into specific areas that full board sessions can't. Your bylaws should detail what standing committees your organization has, their scope and authority, and the requirements of their operation: from whether they require a chair/co-chair to how they are expected to record their activity.

Keep your bylaws lean by defining only your minimum required committees. You can always add more committees and task forces without adding them to your bylaws. Make sure you review your overall committee structure every few years to verify that it reflects where your organization actually is and what it needs. We take a closer look at different committees — and how to operate them well — in Chapter 11.

Identifying indemnification

Your indemnification clause is one of the most important provisions of your bylaws (and likely one you've never read). It outlines the organization's obligations to cover legal fees, settlements, and other costs that directors, officers, or employees incur in the case of legal action because of their service. It provides an additional shield from personal liability, making recruiting and retaining board directors easier.

TIP

Indemnification is not enough. Your organization must also pair this provision with valid Directors and Officers insurance, as well as General Liability, to fully address the risk of personal liability risk. Check out Chapter 17 for more about what insurance you need to protect yourself and your organization.

Addressing administrative processes

Your bylaws are home to a litany of administrative provisions that, though not as exciting, are every bit as critical as the other components. These items include how to amend your bylaws, the terms of your fiscal year, budget adoption requirements, audit requirements, and how to dissolve your organization.

REMEMBER

Policy requirements for record keeping and documentation, conflict of interest, and whistleblowing should also be required by your bylaws, but the complete language for these policies should live in your policy manual (see Chapter 16).

Writing and Revising Your Bylaws

Your organization's bylaws are a living document, and you need to regularly review, update, and amend them to reflect the group's evolving mission, context and legal requirements. By "regularly," we mean at least every few years.

Starting from scratch versus inheriting bylaws

Most boards fall into one of two camps: those who are building their bylaws from the ground up and those who have preexisting bylaws from whoever came before them.

» Starting from scratch is relatively easy. You have a blank slate and the opportunity to be intentional from the beginning.

- Inheriting bylaws is an entirely different challenge. The document you inherit may be poorly written or simply never have been updated to reflect how the organization actually works today. In some cases, boards have operated in violation of their bylaws without ever knowing.

Either way, the move is the same: Read them, understand them, and make sure they actually work for your organization.

Amending bylaws

During the life of an organization, many good, valid reasons to amend the bylaws pop up, including adding staff for the first time, changing the size of the board, strengthening or adding term limit policies, updating how meetings or votes can be held, and changing administrative procedures.

The first step to updating your bylaws is . . . to check your bylaws! Most explain procedures for how to propose changes, including a required notice period and how many votes are needed for approval.

TIP

If you're responsible for proposing a change, create a working copy of your bylaws and mark up your proposed edits so directors can see what you're adding or removing. Add the item to the agenda of your next board meeting, open the floor for discussion, and call for a vote.

REMEMBER

After the board has approved the amendment, make sure the vote is documented in your meeting minutes. Save a clean, updated version of your bylaws dated with the effective date in a location all directors can access. Keep both the final version and the redline for your records and as part of your audit trail.

Consulting a lawyer

In most cases, your board can manage routine bylaw updates without legal support. That includes things like clarifying language, updating committees, adjusting meeting frequency, or aligning with common practices.

TIP

As a rule of thumb, if a proposed change affects how power is exercised, such as how decisions are made or how the organization is legally defined, you probably want to pick up a phone and call a lawyer. That includes altering quorum or voting rights, the membership structure, or officer powers or making large scale changes across multiple sections.

Putting Bylaws into Practice

Your bylaws are your governance manual, not your operating manual. They outline the rules of the game (who has authority, how decisions get made, what protections exist), but they can't (and shouldn't) answer every question that will likely come up in the life of your organization. The following sections discuss what to do when you need more specificity than your bylaws to provide and how to take action when you find a gap in what your bylaws cover.

Distinguishing between bylaws and policy

Your bylaws and your policies are the key governing tools of your board.

- *Bylaws* are the rules, providing the broader framework for legal action for the organization. They're adopted at the time of formation and are amended as needed. For example, a bylaw defines that the board of directors must meet at least once every year.
- *Policies* are guidelines that support day to day activity, drilling down into more specific detail pertinent to the organization. They tend to change more often and are easier to modify than your bylaws. For example, a policy defines that you will collect updated conflict of interest forms every January.

TIP

If you're trying to figure out whether something belongs in your bylaws or your policy manual, use the following framework:

- **Stability:** By design, bylaws should be hard to change. If something needs to be able to evolve more frequently as the organization or board grows, it belongs in policy.
- **Authority versus execution:** Bylaws establish who has the power to do something, whereas policy outlines how that power is exercised on a day-to-day basis. If you're writing a rule that grants or limits authority, it's probably a bylaw. If you're describing how the work is getting done this year, it's a policy.
- **Legal exposure:** Bylaws create legally enforceable obligations and protections. Policy governs internal behavior but doesn't usually carry the same weight. If you need something to be flexible, put it in a policy.

Acting when the bylaws are silent

Imagine this situation: The treasurer suddenly gets ill and is unable to fulfill their duties for an extended period of time. Your bylaws outline how to remove a treasurer and elect a new one but not how to navigate a temporary absence. Can you appoint someone to fill in? Can the president sign checks in the meantime? What do you do?

REMEMBER

Your bylaws can't possibly cover every single scenario your board may face. Gaps are inevitable, and finding one doesn't mean that you're stuck or that no one's accountable. Instead, you need to interpret what your bylaws *do* say and apply professional judgment to fill the gap.

Robert's Rules of Order (PublicAffairs) offers a set of principles for interpreting governing documents when ambiguity arises, including the following:

- If it's clear, follow it. If you want to do things differently, you can't just vote to do so. You'd have to amend the bylaws.
- No interpretation can conflict with another bylaw.
- When in doubt, pick the interpretation that causes the least damage or interference with other bylaws.
- When a specific rule and general rule conflict, the specific one wins.
- If something isn't written out or included in your bylaws, it doesn't mean it's permitted.
- Penalties can't be increased or decreased without amendment.

TIP

When your bylaws are truly silent, make sure to document your reasoning for your chosen action, proceed in good faith, and inform the full board. If the gap comes up again, that may be a sign your bylaws need an update. Flip to the earlier section "Amending bylaws" for more on bylaw updates.

Avoiding Common Bylaw Pitfalls

Bylaws don't have to be complicated to cause problems. The most common issues boards face come down to a few avoidable mistakes. Watch out for the following:

- **Ignored:** Your organization has bylaws, but no one ever looks at them. Yikes! As we say throughout the chapter, your bylaws are one of the most important board documents. Ignoring them is one of the easiest ways to end up in trouble. Ensure everyone has access to the active copy and consider adding a bylaw orientation to your onboarding.

- **Generic:** You can find fantastic free templates your organization can use as a starting point for writing or improving your bylaws. But however tempted you may be to copy and paste them or adopt them as-is, remember that generic provisions rarely reflect your specific context or needs. If you draw on these resources, make sure you tailor them specifically to your mission, beliefs, and operations as well as the requirements of your state.
- **Hyper-detailed:** If the bylaws state your board meetings need to happen on the second Tuesday of every month at 7:00 p.m., changing the time or date to meet shifting needs becomes a compliance risk. Your bylaws should be written flexibly: Define principles and leave room for interpretation. Use ranges rather than specific numbers. Separate operating policies and procedural stuff into a separate manual.
- **Vague:** On the other hand, being too vague comes with its own risks and can lead to disputed elections, power struggles, decision paralysis, and legal exposure. Make sure to test your language after drafting a provision: If two or three people read this wording, would they come to the same conclusion? If not, maybe revisit your language.
- **Incomplete:** Failure to align your bylaws with state and federal regulations can lead to serious repercussions including legal liability and loss of tax status. You may be required to meet a wide array of provisions, including regulations on voting, director and member rights, liability and conflict of interest, and dissolution. If you're writing bylaws from scratch or making big changes, consult with a lawyer.

IN THIS CHAPTER

» **Understanding why you need a board-level workplan every year**

» **Figuring out how to start from square one**

» **Engineering a workplan that drives your board toward success**

Chapter 9
Creating Your Board's Annual Plan

Let's face it: Nonprofit boards are busy! Every year is chock-full of board meetings, project deadlines, community gatherings, and many other obligations and responsibilities. It's easy to overlook something, especially as a group of volunteers — and especially as your organization grows.

In this chapter, we examine how to create an annual workplan for your board. A workplan is a useful tool that's critical for shaping and driving board activity every year, from highlighting deadlines for key filings to mapping out what must happen for your organization to enact key parts of your strategy and execute your mission. As the saying goes, if you fail to plan, you're planning to fail.

Planning Your Year Is Nonnegotiable

Every year your board has meetings and events to run, a variety of responsibilities to fulfill, and compliance requirements to meet. When you don't have a plan for how the year unfolds, meetings will get booked at the last minute, critical decisions will be rushed, and important governance and strategy work will get short shrift or be skipped entirely.

An *annual workplan* is a key governance tool that facilitates accountability and helps ensure the board's activities support the organization's goals. It also specifies what will get done, when, and by whom during your fiscal year, and serves as a template to track the board's work. Some things in a comprehensive workplan include:

- Board meeting times, dates, and locations
- Committee meeting times, dates, locations, membership, and key deliverables
- Regulatory and legal deadlines and responsibilities, such as tax filings, annual reports, and insurance renewals
- Financial oversight milestones, including budget approvals, audit requirements, and IRS Form 990 submissions (see Chapter 3)
- Strategic plan milestones and projects
- Other board responsibilities, including anything from fundraising events to advocacy work and public relations

Because board directors are volunteers, their time and bandwidth likely vary throughout the year. A well-built workplan respects that reality. It distributes tasks strategically across the calendar year, so work doesn't pile up in one quarter. Additionally, by giving advance notice of what's expected of them, it sets them up for success by allowing them to plan their time in advance and flag conflicts early.

TIP

A workplan can also be a valuable recruiting tool. Prospective board directors want to know what they're signing up for in terms of time commitment and workload, and it can give them a realistic sense of the larger work of the board. Sharing your annual workplan ensures that candidates are prepared for the challenge before making the leap.

REMEMBER

When done well, your workplan becomes the single source of information that your board can return to in every meeting to check progress, flag things you've missed, and confirm that you're spending your time on the right tasks.

Looking at Who Owns the Planning Process

Setting the annual calendar is a collaborative effort between the organization's key leaders, and the process itself can be just as valuable as the final product. Sure, creating your workplan takes time, but it can be a rich, collaborative conversation between the nonprofit's board and staff that aligns the organization around strategic goals, clarifies priorities for the year, and ensures everyone understands who is ultimately responsible for what.

Board chair and executive

The board chair, in partnership with the CEO or executive director (if there is one), provides the overarching leadership for the workplan. Together they are the prime architects of the plan, bringing complementary perspectives to their work: The chair is focused on governance, and the executive shares relevant information about organizational deadlines and staff capability.

Once the plan is adopted, the chair develops meeting agendas that advance the workplan and keeps the board working toward strategic goals and priorities. The executive supports this work by providing necessary reports and updates, informing board directors of opportunities for participation, and serving in an advisory capacity on committees.

Board secretary

The board secretary plays a critical role in the execution of the workplan by managing documentation and overseeing logistics. This includes coordinating board and committee meeting dates, ensuring materials from meetings and projects are properly saved and stored, and monitoring key filing and compliance deadlines.

Committee chairs

Committee chairs create their own committee-level workplans, which should feed directly back into the broader board-wide workplan. Committee workplans should include project and planning details for assigned deliverables and deadlines. Committee chairs should coordinate with the board secretary to schedule meetings, as well as ensure minutes are taken, work is assigned and accounted for, and critical conversations are brought back up to the boardroom.

Full board

Once a draft workplan is assembled, the full board must have an opportunity to weigh in before the plan is finalized. Create a shared document for directors to review and comment on, or schedule a presentation where directors can discuss the plan and ask questions. This step helps build ownership of the plan and may reveal oversights or blind spots. At the end of the day, putting together a workplan is a team effort.

Starting Your Workplan from Scratch

If your board hasn't made a workplan before, it can feel intimidating to start. But your first plan doesn't need to be complicated. All you need is a calendar with the dates, times, and location(s) of regular board and committee meetings, as well as key compliance deadlines, such as your IRS Form 990 submission deadline. Then, review your bylaws to ensure you haven't missed anything else that's critical to your mission.

From there, add in a little more detail every year, including setting priorities or assigning projects for each committee, scheduling board participation in major fundraising campaigns, or laying out plans for overseeing other strategic initiatives. Your first plan doesn't have to be perfect; it just has to be in place. The following sections provide some guidance for getting started.

Mapping out the planning process

The best time to build your workplan is in the final quarter of your fiscal year. Here's a guide for timing the work so you don't end up starting your next fiscal year without a plan in place:

- **Weeks 1–2:** Reflect on the past year. Gather progress reports on the strategic plan, review committee accomplishments, get operational and financial updates from your executive leadership, and figure out if your board needs to address any issues in the upcoming year.
- **Weeks 3–4:** Seek input from committee chairs. Either meet with chairs individually or hold an executive session to discuss priorities for the year ahead. What worked last year? What did you miss? Where do you need more support?
- **Weeks 5–6:** Meet with executive leadership to review the organization's priorities against operational and programming realities. Pick out opportunities for board engagement and highlight fundraising campaigns or asks for board participation.
- **Weeks 7–8:** Build the draft calendar and workplan. Lock in all recurring dates with your secretary; layer in known deadlines and key projects; and add in programming touchpoints, recruitment timelines, board education opportunities, and social activities. Don't forget regular holidays and other known conflicts.
- **Weeks 9–11:** Circulate the draft plan for review by the board. Give directors an easy way to flag issues and ask questions or offer changes. Set a very clear deadline, so final approval isn't held up.

» **Week 12:** Bring the final workplan before the board, walking directors through any high-level details one last time, and then call for a vote of approval. Once the plan is passed, distribute it to directors.

TIP

Before finalizing your workplan, run through these reflection questions:

- Is any committee carrying an outsize share of the work, and if so, how can it be redistributed?
- Is any individual board director assigned too much work?
- Are meeting *cadences* (how frequently you hold them) still reasonable, given all the work you have planned?
- Is any quarter overloaded to the point that the board may struggle to meet or miss deadlines?
- Did you forget any of the core elements of a workplan? (See the later section "Covering the Core Elements of a Board Workplan.")

REMEMBER

The goal is to create a workplan that's ambitious but achievable by a group of volunteers. Distribute the work fairly and respect people's time while also being aware of the fact that all this work has to happen after hours for most folks.

Covering the Core Elements of a Board Workplan

A strong annual workplan goes beyond just listing meeting dates and compliance deadlines. It captures every recurring responsibility the board carries, organized across the year in a way that ensures the workload is manageable. While all boards must meet some universal legal requirements, every organization will have different governance responsibilities, committee activities, public events, programming details, and strategic priorities. The following sections outline essential components for your workplan.

Meeting dates

All full board meetings should be calendared *before* the start of the year, with times, dates, and locations confirmed in advance. The same should be done for meetings planned by any active committees. The earlier the meeting calendar is set and distributed, the less likely conflicts arise.

TIP

In Chapter 8, we talk about common meeting cadences and minimum requirements, and recommend that you start your scheduling by looking at your bylaws to determine your minimum required activity.

We also recommend trying to adopt a regular meeting cadence that directors can easily follow, whether it's quarterly, every other month, or monthly. Meeting more than once a month as a full board will be unmanageable for most directors. The same goes with committee meetings — adopt a cadence reflecting the volume of work that needs to get completed.

Annual retreats

Consider adding a retreat to your calendar. Unlike a regular board meeting, a retreat gives directors dedicated time to step back from the regular work of governance and engage more deeply on specific strategic priorities or the work of the organization. It's also an opportunity to provide continuing education opportunities for your board.

Retreats can be especially valuable during strategic planning cycles, leadership transitions, or other major organizational milestones where focused conversation can strengthen engagement in the boardroom. That being said, don't wait for a big moment to justify a retreat. Build one in to your calendar every year.

TIP

We highly recommend working with a third-party facilitator to run your next retreat. A professional can consult with your board leadership to clarify goals for the session, shape the agenda, and ensure your retreat is an interactive, high-value use of everyone's time.

Board socials

Don't forget to include the fun social events too! Many people join boards not just for the mission but to build and connect with their community. Whether it's an end-of-year holiday party or a musical program or play you're all going to see together, these experiences can deepen the connection among board directors and foster a serious sense of trust and belonging that will only help in the boardroom. We talk about ways to engage your board in Chapter 7.

Compliance, finance, and legal deadlines

Like all nonprofits, your organization has a set of recurring nonnegotiable deadlines each year. Inserting these dates into your workplan ensures your board will have adequate time to fulfill its part of the organization's financial and legal obligations. While every organization will customize its approach to oversight, most boards will want to include dates for filing federal taxes and financial reports (Form 990), filing annual state reports and solicitation registrations, renewing insurance policies, submitting regulatory reports specific to your organization or sector, planning and approving the budget, completing an audit, scheduling financial reviews (for example, quarterly or midyear), and reviewing and updating governance policies.

TIP

If your organization has a CEO or executive director, they likely have systems in place for tracking many of these deadlines and obligations. Partner with them to familiarize yourself with these tracking systems and to find the right touchpoint for board reporting.

Committee activities

Just as the board should have a workplan, so should each of your committees. These plans should mirror the structure of the larger annual workplan and provide more detail about key projects, responsibilities, and deadlines that individual committees deal with over the course of the year. The committee-level plans are folded into the broader annual workplan, with overlapping deadlines and other conflicts being identified and resolved.

Critical board maintenance work

In addition to the work it does to further the organization's mission, the board has to work on itself, and it's easy to underestimate just how much time and coordination this type of internal maintenance takes.

Much of this work can be assigned to a specific committee to develop and deliver. The following sections highlight three areas of board maintenance that cannot be ignored or overlooked: board recruitment and orientation, conflict of interest management, and continuing education.

Recruiting and onboarding

Recruiting and onboarding new board directors is often more demanding than you expect. A form of hiring, it involves searching for and identifying candidates, conducting interviews, arranging site visits, and preparing new directors to serve. The process can stretch across months and nearly every director of your board may play a part, so it's critical to clearly chart it in your calendar. For a full breakdown of the process, see Chapter 6.

Updating your COI reports

As we note in Chapter 3, you have a legal duty to ensure that board directors are operating with the best interest of the organization in mind. Conflict of interest (COI) management is a key way to achieve this. Every board director should revisit and update their COI report annually, not just when things change. Marking a specific due date on the calendar ensures that directors don't forget to complete these reports. See Chapter 16 to read more about COI management.

Continuing education

Continuing education is the cornerstone of effective and ethical governance. Whether you include a guest presenter at a meeting, read and discuss a chapter from this book, or plan a learning session at your annual retreat, make sure education is a thoughtfully planned part of your year. Leverage the information gathered from your annual board self-assessment to identify knowledge gaps and pick topics that can benefit your whole board. See Chapter 18 to find out more about self-assessment.

Executive oversight responsibilities

If your organization has an executive leader, conduct an annual performance evaluation. That process, including the preparation, collection of feedback, and formal presentation of the review to the executive, needs to have dedicated time on the calendar. See Chapter 19 for more on how!

Fundraising campaigns and events

The board plays an important role in fundraising, including helping cultivate donors, attending events, and being an ambassador for the mission in their communities. By including fundraising touchpoints in your workplan, you are setting clear expectations and ensuring you get the level of participation your organization needs to be successful. Some common fundraising touchpoints that directors should be aware of, and prepared to support, include annual fundraising campaigns and events (like galas), stewardship moments (like thank-you calls or letters), deadlines for making personal contributions, and grant deadlines.

Programming highlights

To be a great board director, you need to be personally connected to the mission, and one of the best ways to make this connection is through programs your organization runs. Getting out of the boardroom and into the trenches has a way of deepening your commitment and reminding you why you signed to serve.

AVOIDING OVERDEPENDENCE ON STAFF

Your board, not the nonprofit's staff, are responsible for fulfilling your legal duties and responsibilities. While you may sometimes need staff support to get a particular task done, the board needs to be able to do most of its own administrative work. This means board directors should be scheduling their own meetings, taking minutes at those meetings, coordinating their communications with each other, and managing board-related documents with the input of organizational staff only as needed.

Your annual workplan should include a curated selection of programming opportunities that allow your directors to engage with the mission directly. The right events will look different for every organization. An arts organization can highlight important performances or exhibition openings. An education nonprofit may invite the board to a showcase of student work. A food bank can schedule a few volunteer shifts. Other opportunities may include open houses and public tours, workshops and classes, community programming like local business fairs and networking events, as well as other outreach opportunities.

REMEMBER

Don't include every program on the board's annual workplan. It's more effective to create a separate program calendar that sits alongside the board calendar so directors can get a fuller picture of organizational programming and find the right activity for them.

Keeping the Calendar Alive

Creating a calendar in January means nothing if you abandon it by March. The value of having a workplan comes in regular using and maintaining it. Here are our recommendations to ensure your document doesn't just get thrown in a drawer:

- Assign a steward, typically the board chair or secretary, who's responsible for reminding the board of upcoming obligations and for updating the plan when new action items are identified.
- Review the workplan in preparation for every board or committee meeting.
- Make the workplan part of every board packet, with a brief update of what's on the 90-day horizon and a celebration of anything accomplished.
- Update the workplan as progress is made, adding action items for the board to work on between meetings.

» Adjust deadlines or deliverables as priorities or resources shift, being realistic when something sidetracks you, and accept changes with grace and understanding. Things happen!

A board that can adapt its plan without losing momentum or sight of its goals is a resilient board. It's critical to maintain a high degree of flexibility and uphold the collaborative spirit that allowed you to build the workplan in the first place. Your ultimate goal is keeping your governance duties organized and your mission impact on track.

REMEMBER

At least once a year, usually during the final quarter, make sure to take time to review your workplan as a whole. What did the board accomplish? What did you miss and why? What should change for next year? This reflection and commitment to doing better with each iteration of your plan is what turns good boards into great ones.

IN THIS CHAPTER

» Understanding why board meetings matter

» Writing solid, accurate board meeting minutes

» Managing Board Meeting Issues and how to troubleshoot them

Chapter 10
Running a Great Board Meeting

Board meetings are where magic happens. It's a moment when the full board comes together to talk about the mission, oversee the strategic direction of the organization, and make important decisions. Not to mention, sometimes there are free snacks.

In all seriousness, board meetings are the backbone of good governance. When well-run, everyone leaves feeling energized and clear on what comes next. When they're not, they waste everyone's time and chip away at both the trust and momentum your organization depends on.

Running a great board meeting comes down to a lot of preparation, collaboration, and creating and upholding the conditions for honest conversation. This might seem like a tall task, especially if the board is not much more than a group of casual acquaintances. But it's more achievable than you might think.

In this chapter, we look at what makes a board meeting effective and what gets in the way. We cover how to prepare useful materials, build an agenda that generates real discussion, and how to take minutes that protect the board.

Defining What Makes a Great Board Meeting

Board meetings are essential for keeping nonprofit organizations focused on their mission. Simply put, each meeting brings together the entire board to discuss and oversee the organization's strategic direction, review its programming and financial performance, and exercise general oversight. In practice, this can involve the following tasks:

- Debating and deciding on strategic priorities
- Reviewing financial matters
- Asking questions about the organization's performance or operations
- Hearing directly from executive staff
- Ensuring compliance with legal and regulatory standards

However, not all board meetings are created equal. A well-run meeting leaves directors feeling energized, with clarity about their next steps and a stronger sense of partnership with each other and the organization. When run poorly, meetings can tank morale, drive dysfunction, and undermine the mission.

Luckily, running a good board meeting isn't rocket science. The next sections cover the three things we think drive the difference between a well-run and a poorly executed meeting.

Focusing on the highest priorities

The most important thing about board meetings is making sure you're discussing the right issues. With the full board in the room, this isn't the time to read off committee updates, debate whether the gala should be a garden party or a black-tie affair, or approve individual line-item expenditures. That's what committees, staff, and email chains are for.

REMEMBER

Board meetings should be where high-level conversations about the organization come to life. Where is the organization going, and why? Do any opportunities or threats facing the organization need added perspective or action? Are there questions that only the board has the authority to answer?

While your organization's stage of maturity and the context of your mission inevitably influence the agenda, never lose sight of the big-picture thinking that's critical to good governance and long-term sustainability. Small organizations or those just starting out may find the boardroom stuck in weedy conversations about day-to-day operations, with loose agendas and limited long-range thinking. Push back against this tendency toward micromanagement and leave the routine reports and operational work in the capable hands of committees and staff. The more attention the board can focus on high-level issues, the stronger the organization will be.

Keeping directors engaged in the conversation

You've made the effort to get everyone in the same room at the same time, so put their time and energy to its highest and best use: discussion and debate. Having the right agenda means nothing if you don't get directors to meaningfully engage with each other on the topics in front of them. Here are ways to ensure meetings provide serious engagement instead of just being status updates:

» Build the agenda around topics informed by the organization's strategic goals and priorities for the year. When possible, include at least one or two reflection questions on the agenda so directors can prepare before the meeting.

» Compile committee updates into a written report that gets sent out in the board packet before the meeting. Instead of having committee chairs read their updates, carve out time for board directors to ask questions.

» Send the board packet out at least five days ahead of the meeting to give directors enough time to read the materials, including talking points or discussion questions. The more prepared board directors are, the more productive and powerful discussions will be.

» Assign someone (for example, the board secretary) to gather questions and feedback before the meeting.

Maintaining confidentiality

Board meetings work best when directors feel free to speak *in draft*, meaning they can float half-formed ideas, ask uncomfortable questions, and push back during discussions without fearing their words will be leaked and come back to haunt them or back them into a corner. Regularly remind directors to maintain the confidentiality of board business and avoid gossip (even with fellow board directors). Gossip and loose talk can erode trust quickly.

WARNING

In the age of video meeting platforms like Zoom and Microsoft Teams and emergent technologies like AI note-taking apps, it may seem convenient to record a meeting for future reference or to allow absent board directors to catch up. Resist that temptation. Recording board conversations comes with serious legal risks and fundamentally changes the dynamic in the room. It's basic human psychology: When people think they're being recorded, they stop speaking their mind and start managing their image. The honest, productive conversation you're hoping to foster will disappear.

Our recommendation? The convenience isn't worth the risks and tradeoffs. Leave AI and video recording out of the boardroom and rely on the secretary to take accurate minutes of each meeting.

Preparing for the Meeting

A great meeting doesn't just happen. It requires careful planning, including deciding who gets to be in the room, where and when the meeting is held, and what information to provide in advance so people can show up and jump right in. A little work on the front end will make all the difference.

Deciding who should attend

It goes without saying: All board directors should attend meetings. But did you know that people who aren't on the board can also attend meetings? In fact, who is and isn't allowed in the boardroom is entirely up to you as a board.

Executive leadership

The executive leader attends board meetings to provide updates and insights on the operational health and day-to-day activities of the organization. They may report on financial performance or mission impact or inform the board of trends in the nonprofit's sector. They don't typically have a right to vote.

Senior staff

Sometimes senior staff may be invited to attend a board meeting to provide direct insight into programs, operations, or potential risks. They're usually there to support the executive and enhance decision-making by adding a functional-level perspective. In large organizations, it's typical to see the entire executive team (the CEO, chief financial officer, chief operations officer, and so on) in the board-room at every meeting, on standby to offer additional information if needed.

Subject-matter experts

You may have a subject-matter expert in the boardroom for many reasons. For example, you may ask legal counsel to advise the board on certain risks, auditors to present their findings, architects to talk about capital building plans, and so on. Carve out a specific amount of time on the agenda for these guests to make their presentation and set expectations, both with them and the board, about how they can best use that time. Once their portion of the agenda is over, they should be excused.

Members of the public

Most board meetings are not open to the public, though in some cases, such as with a government board or city commission, you may be required to do so. You also can intentionally invite the public to a meeting or town hall to build trust.

WARNING

If you choose to have open meetings, be very careful about what you include on the agenda. Confidentiality becomes impossible, and the stakes are much higher for the topics that are discussed. Save controversial issues and legal matters for another time.

Choosing the right format

Choosing a meeting format, including identifying the best times, location, and frequency, is unique to every nonprofit, and will reflect the organization's reach, size, and scope.

Online or in person

The first question is whether you'll be holding meetings online, in person, or a mix of both. Each approach has pros and cons.

In-person meetings are fantastic for building personal connections with fellow board directors and potentially getting on-site where the organization does its work. Nothing can really replace the magic of being in the same room as other people during a conversation. That being said, in-person meetings can present barriers in the form of commuting time and costs.

Web-conferencing tools like Zoom and Microsoft Teams are great for including directors who can't attend in person, but they add a layer of complication to ensuring people can participate properly. If you find out later that a director attending the meeting online couldn't hear, and a vote was taken, the entire vote may be invalidated.

TIP

The board should be capable of navigating the online platforms and tools you use. Before deciding whether to meet in person or online, check your bylaws. Some organizations, such as public boards and government commissions must meet in a physical location that's accessible to the public. And if your bylaws are outdated, you may not be allowed to use web-conferencing platforms. Don't risk invalidating decisions made at your meetings due to an administrative error!

Time and frequency

How often and when you meet will reflect the schedules and social diversity (retirees, parents with young children, working adults, and so on) of your board and staff. A school board may choose to meet in the evening so that both parents and school leadership can attend. A theatre organization that wants to include artists in its board meetings may need to find a time during the day that doesn't conflict with classes or rehearsals. Find a time that aligns with the majority's availability and poll the board at least once a year on the date, time, and location of your meetings.

REMEMBER

Be transparent about the meeting schedule when recruiting new directors. Give access to the annual board calendar (see Chapter 9) as soon reasonable so they can confirm their availability. If meeting times or locations are an issue, it's better to know that sooner rather than later.

TIP

Although directors are not typically paid for their service, many organizations offer reasonable reimbursement for travel to and from board-related meetings and activities, especially when the distance is greater than usual.

Providing clear notice of the meeting

Once you've decided who is going to be in the boardroom during a meeting, you must let them know when and where it will be. This may seem straightforward, but the specifics of the notice are governed by your bylaws and state law. Jump to Chapter 8 to find out how to provide proper notice of board meetings.

WARNING

If you fail to properly give notice within the prescribed time or by a valid method (for example, email), you may end up invalidating the board meeting and any decisions made during it.

Putting together the board packet

We firmly believe that a board packet can make or break a meeting. A well-organized packet gives board directors access to relevant information ahead of time so they can show up at meetings informed, ready to ask questions, and prepared to make decisions. It also sends a signal about what deserves board-level attention. Not everything makes the packet, and not everything should.

Here's what a board packet should include:

- » The meeting agenda, with time allotted to each issue before the board and built-in discussion questions
- » Minutes from the previous meeting, for reference and approval
- » An executive/management report providing a high-level update on the organization's health and progress toward strategic priorities
- » Committee reports, uniformly formatted for easy reading
- » Decision memos, outlining any items requiring a board vote, with a clear recommendation/rationale
- » Financial reports and visual reports
- » Informational material, when needed, to support debate and discussion

Here's what to leave out:

- » Operational details like staff scheduling, program logistics, and the like
- » Raw data without context or analysis (Numbers need narrative.)
- » Documents so lengthy it won't be read (Think one- or two-page docs at most.)
- » Anything else that doesn't require board-level attention

Leveraging the board packet

After assembling the board packet, here are a few things to do, before and during the meeting, to get the most out of the prework. First, send the packet at least five days in advance and ask directors to submit questions to the secretary in advance. At the start of the meeting, the president should briefly summarize each agenda idea to keep people focused. And, throughout the meeting, never repeat or read information in the packet verbatim.

REMEMBER

Directors are expected to read the packet before the meeting as a responsibility of their service. If directors seem unfamiliar with particular issues, push discussion of the topic to another date. Don't reward bad behavior by providing detailed summaries of the info in the packet. Have the board chair follow up before the next meeting, checking in with individual directors to get feedback. Finally, make sure your packet is manageable. If it's 80 pages of dense text on a wide variety of topics, you've created a problem. (Also, we doubt all of it requires board attention.)

Building an Engaging Agenda

The agenda is the foundation of a board meeting. A clear, well-organized, focused agenda will lead to a meeting that feels the same way. An agenda that's overloaded or disorganized guarantees that no work will get done. Although it seems deceptively simple to write an agenda, many boards consistently make mistakes: They pack in too much for one meeting or sequence things poorly or treat the agenda as an afterthought rather than a powerful governance tool.

Setting the agenda (and who owns it)

It's important to start by clarifying that the board president is the leader in the boardroom and responsible for both setting the agenda and facilitating the meeting. In healthy organizations, the president develops the agenda in partnership with the CEO or executive director, ensuring that what gets discussed in board meetings is both responsive to the nonprofit's current situation and reflective of the bigger picture. Neither perspective alone is enough.

The board secretary will often support this process by drafting the agenda for the president. They're usually also responsible for the meeting minutes, and because your board agenda serves as the perfect template for taking minutes, it's a bit of a no-brainer to task them with both duties.

As the board grows, the president may also choose to include committee chairs in agenda preparation. Chairs can provide status updates and flag anything that warrants discussion by the broader board.

TIP

If the goal is to get a board packet out at least five days in advance of a meeting, we recommend getting together with everyone involved in setting the agenda approximately two weeks before to discuss agenda topics and draft meeting ideas. From there, the board president and secretary can finalize the agenda and get it into a board packet for distribution to individual directors.

Structuring time around what matters

When crafting your board agenda, include the following items:

- Begin with a mission moment to remind board directors how the organization's mission has touched their lives outside the boardroom.
- Focus on anything that has changed since you last met and how it has affected the organization. Discuss any risks or decisions that need to be addressed.
- Provide updates on the organization's progress on strategic goals and whether any timelines need to be adjusted.
- Allow time for discussion and questions about written committee reports included in the board packet.

Including an executive session

We recommend that every nonprofit board meeting include an *executive session*, in which the board meets without the executive leader (if you have one) in attendance. This should be a standing meeting, not one that's convened as a reaction to a crisis or as a workaround for hard conversations. It must be a regular, normalized part of how the board governs itself. Used well, an executive session creates space for three important governance conversations:

- **Board self-governance:** This is a chance to check whether board directors are aligned and operating at the right altitude, neither micromanaging the organization nor being too detached. Is your governance helping or hindering leadership?
- **CEO performance and support:** It's also an opportunity to discuss the board's role in overseeing the executive leader's performance. Are expectations clear? Does the CEO have what they need to succeed? Do you have any real-time feedback from staff and stakeholders?
- **Confidential risk management:** An executive session is the ideal forum in which to discuss matters that require confidentiality, such as litigation, investigations, compensation issues, succession planning, and crisis response plans.

WARNING

Don't use executive session to vent about staff or other directors or as a closed-door forum to reopen decisions that have already been made. If concerns are discussed in executive session, they need to be communicated clearly back to the organization or the affected individuals. Executive sessions should never become shadow conversations your executive leader can feel but not see.

Running an Effective Meeting

Picture this: It's the night of the board meeting. You've laid out the snacks and soda. Everyone's name tag and agenda packet are neatly placed on the table. Your quiet conference room or meeting space will be buzzing any second now. Do you feel butterflies? Take a deep breath. Board meetings are exciting moments in time when people who share a love for the organization and its mission come together to create real impact.

To govern your nonprofit effectively, you must ensure that board meetings stay on course. The following sections offer guidance on how to run efficient and productive meetings.

Setting the tone of the meeting

At the beginning of every board meeting, the president should signal that the meeting has begun by welcoming board directors into the space, thanking them for taking the time to serve, and providing a quick summary (around five minutes maximum) of the following:

- What's changed since the board was last together, including recent programming updates and progress on strategic goals
- What's on the agenda for this meeting
- What needs to be discussed and accomplished

This sets clear expectations for the meeting and gives the board something to keep them grounded and focused throughout the meeting. The president can then invite the executive director to make a few brief remarks.

Using a consent agenda to save time

A *consent agenda* allows the board to take care of routine business or check off agenda items that don't require further discussion. It's a time-saving way to dispense with housekeeping tasks and approve the previous meeting's minutes, straightforward staff reports, committee reports, and standard contracts or administrative appointments.

Facilitating balanced discussion

The board president serves as the primary facilitator for the meeting, keeping the discussion balanced and aligned with the agenda topics. Facilitating a balanced discussion includes the following responsibilities:

- Making sure everyone is invited to speak and share insights or ask questions about each topic
- Keeping discussions on track and refocusing directors who trail off topic
- Guiding the board through the agenda and keeping the meeting within the allotted time limit
- Managing the board's altitude so you don't overstep your governance duties and discussions don't get too far into the weeds that board directors become confused or alienated

TIP

If a topic needs further discussion or if it becomes a bit too granular, the president can ask directors to take the conversation *off-line*, meaning they will save it for a post-meeting discussion. Circling back to a topic or addressing individual concerns/questions, although critical, may not be appropriate during a board meeting. Use your best judgment while respecting the time of other board directors. For more about what to do when conversations go on too long or get too detailed, see the later section "Parking an issue in the parking lot."

Keeping committee reports short

Require committee chairs to submit written reports in advance using a standardized template and make sure board directors understand they must read these reports before attending the meeting. During the meeting, the board president should moderate questions about the reports and direct committee chairs to respond to specific questions. Chairs should never read their reports during the meeting.

Voting and recording votes

Keeping a written record of the board's decisions (and who voted for or against each one) is an important task carried out by the board secretary. Votes should follow the process outlined in your bylaws, and the details should be recorded in your meeting minutes. When in doubt, spell it out:

- » Who made the motion? Who seconded, or endorsed, it?
- » All in favor?
- » Anyone opposed?
- » Any conflicts of interest or abstentions?
- » Did the motion pass?
- » Are there any questions?

Parking an issue in the parking lot

Sometimes the conversation wanders off topic or a director monopolizes the discussion. What they're saying is valuable, but it's pulling the group off course as the clock ticks toward the meeting's end. That's where the parking lot comes in. The *parking lot* is a dedicated section of your minutes where you can "park" an idea, discussion topic, or question that isn't on the agenda but deserves further attention. Rather than letting the group chase the discussion around or dismissing it entirely, capture it in the parking lot to be revisited later.

Following up after the meeting

Follow-up after a meeting is as important as the meeting itself. It's your chance to remind directors what occurred and what they're responsible for, strengthening both trust and accountability. Communications should be sent ideally 24 to 48 hours after the meeting and include draft meeting minutes and assignments for board/committee directors.

Recording Good Minutes

The *minutes* outline what the board discussed at the meeting, what was achieved, and any action items that need to be followed up. They also serve as a legal record for your organization. But having good meeting minutes isn't as simple as recording every word that was said. It requires an understanding of the importance of the minutes' function, strong listening skills, and good judgment.

Taking charge of the minutes

While the responsibility for taking minutes typically falls to the board secretary, who serves as the official keeper of the board's records, anyone can perform this task. Before you ask for volunteers, remember that the person who takes on this role will need proper training how to take minutes. Ideally, they start by reading this chapter and developing a solid understanding of best practices before putting pen to paper, so to speak.

REMEMBER

When taking minutes, it's important to understand that you aren't a court reporter. The goal is to summarize, not transcribe. Minutes are a critical legal document that protects the organization's decision-making (and decision-makers) and a strategic tool that can be used by future boards to understand past decisions. Reading previous meeting minutes will help you figure out the note-taking style you'll need to adopt.

Knowing what to include or leave out

All minutes should include the following information:

- **Meeting logistics:** Record the date, time, location, type of meeting (regular or special session), and format (in-person, online, or hybrid).
- **Notice of the meeting:** Document how and when notice was provided to all directors. If notice was waived, include written waivers or consents with the minutes. (For an overview of notice requirements, see the earlier section "Providing clear notice of the meeting.")
- **Attendance:** List every board director by first and last name, and whether they are present or absent. Additionally, make note of any special guests or nonvoting participants, such as staff or community directors. Confirm that you have a *quorum* (meaning the minimum number of directors are present to conduct business), and if anyone leaves during the meeting, note their exit time.
- **Agenda items:** Include a brief description of each issue discussed and any materials reviewed.

CAPTURING KEY DISCUSSION POINTS

When taking minutes, capture the essential context of what's happening without transcribing what people are saying word for word. The goal is to keep an accurate record of the high points of the discussion. This is where your executive judgment comes in. You can use bullet points to note the main considerations like this:

- The board discussed the results of the FY26 audit.
- The director of finance shared insights and analysis on budget forecasting, noting that they anticipate a $25,000 surplus at year-end.
- The board considered multiple facets of the upcoming fundraiser, including staff capacity, timing, contractor expenses, and event rental space, before voting.

When recording motions and votes, write down the exact wording of each motion, who made it, who seconded it, and the vote count. Note any directors that abstained. You don't have to name people explicitly unless they request to be named.

If you need to document any conflicts of interest, list the conflicts and how they're managed (for example, the director refrained from joining the discussion or left the room during the vote). Log any materials that are given to the board to review during the meeting and attach copies to your minutes, unless the information is sensitive or confidential. Finally, make note of any key to-dos from the meeting. Be sure to record who is responsible for what, and when it should be done. The more specific in this case, the better.

Here's what to avoid:

» **Verbatim quotes and attributions:** Because minutes can be requested in legal proceedings and used as evidence in lawsuits, detailed accounts of who said what are dangerous. Beyond the legal risk, attribution tends to personalize and politicize discussions, shifting focus from what the board decided to who dissented. As a result, directors may become reluctant to join the debate and express their true opinions. Directors need to be able to test ideas and change their minds without worrying about their words becoming part of a permanent record. Documenting every turn in the conversation creates unnecessary exposure.

» **Too much or too little detail:** The more detail you attempt to capture, the more likely you are to get something wrong (for example, misattributing a comment or mischaracterizing a position). Overdocumentation can lead to factual errors that may undermine the credibility of your records. But being too vague or omitting critical information can also lead to serious problems. Minutes that say, "The board discussed the budget," without noting what was decided provide no evidence of the board's due diligence.

- **Copy-pastes from presentations:** If the nonprofit's staff presents a 20-slide report, don't reproduce it in the minutes. Summarize the report, attach a copy, and reference it. For example: "The CFO presented the Q4 financial report (attached). The board accepted the report as presented."
- **Personal opinions, judgments, and interpretations:** Leave editorial opinions out of the minutes. Commentary like "The board was frustrated" or "It was a heated debate" is an interpretation, not a factual record, and it can create problems down the road. Don't polish what people said to make it sound better and resist writing down what you think they *really* meant. Stick to the facts.

Making the job easier

The board secretary can do a few things to make the whole minutes-taking process easier, before, during, and after the meeting.

Before the meeting:

- Make a copy of the agenda to use as a template for taking meeting minutes. This ensures nothing gets overlooked.
- Create a checklist of all the board directors and key staff, so you can easily mark people off as they arrive.
- Review and the bylaws. The secretary's job is to help the board navigate the meeting process, and understanding the bylaws, when and how to call a vote, and which procedural requirements to follow are critical responsibilities.

During the meeting:

- Wait until someone is done speaking before summarizing what they said.
- Keep your wording neutral; write, "The board discussed," not "Jane argued that. . . ."
- Mark action items as "ACTION" or "VOTE" highlighted in color, so people skimming the minutes later can easily find critical activity.

- When the board decides to engage in a longer discussion, capture the key points without getting too detailed. For example: The board discussed [TOPIC]. Key points included: [Discussion Point, Outcome], [Discussion Point, Outcome][Discussion Point, Outcome][Discussion Point, Outcome].
- Don't write down small talk or things brought up during breaks.

After the meeting:

- Edit your notes right away. Your first draft isn't your final record, nor should it be, and you want to ensure you have everything covered before you forget.
- Send a draft to board directors within 48 hours. Mark your minutes "DRAFT" and ask directors to review them for accuracy.
- Manage board directors' suggested changes and clarifications. Keep in mind that you're documenting what occurred during the meeting, not individual positions after the fact. Accept any factual corrections and reject added commentary or personal observations along the lines of "what I meant to say."
- Organize your minutes in a folder stored on your computer, ensuring they're clearly labeled (for example, board_minutes_05.21.2026).

Dealing with Common Boardroom Problems

Let's be real: Everyone makes mistakes, and sometimes they create roadblocks, hiccups, and frustration. In our experience, problems usually arise in board meetings because board leadership is unaware of (or sometimes blind to) simmering issues that need to be addressed before they boil over. Here are some common boardroom dysfunctions you may experience and tips on how to address them in the moment. Flip to Chapter 23 for an overview of more dysfunctional behavior to be on the lookout for.

Managing absenteeism and unpreparedness

Board meetings can't be effective if only one-third of the directors show up prepared to conduct business, one-third are unprepared, and the other third don't show up at all. Consistent attendance, well above a *quorum* (the minimum needed to conduct business), is the baseline for an effective board meeting.

But showing up isn't enough. Board directors must be familiar with the meeting materials and prepared to get down to business. Anyone who walks through the door expecting to just sit back and listen to reports contributes to the worst type of meeting: one that could've been an email. Board meetings are an opportunity to engage in meaningful dialogue, strategize, and address big questions, not to catch up on the organization's day-to-day activities. Here's how to make sure directors come to meetings ready to do the work:

- Set clear expectations on attendance and readiness early on, from recruitment through onboarding.
- Deliver the board packet at least five business days before each meeting.
- Track attendance at meetings.
- Follow up when folks miss the maximum number of meetings allowed (see your bylaws).
- Rotate facilitators on the agenda to increase engagement and accountability.

Containing dominant personalities

Everyone has suffered through a meeting where someone dominated the conversation, bulldozed over others, or turned a group discussion into a monologue on their worldview. Here are ways the board can respond when directors with dominant personalities take over:

- Redirect the conversation by gently but firmly interrupting the director to request input from others who haven't spoken on the issue.
- Use the clock to keep the discussion moving, noting the time limits allotted for each agenda item.
- Remind directors that the board's job is not to dissect every issue or micromanage the organization's operations.
- Thank the director for their insight and offer to continue the conversation after the meeting.
- Approach passionate board directors as allies who can inspire others with their energy. Validate their commitment by asking them to encourage their fellow board directors to share their insights as well.

Drawing out quiet directors

On the flip side, some people may not talk at all during meetings, and remain silent for any number of reasons, from introversion or discomfort with speaking in public to lack of preparedness. Help these board directors step into the spotlight:

- Talk with quiet directors before the meeting to get their thoughts on an agenda item. Sometimes people prefer to explore their ideas one-on-one, and allowing them to talk something over in a smaller setting can ready them to share their ideas with the larger group.
- Solicit input from everyone around the table, especially on important topics. Normalizing participation reduces the "social risk" of speaking in public.
- Allow for pauses in the discussion. Silence may sometimes feel uncomfortable, but it can help people gather their thoughts.
- Offer a word of encouragement or praise when quiet directors speak up.

Reengaging a bored board

When board directors become bored and disengage, it's usually because they feel like their time isn't being well spent. Maybe you're using the same agenda and board packet at every meeting, and directors have switched to autopilot because they don't have to think about what's going on. The deeper issue is that you've trained the board to be passive through your reliance on top-down reporting and cookie-cutter agendas, and they have few opportunities to really engage. Try these tactics to reengage the board:

- Energize meetings by posing hard questions, reducing reliance on reports, and inviting various speakers to provide outside perspectives.
- Introduce a big topic for each meeting, a meaty strategic goal or thorny governance issue that directors can substantially explore.
- Switch up the meeting location or format from time to time. Shorten your meetings when your agenda is light or ask directors what they want to talk about during the time that's left. A simple inquiry like "What's on your mind that we never seem to discuss?" can open the floodgates to lively conversations.
- Ask for suggestions about how meetings can be improved.

IN THIS CHAPTER

» **Understanding the types of board committees**

» **Creating and overseeing good committees**

» **Laying out common board committees**

Chapter 11

Building and Managing Effective Committees

Because boards have many responsibilities and limited time, they depend on committees to get work done. *Committees* are small subsets of the board who manage key functions or projects, such as finance or recruitment, on the board's behalf. They're the "doers" of the board, actively taking on tasks and supporting staff collaboratively.

By meeting regularly outside board meetings to explore issues in greater depth, committees create efficiency for the entire board, enabling it to focus on larger strategic conversations. At the end of the day, committees not only support your short- and long-term goals but also provide a meaningful way for directors to contribute their individual skills, insights, and actions toward the organization's success.

This chapter is your one-stop shop on how to run committees that supercharge your board. We explain how to structure committees and their work for maximum impact and get into the details on how to run your executive, finance, governance, and fundraising committees in an effective, empowering way.

Picking the Right Structure

Most boards have permanent and short-term committees to support ongoing functions and respond to emergent needs. They fall into one of two types, depending on the duration of the committees' ongoing responsibilities: standing and ad-hoc. We introduce both in the following sections.

REMEMBER

Regardless of whether a committee is a standing committee or an ad-hoc one, it requires a clear mandate, a charter outlining its roles and scope of responsibilities, and a reporting cadence to the whole board.

REMEMBER

Committees aren't created out of thin air. Your bylaws, which we discuss more in depth in Chapter 8, name what committees are required and should explain how you may form additional committees, task forces, or working groups.

Standing committees

Standing committees are permanent committees with an ongoing, recurring body of work that's essential to the function of the board. Typically, your bylaws explicitly name these standing committees, which are formed when the organization comes into existence. We get into common committees and their best practices later in the chapter.

Ad-hoc committees and task forces

When a board has a short-term project or task, such as planning a gala with the fundraising team or undergoing an executive search, it may form *ad-hoc* ("when needed") *committees* or task forces. Unlike the standing committees in the preceding section, ad-hoc groups form for each unique situation, often with a set time frame, and disband after the project is complete. They're sometimes called specialized committees. Ad-hoc committees are especially useful when your board needs to address an emergent issue or special project such as the following:

- Recruiting an executive leader or CEO
- Facilitating strategic planning
- Planning fundraising events or an annual gala
- Organizing capital campaign planning
- Promoting diversity, equity, inclusion, and accessibility
- Assessing executive compensation

Setting Up Effective Committees

Don't create committees willy-nilly. Before you vote one into existence, check that you have legitimate strategic need for it. Adding a committee means creating a charter for it and carefully deciding who gets to serve where. In the following sections, we take a closer look at laying the groundwork for great committee work.

Seeing what you really need

No one-size-fits-all list lays out what committees your board needs. For one thing, that need may shift at any given time depending on your scale, your strategic priorities, and what's going on in the world. Committees should follow your needs as the organization grows and develops.

In addition to what committees your bylaws require, your board needs to figure out where its limited time and resources are best spent on advancing the work of the mission. Does your organization have a large and complex campus of buildings to manage? Maybe you need a facilities committee. Or perhaps you juggle a diverse array of finance or investment vehicles like endowments, and donor-designated funds. That situation may call for an audit committee separate from your finance committee. We discuss those later in the chapter.

REMEMBER

Committees can burden a board with bureaucracy unless their scope, authority, and strategic value are clear. Committee work also shouldn't duplicate staff efforts or add more work for staff and board.

Formally adding a committee

Most organizations start with common committees such as executive, governance, and finance built in. Adding more requires a board vote. Check your bylaws to confirm the process and votes required to move forward.

TIP

You don't need to update your bylaws with the details of the new committee, but you should capture the vote in your minutes and save the charter (see the following section) in a common place where everyone on the board has access.

Writing a committee charter

Every committee needs a charter! The *charter* is a living guide that clearly outlines the committee's purpose, scope of work, and membership. It keeps the committee aligned with larger organizational goals and everyone clear on their responsibilities, even as the group shifts year over year. A committee charter should include the following:

- **A purpose statement:** This item articulates what the committee is there to do. The more specific it is, the better. For example: The purpose of the governance committee is to oversee board recruitment, onboarding, and executive evaluation.
- **A list of responsibilities and deliverables:** Think of it as a job description that includes things like delivering the budget, reviewing the succession plan, or leading the executive evaluation process (depending on the committee).
- **A list of annual priorities:** These include specific goals or initiatives.
- **An explanation of individual roles:** Identify who the chair will be, who will serve on the committee, qualifications to participate, and any responsibilities.
- **The meeting cadence:** Add projected meeting dates for the year as well.
- **A calendar of anticipated due dates:** This info keeps everyone on the same page about what's needed when.

Writing down these details at the start, and regularly revisiting and revising them, keeps everyone aligned and working toward the same goal.

Assigning members to committees

Committees need at least two members, though three to five is more sustainable. Select members based on relevant expertise, independence, and personal interest. Every director should be required to serve on at least one committee, and you should let them rank their preferences or ask them directly about what interests them.

Reviewing your committees periodically

As your organization's needs and priorities shift, your committees should, too. Every few years, do a fresh-start exercise: Set aside what's always been done and evaluate what the board needs right now. Here are reflection questions you can use when updating and evolving your structure:

- Does committee structure and work directly connect to our current strategic plan and priorities?
- Is any committee doing work that staff, another committee, or the full board is already handling?

- Does every committee have enough meaningful, ongoing work to justify its existence, or could we handle its work in a different or more efficient way?
- What did each committee produce this year? What decisions did it help inform, and what would we have missed if we hadn't had it?
- Do we have more committees than directors to serve on them? Are we asking directors to serve on too many committees?

Managing Committee Work

To get the most out of your committees, you need strong leaders who know how to facilitate, clear workplans each year, and the same standard of meeting hygiene you'd expect in any well-run business.

Defining leadership roles from the get-go

Effective committee management starts with defined and accountable leadership. Every committee should have two key positions, the chairperson and the secretary.

The committee chair

The chair oversees and facilitates the committee's work. Ideal candidates have expertise pertinent to that specific committee, a comfortable understanding of the organization's strategic priorities, and the ability to steer decision-making and hold committee members accountable for the action items they outline in meetings. They also need to be strong, diplomatic communicators who are willing to represent the committee's work to the board. The charter outlines the chair's duties (more on that in the earlier section "Writing a committee charter"), but common ones may include the following:

- Setting and distributing meeting agendas in advance
- Facilitating meetings with purpose; keeping discussions focused and on track' balancing conversations so all voices are heard
- Creating and owning the annual workplan for the committee; assigning action items and tracking progress
- Setting the tone for respectful dialogue and addressing disruptive or inappropriate behavior promptly

» Ensuring minutes are captured at every meeting; reviewing draft minutes for accuracy, completeness, and clarity before distribution

» Reporting on committee activity and providing any relevant context necessary to support board decision-making

» Leading evaluation of committee work at the end of each board year

TIP

Some boards use co-chairs, which can help you deepen your leadership bench. Being co-chair allows another director to get closer to the work while reducing the pressure and reliance on a sole chair to keep everyone on track. It also creates a level of shared accountability for managing the workload and maintaining a presence at every committee meeting if one is absent.

Committee secretary

Many committees underestimate the value of having a designated committee secretary, but this person can play a valuable role in keeping things on track, managing assignments, and creating quality reports for the board. Plus, they free up the chair to focus on facilitating rather than notetaking. Key secretary responsibilities may look like this:

» Partnering with the chair to draft and distribute the agenda and any other support materials for the committee meetings

» Coordinating logistics for meetings including invitations, meeting links (if virtual), dates, and times

» Taking accurate meeting minutes and drafting written reports or requests for the full board

» Collaborating with the chair on evaluating the committee's effectiveness

» Maintaining and updating the committee charter

» Saving documentation of committee work according to organizational policy

Drawing up an annual workplan

Each committee has its own set of ongoing, recurring tasks it needs to complete each year as well as one-time projects. The committee should review these items annually with board leadership and executive management to align them with the organization's strategic priorities. Then it can create a workplan that maps every task and project to the annual calendar, with clearly defined goals or deliverables from the committee. Provide this workplan to the larger board and submit progress reports regularly (often at board meetings). Flip to Chapter 9 for more on how we recommend going about this process.

Setting agendas and writing up the minutes

Just like your board meetings, your committees need an agenda, too. It should include a list of specific topics for discussion, an assigned time slot and discussion leader, and any necessary materials for preparation. You also likely want to keep track of action items from past meetings and a parking lot for things you need to either monitor or address in the future. The committee chair should build the agenda in collaboration with the secretary and any assigned staff leadership.

Meeting minutes serve as the official written record of the meeting, documenting any key discussions, decisions made, and assigned follow-up actions. Committee meeting minutes are important for reporting to the larger board and submitting committee reports to board and executive leadership. How you structure your minutes largely depends on the structure of the agenda. Using the agenda as your template for taking minutes is totally acceptable, though note that your bylaws may specify additional requirements for committee minutes. Check out Chapter 10 for recommendations on how to write effective agendas and take minutes.

Scheduling and running meetings

Committee meetings should occur during the months between scheduled board meetings. This schedule keeps the staff and the board progressing toward their goals. Some groups meet on an as-needed basis, whereas others have standing regular business to attend to. Work with board leadership to determine the best approach to meet your governance responsibilities.

Set meeting length thoughtfully, considering both the agenda and the availability of members. One hour is more than enough for progress updates, discussion, and task delegation. Be vigilant of conversation going off-track. Chapter 10 has details on how to run a great meeting.

Assigning action items after meetings

Committee meetings are only effective when the chair delegates action items and support needs back to the committee members and staff. If committee members volunteer to manage a task for the committee, the chair must record this request and manage the person's progress. Chairs can empower committee members to work with staff on managing action items without causing more work for the staff.

REMEMBER

The committee chair must be neutral when addressing action items, requesting only that staff provide more information, materials, or additional partnership to committee members. (For more on working with staff, see the section "Partnering with staff" later in the chapter.)

Tracking ongoing work

Committee members need to agree on a collaborative method for managing committee tasks and projects. Free online collaboration and project management tools can be useful for ensuring all parties can transparently track goals and progress, but even a simple shared spreadsheet can get the job done. Check with board leadership on what tools are appropriate for your organization, and confirm that members can access them easily. We recommend using Google Sheets or other cloud-based sharing tools for this work.

Submitting committee reports to the board

A *committee report* is a concisely written document detailing progress toward annual goals, discussions requiring full board attention, and recommendations for the board. In some cases, reports are essential to helping the board make informed decisions on specific issues.

TIP

Not everyone is a subject matter expert. Create reports that are accessible for all board directors. That means providing an executive summary, using jargon-free language, and including essential context. Visual aids never hurt!

Partnering with staff

As organizations grow, they often have a staff member with subject matter expertise serve on relevant committees. They can offer professional guidance, provide internal reports and data, assist with research, act as a link to the day-to-day work of the organization, and handle limited administrative tasks.

REMEMBER

Staff supporting a committee aren't there to do the committee's work. They're partners, not direct reports, so don't treat them as such. The committee ultimately remains responsible and accountable to the board for its body of work, even when staff provide substantial assistance and resources.

Rotating your membership

The board should try to rotate committee membership on a regular cadence, ideally every year. Doing so ensures committees see a diversity of perspectives, and directors receive new opportunities to learn, grow, and contribute. It also gives directors a broader understanding of the board's work.

Examining the Executive Committee

The *executive committee* is responsible for overseeing and coordinating the board's work. It streamlines issues the full board needs to address and moves work forward between full board meetings. This committee is especially useful in larger organizations and boards that require more frequent action between meetings.

REMEMBER

When determining whether your org needs an executive committee, check your bylaws, consider the size of the full board, whether your board can respond nimbly to emergencies or time-sensitive issues, and how frequently your board meets.

Addressing the committee's authority and makeup

The following list outlines the common responsibilities and projects of the executive committee:

- Exercising board powers between full board meetings as permitted
- Monitoring the executive's performance, conduct their performance review, and make recommendations to the board regarding performance expectations and compensation for the upcoming year
- Serving as a sounding board or source of advice for the executive on personnel and operating matters
- Leading annual planning for board work (see Chapter 9), reviewing and approving each committee's goals and objectives
- Making recommendations for committee structure and membership

- Making recommendations on policies, procedures, and so on
- Creating agendas for full board meetings, including determining whether an executive session is necessary
- Responding to legal, financial, or reputational emergencies on the board's behalf
- Reporting its activities to the full board and keeping records of actions

WARNING

Here are some things the executive committee should *not* have the authority to do on the board's behalf:

- Amending or repealing bylaws
- Appointing or terminating board directors, filling vacancies on the board, or approving compensation for board directors
- Authorizing major financial transactions or entering into significant community partnerships, mergers, or acquisitions
- Taking any action that requires a majority of the board

The bylaws indicate who's on the executive committee; typically, it's the board officers. On very large boards, the chairs of committees and the most recent past president may be included.

Avoiding falling into shadow

WARNING

The biggest mistake executive committees make is becoming a *shadow board*, where the committee operates outside its authority, advances serious or substantial issues without appropriate input on from the full board, and fails to report back on its work in a timely or transparent manner. In its worst state, it can look like a small group deciding what the organization should do and then backchanneling conversations to build support before the full board ever has a chance to weigh in. This behavior erodes trust with the board and leads to disengagement and liability. The antidote? Stay on the side of transparency and communication, reserving independent action for situations where speed or confidentiality requires it.

Figuring Out the Finance Committee

The *finance committee* serves as the financial governance backbone for your board. Chaired by the treasurer, the committee works in close partnership with management to provide a level of detailed oversight that simply isn't possible in a full board setting. We'll be real: You can't dig into the details of a budget variance or debate the details of policy with 15 people around the table in a two-hour meeting that also covers strategic updates and program reports. Here are the finance committee's common responsibilities and projects:

- Ensuring complete, accurate financial records are maintained; reviewing budget against actuals and understanding variances
- Presenting accurate, timely financial reports to the board on a quarterly or monthly basis and offering an opinion on overall performance
- Overseeing budget preparation and financial planning; setting long-term goals in alignment with strategic priorities
- Safeguarding the organization's assets; putting risk management provisions into place (see Chapter 17) to protect against loss
- Helping the board understand the finances by communicating with limited financial jargon and answering all questions, no matter how simple
- Reviewing and recommending financial policies to the board, including ensuring adequate internal controls
- Making sure the organization has adequate insurance coverage and that it meets all required federal, state, regulatory requirements

REMEMBER

The finance committee doesn't make final decisions; it recommends them to the board. Depending on the complexity or nature of the organization's work, the committee may have the power to authorize a level of expenditure.

Unlike other committees, this one requires actively recruiting people who bring proven financial expertise — ideally CFOs, accountants, and senior leaders who have managed significant budgets, plus bankers and investment professionals. Conflicts of interest also call for a higher level of scrutiny. Vet prospects for ties to vendors, auditors, or institutions you use, and watch for anything that may color or call into question their judgment.

In very early-stage organizations or those with budgets under $50,000, the board treasurer or finance committee may be asked to step in and help handle day-to-day financial tasks. This move is understandable, especially when staff capacity is limited, but it appropriate long-term. As the nonprofit grows, it should seek to separate governance from operations as soon as possible.

Planning your financial year

If your fiscal year is your calendar year, here's an example of a calendar of standing activities your finance committee may follow. For details on the Form 990 mentioned in the table, head to Chapter 15. We also again include a template for a calendar in the Online Appendix.

January Review and present prior year budget versus actuals. Review and present Q4 financials from prior year.	**February** Confirm audit engagement for year just closed. Ensure Form 990 preparation is initiated after books are closed.	**March** Conduct financial policies review, earmarking any policies that need update and bringing to board for review. Ensure 990 work is on track.
April Review and present Q1 financials. Review draft 990.	**May** Ensure 990 is submitted by deadline (May 15) or extended to November.	**June** Perform mid-year financial check-in. Review cash position and budget variances. If major changes exist, consider a reforecast.
July Review Q2 financials.	**August** Begin preliminary budget work and high-level discussions about next year's goals.	**September** Advance budget development in earnest, with committee providing input to executive. Review and approve insurances.
October Review Q3 financials. Present proposed draft budget for full board approval. Take back any feedback for further edit.	**November** Present final budget to board to secure approval. Review reserve levels heading into the new year.	**December** Review year-end financial projections. Perform annual investment review.

Finding finance committee resources

You can find a wealth of easily accessible and freely available resources on nonprofit finance and accounting. Here are just a few:

- **Chapters 15, 16, and 17:** Get a high-level overview of important financial concepts, risks, and policies every board should have.
- **The Certified Nonprofit Accounting Professional credential course offered through BDO CNAP:** You don't need to be eligible for the credential to still be able to take the course and benefit from its knowledge.

» **Nonprofit finance certificate programs at your local university:** Many colleges now offer coursework both in person and online at an affordable price.

» **Free financial courses from Nonprofit Ready:** Find them at www.nonprofitready.org/.

» **Free resources from Nonprofit Finance Fund and Jitasa Group:** Head to nff.org/ and www.jitasagroup.com/.

TIP

The board treasurer should participate in additional professional development to deepen their personal understanding of nonprofit finance, whether that's getting a professional credential or reading through a small library of books.

Getting the Skinny on the Governance Committee

The *governance committee* is typically responsible for sustaining the overall health of the board. That includes recruiting and onboarding new directors, providing education, evaluating performance, and maintaining the essential legal documents powering the organization.

Here are the common responsibilities and projects of this committee:

» Maintaining and updating essential governing documents such as bylaws and core policies like conflict of interest, whistleblower, and document retention

» Creating and maintaining a board handbook with governing documents, policies, and procedural information

» Facilitating the annual or biannual board performance assessment process, reporting findings to the full board, and identifying areas for further education and development (as we outline in Chapter 18)

» Leading board education on governance, whether by drawing on internal expertise or external consultants

» Leading board recruitment by identifying prospective directors, managing the interview and selection process, and recommending candidates to the board

» Onboarding new directors and helping them understand their responsibilities

» Maintaining up-to-date board materials, including a matrix of board skills and directory of contact information, board terms, and attendance records

TIP

Nonprofits with large boards or significant board activity may establish a nominating committee to focus exclusively on recruitment and membership management year-round. This approach is especially valuable when the board has a lot of competing priorities because recruitment is time-intensive, and cultivating prospects can require sustained effort over multiple years.

Ideal governance committee members bring expertise in governance, policy, and organizational leadership and experience serving on other boards or in nonprofit leadership. This group includes lawyers, nonprofit executives, human resource professionals, and policymakers. They need to bring the highest standard of ethics and integrity and be dedicated to deep, continuous self-education.

Planning your governance year

The following is a sample governance committee calendar.

January Update the board directory. Conduct a skills/expertise survey to figure out what you need for next recruitment cycle.	**February** Update the board job description based on gaps identified. Host an educational session or provide educational materials on a select topic.	**March** Launch the recruitment cycle for new directors. Begin sourcing and cultivating prospective board directors.
April Interview candidates for the board.	**May** Interview candidates for the board. Recommend a slate of new directors for approval.	**June** Say goodbye to directors who terms are ending at the end-of-year board dinner. Launch/conduct the annual board self-evaluation.
July Use self-assessment results to develop board education plan for coming year.	**August** Finalize the board calendar and orientation materials for new directors.	**September** Have welcome dinner and orientation as new board year begins. Shift review work to policies and bylaws.
October Focus on policy review, updates, and special governance projects.	**November** Focus on policy review, updates, and special governance projects. Check in with new directors.	**December** Wrap up loose ends for the year.

Finding resources for governance

If you're looking to strengthen your governance expertise, start with Chapter 3 for a deep dive on the board's legal duties. Chapter 8 covers your bylaws, where you'll spend considerable time. Chapter 6 is essential reading for running a strong recruitment and onboarding process, while Chapter 17 covers the common policies you're responsible for maintaining. Finally, Chapter 18 offers guidance on running a useful board performance evaluation.

Feeling Out the Fundraising Committee

A *fundraising committee*, sometimes called the *advancement committee* or *resource development committee*, helps the organization raise the money it needs to do its work. The committee support planning and implementation of fundraising strategies and works alongside executive leadership, staff, and volunteers to cultivate donors, organize events, and plan for long-term needs. The scope of this committee can vary depending on the organization's scale and complexity and the maturity of its fundraising program. Here are the common responsibilities and projects of this committee:

- Identifying and cultivating prospective donors, sponsors, and supporters
- Collaborating on and approving fundraising plans
- Setting policies for ethical practices including gift acceptance, donor relations, sponsorship agreements, planned giving, and endowments
- Shaping fundraising events that promote the organization's mission in partnership with staff
- Establishing written expectations and training directors on how to participate in fundraising and giving while serving on the board
- Identifying opportunities to advocate for funding and lending a voice to donor communications, public relations efforts, and strategic communications
- Introducing the organization to potential business, civic, and philanthropic leaders in the community

Finding the right members for the fundraising committee

Fundraising committees are a unique group of proactive doers and compelling storytellers able to jump in on helping create opportunities for donors.

Directors who are a great fit for this communities are:

- Ambassadors who can talk naturally about the organization's impact and mission and are comfortable meeting new people
- Connectors who have a large networks and love making introductions
- Hand-raisers who are willing to roll up their sleeves and do things that are new and challenging
- Learners who are ready to grow as fundraisers and advocates for the organization
- Givers with their own track record of making personal gifts or contributions to your nonprofit (or others)

WARNING

You don't need to fill the fundraising committees with your top donors. To create an inclusive culture of philanthropy, you need a variety of people who give at different levels or in different ways.

Steering clear of fundraising committee pitfalls

The following tips help you avoid some of the most common mistakes fundraising committees make:

- **Don't make donors promises you can't keep.** When in doubt, under-promise or under-share and then follow up later with accurate information, especially if it's about impact or financials.
- **Don't get over-involved with event logistics.** Leave logistics to the organizer. Committee members are most valuable when helping shape the guest list and figuring out who should connect with whom.
- **Don't solicit donations without coordinating with your executive leader.** Before anyone goes asks for money, the organization needs to be aligned on who it's approaching, what it's asking and for how much, and what the donor's history is. Uncoordinated fundraising can create confusion, put relationships at risk, and open the organization to liability.

- **Don't treat donors like ATMs.** Donors are real people who pay attention to your organization's culture and how they're treated. Lead with respect. Be mindful of personal bias. Appreciate gifts as investments in your mission.
- **Don't break confidentiality.** This committee gets access to sensitive information, including donor history and giving behaviors. Look at donor data in aggregate, and treat personal information with care.
- **Don't criticize without consideration.** Good fundraising strategy is built to reach a wide range of audiences, and not everything is designed for you. What doesn't resonate with you personally may connect with someone else.

Considering Additional Committees

Every organization has a different mix of committees that's shaped by its unique mission, priorities, and resources, and that may mean including some extra committees beyond those we cover in the preceding sections, such as:

- **Audit or investment committee:** We note earlier in the chapter that as an organization's financials grow more complex, the board may create secondary committees for deeper expertise and time than a general finance committee can provide. An *audit committee* often forms when an audit process becomes substantial or unwieldy enough that it requires dedicated oversight. This group selects the auditors, initiates the process, monitors progress, and guarantees everything proceeds on track. Beyond the audit itself, the committee partners with staff to strengthen internal controls so that the audit goes off without a hitch. An *investment committee* forms when an organization holds significant capital or investments and is responsible for developing investment policy, monitoring performance, and conducting deeper due diligence for the benefit of the board.
- **Executive performance and compensation committee:** If the board manages the executive performance process internally, a task force may design the process, conduct surveys, benchmark compensation, and coordinate the board response. You can read more about dealing with executive performance in Chapter 19.
- **Facilities committee:** A *facilities committee* is appropriate if your organization owns or manages buildings, land, or significant equipment. This group focuses on overseeing long-range needs and risk management and can help through a renovation or potential move into a new space. You need engineers,

architects, real estate professionals, contractors, and the like to join. If your organization merely rents space, the scale of work probably won't rise to requiring board involvement.

- **Communications committee:** You most commonly see *communications committees* in smaller organizations that lack dedicated marketing or communications staff; the committee steps up to take on day-to-day tasks related to raising awareness and promoting the mission. In larger organizations, this committee is rarely necessary at all after dedicated communications staff is in place, though a task force may pop up for occasional support on public relations and press work.
- **Advisory committee:** *Advisory committees* are composed of community stakeholders that provide feedback or specialized expertise to help the board fulfill its directives. Very carefully consider before forming an advisory committee, and follow the same best practices for regular committees, including having a charter, a chair, regular meetings, and a method for reporting to the board.

REMEMBER

An advisory committee presents added needs, including a recruitment model, a more substantial onboarding processes, and a plan for long-term management. Keep in mind that unlike the other committees we mention in this chapter, advisory committees typically don't have any formal legal responsibilities or fiduciary duties. Clearly communicating the scope of authority to participants is critical in order to avoid frustration down the line.

These are just a sampling. Technology, education, curatorial, event planning, strategic planning . . . the list goes on. The only real limits on what can and can't be a committee are your capacity, your priorities, and the mission.

4 Fulfilling Your Responsibilities

IN THIS PART . . .

Plan for your organization's future with a strategic planning process.

Become a team player in fundraising.

Examine the different ways nonprofits can (and can't) legally engage in political advocacy.

Get comfortable reading, interpreting, and asking questions about your organization's finances — no prior experience required! Develop a policy and procedure manual that covers all your bases, from the nonnegotiables to the nice-to-haves.

Recognize the six categories of risk every nonprofit faces, including those beyond your control, and create a plan to reduce your exposure.

Evaluate the board's overall effectiveness and performance and use the results to drive education and development.

IN THIS CHAPTER

» Developing the foundation for a strategic plan

» Engaging your board in the planning process

» Recognizing the green and red flags of a strategic planning process

Chapter 12

Strategic Planning: Finding Your North Star

You can't drive your car for very long without having some kind of destination in mind. Sure, you may enjoy the view for a while, but eventually you'll run out of gas or get lost or end up somewhere you never intended to be.

The same is true for your organization: As you gather people and resources to support your cause, sooner or later you'll have to ask yourself, *Where are we going and how do we get there?* Your strategic plan is the answer. It serves as the road map for your organization, outlining where you want to go, which roads you'll take, where you'll stop along the way, and what you'll need to reach your destination.

In this chapter, we explain the ins and outs of strategic planning, from who should be involved to how to get it done, and ways to keep the plan alive when the world is rapidly changing.

Understanding Why Strategic Planning Matters

A *strategic plan* is a comprehensive framework that outlines your organization's goals, how you'll achieve them, and milestones along the way. When done well, it serves as your organization's North Star, pointing your board, staff, and community toward a common destination.

These multi-year documents focus on a few specific strategies that further your mission, broken down into time-bound goals and actionable steps, grounded in the organization's current capabilities, budget, and available resources. But the benefits go well beyond having a shared vision at the top. Your plan can also help your organization:

- **Better understand the landscape around you.** Laying out a strategic plan forces you to examine your environment, including what's working (or not) for other nonprofits in the same sector, what makes your organization unique, and whether your programming is still meeting a genuine community need.
- **Connect to your community.** Create real buy-in, both internally among staff and board, and externally with the people you serve, by bringing in many voices during the planning process.
- **Simplify decision-making.** By focusing on what matters most, your strategic plan can provide the clarity you need to say *yes* to things that move the mission forward and the confidence to say *no* to opportunities that may derail you.
- **Measure your progress.** Taking time to define what success looks like from the beginning means you'll be measuring the right things and know when you'll achieve them.
- **Be proactive.** The planning process should push you to think beyond what you're trying to achieve and look closer at what may go wrong. This helps you feel more prepared if the environment shifts economically, politically, or socially.
- **Strengthen public trust and transparency.** Sharing an easy-to-read strategic plan with your organization's staff, beneficiaries, and funders can inspire trust and a sense of accountability.

In short, your strategic plan is one of the most powerful tools your organization has for turning your vision and mission into reality.

REMEMBER

One size does not fit all. Your plan should be unique to your organization, your mission, the community you serve, and your budget. You can learn a lot by looking at what other organizations have done, but just because an approach works for them, that doesn't mean it will work for you.

Setting Up the Logistics of Strategic Planning

The strategic planning process can be quite time-consuming and complicated, depending on the size and complexity of your organization. Before you get started, your board needs to consider and discuss the logistics covered in the following sections.

Deciding who gets a say

While the board holds ultimate responsibility for the strategic planning process, an effective strategic plan brings together diverse internal and external voices. Identify early how and when to engage with each of these key groups and communicate your expectations of them. Deciding who gets a say requires you to balance inclusion with efficiency: Too many people slows the process down and make it hard to manage, too few may result in a plan full of blind spots that doesn't get much buy-in.

Board directors

Every director has something to contribute to the strategic planning process, whether professional insights, historical knowledge of the organization, community perspective, or subject-matter expertise relevant to your mission.

REMEMBER

Everything you bring to the table — your cultural and professional background, your identities — has value. You were invited to serve for this reason. Speak up, share candid feedback, ask difficult questions, and offer a perspective that others may not see. That's exactly what the strategic planning process needs.

Management and staff

For a strategic plan to be truly effective, it needs to be the result of collaboration between the board and the nonprofit's executive leadership and staff. Management and staff are your local experts, bringing knowledge of day-to-day operation, community partnerships, staff capacity, and sector trends. Staff also have the best sense of what is working, what isn't, and what the organization can realistically take on.

Board-staff collaboration should be straightforward, ego-free, and focused on moving the organization forward. Although working together presents challenges, a cooperative attitude ensures both groups are fully aligned behind the final plan.

Community members, funders, and others

Program beneficiaries, community members, volunteers, program partners, and donors offer an outside perspective. Gather input by hosting town halls, surveying the community, interviewing program participants, and having focus group discussions. Broader involvement ensures that you have community support when you finally release your plan.

Considering how long it will take

Small organizations can complete the strategic planning process in three to six months, while very large and complex nonprofits may take more than a year. Factors that affect the timeline include the extent of external stakeholder involvement, your teams leadership and decision-making abilities, the scale of proposed change, the strength of your facilitator, and whether a clear vision is already in place.

TIP

Timing also matters. Kicking off planning during a busy season can slow progress or divide board attention. Conflicts aren't always avoidable, but being aware of them helps you plan accordingly.

Determining who is running the show

Every strategic planning process needs a strong facilitator: someone who can be objective, keep the process on track, mediate difficult conversations, and ensure the plan reflects the collective goals of the entire board rather than one director.

TIP

Some organizations ask the executive leader, board president, or director with relevant expertise to facilitate. Large boards may form a task force. While it may save you dollars, it costs you in efficiency and objectivity.

We recommend bringing in a third-party consultant as a skilled facilitator can keep the process more neutral and paced than an internal leader. That said, consultants can be expensive, with some charging six figures, depending on project complexity. Here's how to find the right fit for your budget:

» **Ask around!** Reach out to other boards for referrals. Word of mouth is the best method for finding quality consultants.

» **Review a consultant's track record.** Keep a list of past clients to ensure they have worked with nonprofits similar to yours.

» **Avoid consultants who speak in jargon.** A good consultant should be able to speak to your organization's needs without alienating you.

» **Have a clear budget, timeline, and deliverables.** A six-figure contract may be out of reach, and a 90-page plan isn't realistic for anyone to implement.

Deciding how far to look ahead

Strategic plans can cover any length of time from a year to a decade or more, but a three- to five-year plan tends to be the sweet spot. Increasingly, organizations opting for one to three years plans.

After the disruptions by COVID-19 and amid the rapidly shifting economic and political landscape, many have found that focusing on a closer horizon allows them to stay more responsive to their communities. Ultimately, the right time span is the one that's most realistic for your goals and the most responsive to the environment you're working in.

Establishing the Keystones of Your Plan

Before diving into strategic planning, your organization needs to be crystal clear on three things: (1) your mission, (2) your vision, and (3) your core values. Together, these form the foundation on which everything else is built.

Crafting a strong mission statement

Your *mission* is the core reason your organization exists and the heartbeat of your entire strategic plan, influencing every decision you make. A strong *mission statement* is a concise sentence that explains the need your organization is trying to meet, the people you serve, and the reason it matters.

It should be both aspirational and functional, and easy enough to remember that anyone can recite it. Most important, it explains the *why* of what you do, not the *how*. The how is what your strategic plan is for.

REMEMBER

Keep it simple, silly! Your mission statement is easy to memorize and say out loud. Too much jargon or a laundry list of programs makes it difficult for funders to understand your "why." Here are examples:

> **Weak:** Our mission is to plant trees and clean up beaches in our community.
>
> **Strong:** We strive to preserve the natural world for future generations to enjoy.
>
> **Weak:** We offer affordable painting classes, pottery workshops, and gallery exhibitions for all.
>
> **Strong:** We strengthen our community by making the arts accessible to everyone.
>
> **Weak:** We provide temporary housing and shelter for unhoused individuals, including children.
>
> **Strong:** Our nonprofit strives to ensure that every family experiencing houselessness is provided with the housing, education, and skills necessary to live their fullest lives.

Knowing your vision and how to achieve it

If your mission explains why you exist, your *vision* describes what the world will look like when it succeeds. Your mission is the *work*. Your vision is the *change*. A strong vision inspires board, staff, donors, partners, and volunteers to move together toward a shared future. It is a North Star that guides long-term priorities beyond short-term wins. Here is an example:

> **Mission statement:** Our mission is to provide individuals with the knowledge and ability to address climate change's most critical issues and work toward building a safe, sustainable future for all.
>
> **Vision:** A world where climate change is never an issue.

REMEMBER

Your vision can also help you make hard decisions. When two program options both align with your mission, the vision breaks the tie. What choice gets you closer to the future you're trying to create?

Outlining your values

Values are underlying principles that guide how your organization works and what it stands for. They shape organizational culture by setting the expectation for how the board, staff, and volunteers show and up work together. They also support consistency and make decisions easier. A few examples of values include:

- **Collaboration:** We believe in working together, because a cooperative group effort creates better outcomes for our community.
- **Transparency:** We explain our decisions and share information openly.
- **Equity:** We actively cultivate a diverse workforce and seek to remove barriers to ensure everyone has what they need to succeed.

TIP

Define your values before undertaking strategic planning as they directly shape the process. An organization that values collaboration will seek input from the people it serves. An organization that values transparency may decide to share a draft of the plan before finalizing it.

Phase 1: Assessing the Organization's Current State

Before your board jumps into dreaming up where you want to go, establish a fact-based understanding of where your organization currently is now. A shared understanding of the factors influencing your organization's health and effectiveness will streamline decision-making throughout the process.

Doing a SWOT analysis

One of the most widely used tools for building this common ground is to conduct a *SWOT analysis*. SWOT, which stands for strengths, weaknesses, opportunities, and threats, serves as a comprehensive framework for looking at your organization's internal capabilities and external factors. Here's a breakdown of how it works:

- **Strengths and weaknesses:** Look inward at internal factors, including the organization's financial health and performance, operational processes and technological savvy, culture, talent, programs, and resources. What are you good at doing, and where do you struggle?
- **Opportunities and threats:** Look outward at the external factors that may impact your choices, including trends in technology, competition for resources, economic and political factors, legal considerations, and social trends. What can help you fulfill your mission, and what may get in the way?

TIP

Before your first SWOT session, spend time independently reflecting on the SWOT framework. Using Figure 12-1 as a guide, come up with four to six ideas for each aspect of SWOT and bring your notes with you to the table. Focus on what is most important, be specific, and stick to what you've personally observed, not rumors or assumptions. If this is your first time doing a SWOT analysis, here's a little advice:

- **Keep it simple.** You're not trying to solve problems yet; you're naming what you see. A few observations are better than a long list of issues.
- **Be honest.** This exercise only works if people share what they actually see and think.
- **Avoid blame.** Focus on challenging situations and patterns, not individuals. Every organization struggles with something. This is not about pointing fingers.

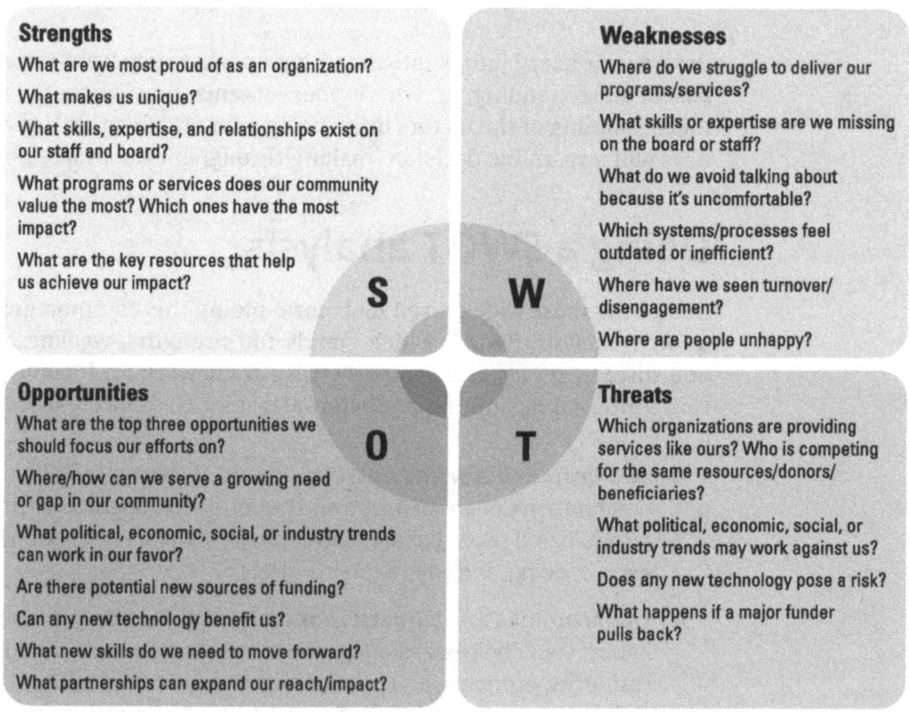

FIGURE 12-1: A typical SWOT framework.

Conducting a comparative analysis

A *comparative analysis* is a structured evaluation designed to compare your organization's programs and services against those offered by nonprofits that are similar in size, budget, or mission. A comparative analysis can provide valuable information such as:

- How your programs and impact compare to those of peer organizations
- What needs are already being met in your community and where you can fill any gaps
- Things other organizations are doing well that you may want to adapt to your mission
- Insight into what's "typical" for staffing, budget, or growth at your stage

Debriefing everyone

By the end of this stage, everyone should have a shared understanding of the current state of the organization. The board and executive leader should sit down together and talk through the results of the SWOT analysis, comparative analysis, and board assessment, and openly address any challenges or conflicts before moving forward.

HOW TO GET THIS WORK DONE

When you're evaluating your organization, the SWOT assessment and comparative analysis are the foundation everything else is built on. Being thorough and getting the facts right is key. Smaller organizations with strong internal trust can absolutely do the work in-house, but larger ones may find it harder to carve out time for these tasks and stay objective. More people means more perspectives to gather and more dynamics to navigate.

Ask if you have the capacity to take on this work and do it well. Can you have hard and honest conversations about your organization? Is there any history or conflicts that might get in the way? If the answers to any of these questions give you pause, consider bringing in outside help. A third-party consultant can provide structure, neutrality, and a fresh perspective on issues insiders have learned to work around.

Phase 2: Visioning for the Future

With your assessment of the organization complete, it's time to reach for the stars. *Visioning* is one of the most exciting parts of strategic planning, where you get to think boldly about the future you want to build.

This stage can feel overwhelming, so remember: You don't need to answer every question about where you're going or solve every problem *right now*. The goal of this stage should be to get aligned on the big ideas and aspirations that will guide the more practical work of setting strategies and goals.

TIP

Consider trying the collaborative in-person conversational format known as the *World Café method* for your visioning session. Set up several tables around the room, each with a different question that prompts your planning team to envision the organization's future and paper or sticky notes for capturing their thoughts. Participants choose a table to start at, spend 10–20 minutes discussing the question for that table, and then rotate freely to the next one (no need to stay with the same group). The key is that everyone's notes stay at the table, so each new group can build on what the last one left behind. At the end, a facilitator can move between each table and share the ideas and themes that emerged. It's simple, energizing, and brings a lot of voices into the conversation. Here are questions you can explore:

- It's five years from now, and our organization is on the cover of *The New York Times*. Why?
- If we received a $10 million gift, no strings attached, what would you want our organization to do?
- What would we pursue if we knew we couldn't fail?
- If we could do only one thing in the next five years, what would have the greatest impact?
- Is there anything that, if left unaddressed in the next five years, would cause our organization to shut down?
- If we didn't exist, what would be lost?

You don't need to spend too much time answering each question. The goal is to get everyone aligned on the big ideas and aspirations that will ground the more practical work of setting strategic goals.

Phase 3: Identifying Strategic Goals

Now comes the work of turning your vision into a plan of action. After assessing the state of your organization and brainstorming your vision, you may have a very long list of ideas. On the one hand, that's great! It means people are engaged in the strategic planning process. But on the other hand, a strategic plan that tries to accomplish everything will accomplish nothing. This phase is about making choices. Aim for three to five clear top-level goals your organization can realistically achieve in the time frame you've selected.

Narrowing down your goals

Struggling to narrow things down? This is where an organizing tool like the Pyramid Principle (Figure 12-2) can help. You can break down your goals like this:

1. **Start at the top.** Sum up what you're trying to do in the next three to five years in a single sentence. For example, are you trying to expand your impact and grow your organization over the next five years? Stabilize and shore up the foundation? Become self-sustaining? Pivot to meet new needs? This summary should come directly from your visioning conversations. The goal is to have a simple, top-level story that all your priorities lead up to.
2. **Group similar ideas together.** Gather all your ideas for reaching each top-level goal (sticky notes work great for this) and start grouping similar ones together. Look for shared themes. For example, hire more staff, improve professional development, and evaluate use of consultants would all fall under the goal of building your organizational capacity.
3. **Craft your strategic goals.** Look across different clusters of ideas and identify three to five that will have the highest chance of getting you to your top-level story. Give each one a heading or title — something that's direct and instantly understood, broad enough to cover multiple initiatives, and specific enough to guide further decisions. If two headings sound similar, merge them together. These are your strategic goals.
4. **Make sure your strategic goals are clear.** Before moving forward, test the clarity of each goal. Would a new board director or outsider reading your plan be able to understand it? Would staff recognize your goals in their work? Take the time to get this right.

5. **Let go of the rest.** Not every idea can make it into your strategic plan, nor should it. Developing your ability to discern what's most important is an essential skill of leadership. A strong board needs to learn how to say "not now" as clearly as it says "yes, today!"

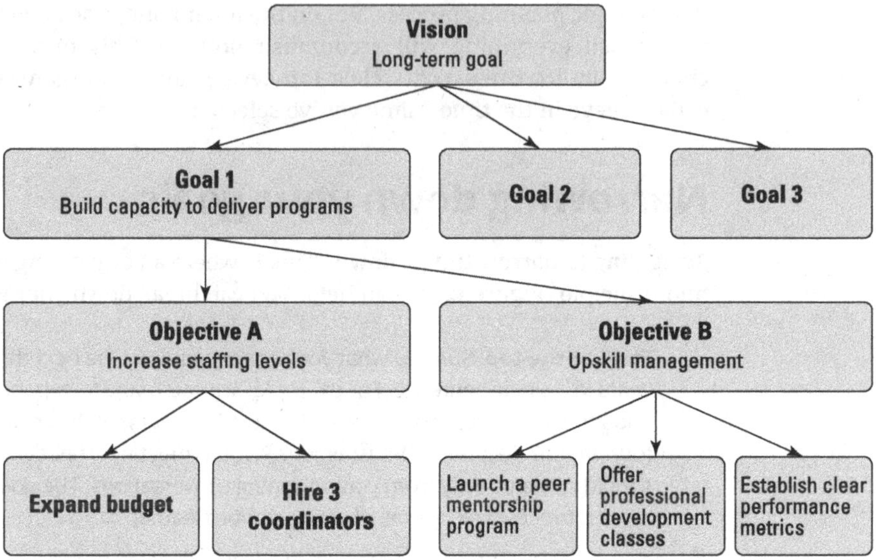

FIGURE 12-2: The Pyramid Principle.

Recognizing common goals

Here are common categories of strategic goals that organizations tend to identify:

- **Programmatic excellence:** Are your programs effectively serving your community and advancing your mission? These goals focus on sustaining or growing your reach and impact over time.
- **Financial sustainability:** Are your finances healthy and well-managed? These goals address budgeting, revenue, compensation, and forecasting.
- **Community engagement:** How does your community see you? These goals focus on building your reputation and visibility through word of mouth, public relations, and marketing.
- **Leadership and governance:** Is your board well-structured and functioning effectively? These goals address board development, succession planning, and executive leadership.

» **Advocacy and policy:** Is your organization positioned to influence systemic issues and policy gaps affecting your community? These goals address policy work and thought leadership.

» **Culture:** Is your organization fostering shared values? These goals look at how the staff, board, volunteers, donors, and community members grow together.

Phase 4: Developing Tactics and Action Items

Once your strategic goals are set, the next step is to break each one down into specific tactics and action items that will get you there. Here's a reminder to help you separate the steps:

» **Strategic goal:** A direct statement about what you're trying to achieve. Limit your strategic plan to three to five goals.

» **Tactic:** A specific initiative or activity that can help you achieve your strategic goals, with a time-bound, measurable outcome or output. Aim for no more than five to eight tactics.

» **Action item:** Day-to-day tasks assigned to a specific staff member to help implement the tactic. These will evolve on a quarterly or annual basis as your organization progresses toward these goals and resources, time, staff capacity change. The board and executive leadership should define strategic goals and tactics together. From there, executive leadership and staff will develop the action items that provide the ground-level details of how the work gets done. This phase is typically overseen by executive leadership rather than the board. It's detailed, in-the-weeds work, but it produces the comprehensive workplans that will drive execution.

REMEMBER

More isn't always better. Too many tactics, and staff may end up being pulled in too many directions. Aim for no more than five to eight major tactics per strategic goal (see Table 12-1).

TIP

Plans are meant to evolve. You may hit unexpected financial or staffing challenges, or an external roadblock that forces you to rethink a goal. Don't get hung up on it. The ability to adapt while staying focused on the bigger picture is exactly what good strategic planning is designed to support.

TABLE 12-1 **Strategic Goal 1: Increase Program Reach**

Tactic	[YEAR] Action Item	[DUE DATE FOR EACH ACTION ITEM]
1.1 Identify barriers to access.	1.1.1 Conduct focus groups with current and former participants. 1.1.2 Survey community members. 1.1.3 Analyze and present findings.	1.1.1 Deadline – [DATE] 1.1.2 Deadline – [DATE] 1.1.3 [. . .]
1.2 Launch one new program site in an underserved neighborhood by June 2030.	1.2.1 Research and identify target neighborhoods. 1.2.2 Secure a community partner location. 1.2.3 Hire and train staff.	
1.3 Develop a digital program option for participants unable to attend in person.	1.3.1 Assess current technology. 1.3.2 Pilot virtual program. 1.3.3 Evaluate and refine program based on feedback.	

Phase 5: Adopting Your Plan

The final step in strategic planning is to bring the plan forward for full board approval. Larger organizations may invite key stakeholders back to the table for final comments; smaller ones may do one or two rounds of edits before voting on the finished plan. Either way, schedule a dedicated meeting to walk through the plan together, with key staff on hand to address operational questions.

Once all questions have been answered and all issues are addressed, vote, approve your plan, and celebrate! Getting a strategic plan across the finish line is no small feat. Take a moment to honor your accomplishment.

Keeping the Plan Alive

It's easy to pour energy into developing a strategic plan only to have it slowly fade into the background once the excitement wears off. Think of how you make New Year's resolutions: You create your plan, spend a few days or weeks going to the gym or eating better, and then crash out by February. Strategic plans require the same discipline to maintain as they do to create. Here is how your board can keep your plan alive:

- **Create a mechanism to track your progress.** This may be a dashboard or a scorecard on your website or an executive report that gives the board a consistent view of progress toward strategic goals on a quarterly or annual basis.
- **Revisit goals at every board meeting.** Initiate conversations about how goals are moving forward, what support the board can offer, and any potential risks/pitfalls that may come up.
- **Draft board agendas to allow time to present new info on strategic goals.** Because you will revisit the progress toward strategic goals at each meeting, plan to give the board a heads-up about upcoming milestones and goals during the new business portion of the agenda. This can be a quick refresher on what's coming up with regard to implementing the strategic goals to get board directors thinking of questions regarding progress toward goals and how they may support them before the next meeting.
- **Educating new board directors.** Recruitment never stops, even when you're in the middle of strategic planning. Be sure to orient any new directors on the organization's goals and objectives during their onboarding. Providing an overview of the full plan and key milestones will help them understand their role in monitoring progress.
- **Share your plan with the community.** Many nonprofits post their strategic plan publicly or announce its release. This builds trust, strengthens accountability with funders and partners, and can attract new supporters excited about your future.

REMEMBER

Even the best strategic plan is just that — a plan. Detours happen. Conditions change. Unexpected challenges inevitably arise. A good strategic plan isn't about predicting every single thing that may occur. The board and the organization's executive should review the plan regularly, assessing progress and adjusting expectations or tactics as needed. Flexibility is key to long-term success.

REMEMBER

Strategic plans eventually come to an end, and the next round of planning needs to start anew. Each new cycle is an opportunity to bring in fresh perspectives and keep your organization grounded in the evolving needs of your community.

Recognizing Green Flags in the Process

Every strategic planning process is a little bit different, but the ones that tend to succeed and energize an organization share a few common green flags. Consider the green flags covered in this section signals that your organization is likely on the right track.

Trusting and collaborating with staff and leadership

For your strategic plan to be successful, the board must recognize and trust the expertise of the nonprofit's executive leadership and staff. These subject-matter experts working on the ground are responsible for bringing the plan to life. Healthy collaboration ensures the board understands what the organization needs to execute the plan and where they can offer meaningful support without overstepping into day-to-day operations.

Listening to your community

Organizations that actively seek input from the people they serve build strategic plans that have greater relevance and impact. As a board director, you have a unique role in making this happen. Share what you've heard from neighbors, colleagues, and community members, and offer perspectives that may be unrepresented. One of the most powerful contributions you can make, far beyond a financial gift, is amplifying the voice of the community you represent.

Maintaining honesty about organizational capacity

Ambition is necessary for mission success, but so is realism. If you have three full-time staff members or are a start-up nonprofit with a small budget, your strategic plan needs to reflect that reality. The strongest plans are those that strike a balance between inspiring the organization forward and staying grounded in what's achievable. Here are a few questions to help you reflect on your goals while keeping it real:

- Do we have the staff capacity to execute this plan?
- Is this plan fundable? Do we have the resources we need?
- Have we asked the people responsible for doing the work if it's actually doable?
- If everything went sideways, which of these commitments could we still honor?
- Are we building in enough time to get these things done?
- Do we need to stop doing anything we're currently doing in order to take this on?

Staying focused on your mission

It's easy to get carried away with exciting new ideas or feel the pressure to do more, more, more! Keep returning to the guiding question: Does this plan serve our mission? Staying focused on your mission requires a degree of self-awareness and selflessness, as well as a willingness to let things go.

Your own preferences, opinions, and instincts matter, as we've been saying, but they should always be in service of the organization's mission. When you find yourself advocating strongly for a particular direction or idea, ask yourself if you're speaking from your own perspective or for the community the organization exists to serve. Those aren't always the same thing.

Watching Out for Red Flags

Strategic planning can quickly get complicated. This section highlights some red flags to look out for that can undermine long-term success.

Doing too much

A 50-page strategic plan packed with dozens of tactics and no priorities is a sure sign of trouble. When everything is a priority, nothing is a priority, and both the board and the organization's staff will feel the tension of being tasked with too much to handle. The most effective plans are short and ruthlessly prioritized. A few things done exceptionally well will always be better than a long list of things done halfway.

Overstepping into operations

As a board director, your role is to define where the organization is going and to hold it accountable for getting there. How the work gets done is the responsibility of staff. It can be easy to blur this line, especially during planning conversations when ideas are flying and everyone is engaged in making connections to turn your goals into reality. However, once the plan is adopted, there's a meaningful difference between asking, "Are we making progress toward this goal?" or offering up a possible solution or alternative approach, and dictating how the work gets done.

For example, if a goal in your plan is to increase program enrollment, your job is to track progress toward the target number, not to tell the program director how to get the numbers up. Whether they achieve the enrollment increase through social media, community partnerships, or other outreach strategies, it's their call to make, not yours. Unless you're assigned to execute a part of the strategic plan, step back and monitor the staff's progress.

Forgetting the financials

Every strategic plan needs a budget to back it up. People, programs, and resources all cost money. A strategy without financial backing is an incomplete plan. Projecting revenue and expenses over multiple years is hard, and assumptions don't always hold. The goal isn't perfection, but you must have a conversation about what every commitment in your plan will cost, how it will be funded, and what resources it may generate for your organization. Create a proforma (aka financial projection) to revisit each year.

Assuming the best without measuring success

A wise executive leader once said, "Hope is not a strategy." A plan without measurable ways to track progress is just a list of good intentions. From the start, work with staff to define what success looks like and how you'll know when you've achieved it. Be realistic about what can be measured and how often you should check progress.

TIP

You don't need to figure out how to track progress alone. Similar organizations are usually happy to share how their organization measures success. You may be surprised at how much you can find out by asking around.

Knowing When to Abandon Your Plan

It's rare to have to throw out your strategic plan entirely. More often, you just need to adjust it. A program underperforms, a key staff member departs, a grant you applied for doesn't come through — these are all bumps in the road, not forks. It may require a tactical adjustment, but your plan's overall direction should stay the same.

Even so, there *are* moments when an adjustment isn't enough, when the necessary changes are so large that you end up going in a different direction, when the best decision for the organization may be to scratch the current plan and start over. Here are a few situations where it may be time to reassess your strategic plan entirely:

- **A major external event:** Something that's out of your control may disrupt your operations and rewrite the environment you're working in. Think a global pandemic, a natural disaster, or a political shift so significant that the plan you built no longer makes sense.
- **New executive leadership:** It isn't uncommon for strategic plans to shift with fresh leadership, especially if your organization is experiencing some type of distress (for example, a significant loss of funding or volunteers) or isn't seeing the results it had hoped for from its current plan.
- **A dramatic shift in community needs:** The people you serve may face fundamentally different challenges than they did when you wrote the plan. For example, a rise in houselessness in a city may increase the demand for a houselessness nonprofit to build shelters to help accommodate the community's need.
- **A catastrophic loss of funding or ability to carry out the mission:** Losing a major donor or several key staff members may change what your organization can realistically achieve.
- **Flaws in the plan:** Perhaps you discover that the plan was built on faulty assumptions, or lacked community buy-in, or didn't bring the proper focus to the work. Continuing to execute a flawed plan is a waste of donor dollars and public trust.

REMEMBER

Your goal should never be to follow the strategic plan perfectly. The goal is, and always should be, to serve your mission and the community counting on you. Keep your North Star in sight, don't get pulled off on too many side quests, and you'll find your way there.

IN THIS CHAPTER

- » Knowing how fundraising works in your nonprofit
- » Understanding how board directors can give
- » Teaming up with the fundraising staff
- » Evaluating successful fundraising performance

Chapter 13 Fundraising for Your Mission

Fundraising is the lifeblood of a nonprofit. The fact that volunteers, donors, and funders voluntarily choose to invest in your mission is one of the many things that make nonprofits special. As a board director responsible for overseeing the financial health of your organization, you'll likely find yourself playing some part in raising funds.

It's okay to be a *little* afraid of fundraising. Asking people for money can be scary — nobody wants to face the possibility of rejection. But here's the thing: Fundraising isn't just about money; it's about building relationships and resources that support your mission. As a board director, your role is to partner with staff to share the organization's stories and successes in a way that attracts potential supporters, resources, and gifts that help further the mission and keep the organization going.

In this chapter, we break down the ways nonprofit boards can participate in fundraising, how individual board directors can support staff in building donor relationships, and the key metrics for nonprofit fundraising success.

Looking at Various Types of Contributions

Fundraising is an essential function for keeping a nonprofit organization healthy. While your board can play a key role in raising funds for your organization (see the sidebar "Fundraising: The role of the board"), your main responsibility is sound financial governance, which includes keeping a strategic eye on the funds raised through donations, bequests/wills, capital campaign gifts, grant funding, and other channels. As a board director, you should understand the various ways funds may flow to your nonprofit and your role in making them happen.

Donations

Donations are voluntary gifts of money, services, or goods made either one time or on a recurring basis. Donations take many different forms, including:

- **Cash gifts:** A donor may write a check, click the Donate button on your website, or give money at a fundraising event.
- **Planned or legacy gifts:** These are gifts that a donor arranges during their lifetime to be given to the organization later, usually after their death. For example, your organization may be named as the recipient of a monetary gift in a will or listed as a beneficiary of a life insurance policy.
- **Appreciated assets:** These are donations of stocks/securities, bonds, or cryptocurrency directly to your organization.
- **In-kind gifts:** Examples of this type of gift are a local restaurant donating food for a reception, an office store donating paper and pens, or a company offering free office space to a nonprofit. In-kind gifts also can be *pro bono* (voluntary) legal or financial services provided by a law firm or bookkeeper (see the later section "Expertise" for details on pro bono services).

TIP

In-kind gifts offset costs you would otherwise have to incur to operate and save your organization money. Be sure to ask your local business leaders about the in-kind support they offer nonprofits.

Grants

Grants are funds formally donated by governments or foundations to support the programs and operations of nonprofit organizations. Grants may be used for the following purposes:

- General operating grants cover a nonprofit's day-to-day expenses, such as employee salaries and benefits, rent, or equipment and materials needed to function properly.
- Some grants are earmarked for programming costs, including materials and staff that support the nonprofit's programs.
- Capacity building grants are meant to strengthen a nonprofit and its staff and increase efficiency. They may provide money for an organization's staff and board directors to attend trainings and workshops or to upgrade technology and tools used by the nonprofit.
- Capital improvement grants often come in handy during the early stages of a *capital campaign*, a multiyear fundraising effort by a nonprofit to expand its programs and capacity by building, buying, or renovating a facility from which it can operate.

Restricted and unrestricted gifts

It's critical for board directors to understand the difference between a restricted gift and an unrestricted gift. When someone makes an *unrestricted* gift, the organization can use the money, goods, or services for any purpose it deems the best and highest use.

FUNDRAISING: THE ROLE OF THE BOARD

As a board director, your job is not to master every type of giving, but to have a working understanding of what kind of money flows through your organization, what your obligations are at this point in the organization's life cycle, and how to be an informed partner to your fundraising leaders.

Generally, most boards are asked to participate in their nonprofit's fundraising. This looks different for every board and every individual. Maybe you make a financial gift to support the organization's programming. Perhaps you volunteer to serve on fundraising committees, introduce fundraising staff to potential funders, such as businesses and foundations you have connections to, or participate in fundraising events. The point isn't to do *all* these things or write the biggest check; it's to show up in a way that works best for both you and the organization.

On the other hand, a *restricted* gift comes with conditions set by the donor, meaning the funds must be used for a specific purpose, program, or period of time according to the donor's wishes. For example, a donor may restrict their gift to funding youth swimming programs. This means you cannot spend any of the money on running, or say, art classes.

TIP

You can read more about financial controls and risks associated with restricted gifts and other forms of contributions in Chapter 15.

Exploring the Four Ways Boards Give

Your fundraising duties as a board director will usually focus on promoting a culture of philanthropy and engaging in specific activities aimed at developing funding sources and opportunities throughout the year. But what that looks like in practice will evolve as your organization grows.

In smaller organizations without paid staff, board directors may be asked to help draft grant proposals, plan fundraising events, and even ask for donations. However, as the organization grows and builds its staff, most of these operational tasks will move into their hands. At that point, your role will shift toward making personal donations, supporting fundraising events, opening doors to new connections, and serving as an ambassador in the community. You can find creative ways to get involved at any stage of organizational maturity in the later section "Working Alongside Staff."

The following sections explore the four ways boards give.

Time

Time is the most valuable thing you can give to your organization, and you're already making a major commitment by volunteering to serve on the board. Between attending meetings and working on committees, fulfilling your governance responsibilities (more on that in Chapter 4), and sharing the joy of your nonprofit's mission in your community, the hours add up. This investment of time is a significant gift that's critical for the organization's long-term functioning. Your time investment is also part of sharing your expertise and leveraging your connections.

Money

While money isn't the be-all and end-all for board giving, it's a meaningful, concrete way to demonstrate your investment in the organization's health. No matter the amount you pledge, becoming a donor signifies that you personally stand behind the mission. You can give an annual monetary gift or spread your gifts throughout the year, donate at fundraising events, or direct your giving to specific programs.

Pledging your support

The primary way boards support fundraising is through their own financial giving. In fact, the best practice is to ask all board directors to commit to making monetary donations in some capacity, because when the entire board shows it's invested, it sends a powerful message to funders and the community.

To achieve this, individual directors should pledge their annual giving ahead of time. Pledging a gift helps you anticipate how and when you will be supporting the organization throughout the year. This way, you are never surprised by a fundraiser, and the organization knows what it can expect in terms of revenue.

TIP

If your organization has an executive director or CEO, look for an opportunity to discuss your plan for giving in a more direct and strategic way, such as pledging your gift over multiple years, increasing your gift over time, or preparing to give a major gift for an anticipated capital campaign in five years.

At the start of each year, all board directors should self-identify their giving plan by filling out an annual pledge form (see the Online Appendix for a sample). This should cover things like:

- How much you plan to give
- How your donation will be funded (check, cash, or distributions through stocks, IRAs, donor-advised funds, or annuities)
- Which programs/initiatives/events you wish to support (unrestricted giving, event sponsorship, specific programming)
- When you plan to give the gift (once on a specific date, monthly, at an event)

Dispelling the give/get model

Historically, many nonprofit boards have operated under what's known as a *give/get policy*, which sets a minimum donation amount each individual board director is expected to give or, if they're unable to meet the minimum, an expectation that they'll get enough donors to make up the difference.

WARNING

While a give/get policy can motivate some directors to donate personally or bring in new donors, it also creates a problematic culture that measures the value of what individuals bring to the table primarily in dollars. Money is necessary for keeping the lights on at a nonprofit, but it also can be a barrier for many people who want to become involved in your organization's work. Be aware of this when you're developing a board giving policy.

Board directors should always be free to give any amount they feel most comfortable with. If you're having a hard time self-identifying a dollar amount, ask your director of fundraising about the nonprofit's *median gift amount*. This middle point of your organization's total donations is a good starting place to help you figure out a comfortable giving amount.

TIP

Don't forget to check if your employer will match your gift. It's becoming more common for private companies (and some public entities) to offer a donation-matching program as an employee benefit. Talk to your HR manager or the people/culture team at your workplace to get more information.

REMEMBER

Fundraising is a team sport, and everyone on a board contributes in ways that align with their resources and abilities. That being said, peer pressure is a real thing, even on boards. Someone will always have more time or money on their hands than you do, which may cause you to feel insecure about the amount you can contribute. It's important to remain true to what you're ready, willing, and able to give. Focus on the strengths and insights you bring to the table. Pledges can always be altered based on your personal and financial circumstances; be sure to update the organization if you anticipate any changes in your giving.

Expertise

What do you do in your day-to-day life? Maybe you run a bookkeeping business or advise companies on employment law or manage a large team. Whatever your background, the skills and knowledge you've built over your career can benefit your organization.

Leadership experience, strategic thinking, financial acumen, legal knowledge, and communication proficiency are all transferable skills that can help guide your organization to sustainable success. Have a conversation with your board chair and executive director to discuss how your expertise can help the organization move forward.

REMEMBER

Donating your professional services is considered an *in-kind gift* to the organization. To document your pro bono work properly, create an invoice reflecting what you would normally charge, with the full amount discounted to zero. This helps your organization understand what they would've otherwise had to pay and serves as a useful planning tool. It also helps them issue you an accurate letter to acknowledge the contribution.

TIP

Unfortunately, the IRS doesn't allow you to deduct the value of your time or services on your taxes because it's considered a financial contribution. But you *can* deduct any unreimbursed out-of-pocket expenses you incur. Keep your receipts and consult a tax advisor to understand the rules that apply to your situation, especially if you provide a substantial amount of pro bono work.

Connections

Being connected to the community your nonprofit serves is enormously helpful. This includes both who you are and whom you know. Don't worry, your role isn't to speak for everyone or to everyone. Instead, you can bring context, share stories, and help the board consider how their decisions may affect the community.

For example, if you're a parent serving on a school board for the district where your child is a student, your relationship with other parents and the kids will provide insights into those communities that can help the board make better decisions.

Beyond your community ties, think about your wider network: the colleagues, business partners, or community leaders in your circle who may be interested in your mission. These are potential donors, volunteers, sponsors, or advocates for your nonprofit — the people you can introduce to your organization who may turn out to be some of its most important supporters.

TIP

Two specific ways you can leverage your connections to support fundraising are through *peer-to-peer giving*, where you invite your community to give to the nonprofit alongside you, and *friend-raising*, where you help cultivate new friendships between the organization and people in your personal network.

Peer-to-peer giving looks like this: As your organization's annual fundraising event — say, a gala, 5K, or golf tournament — approaches, you share details about the event and talk about it in your circles, inviting friends or work colleagues to attend or pledge a donation. Or, during a fundraising campaign, you can post the information on your social media, talk about your service with friends, and invite others to give to the cause alongside you.

Sometimes, all it takes is a call to action or request for support. You may need your friends to help out. For example, you may invite a friend to volunteer at a food distribution event with you to see your organization's programs in action, giving them firsthand experience with the mission. From there, they can begin building a relationship with the organization, not necessarily through donating money, but through volunteerism.

Getting creative with your giving

You and your board can give your time or money, leverage your expertise, and share and inspire connections in many creative ways. If you have staff, work with them to find the right giving strategies for your organization. Here are just a few ideas to spark your thinking:

- Host a dedicated *day of giving*, where the board can reach out and inspire others to give by telling their story.
- Organize house parties and friend-raisers that bring your networks together to learn more about the organization.
- Set up a volunteer day on which board directors can bring in family and friends for some hands-on experience with the mission.
- Reach out to lapsed donors to personally invite them to an upcoming event.
- Thank current donors personally for their gift/lifetime of giving. A handwritten note or a quick phone call can mean more than you think!
- Share stories and program highlights on social media, LinkedIn, or other online platforms. Include a picture from a recent program you attended or other visual materials. Highlight impact numbers and stories to your audience, including how *you* are inspired by the nonprofit's work.

Working Alongside Staff

As your organization grows, your board will need to shift its mindset and approach to fundraising, moving away from doing the day-to-day work and toward supporting the staff who take over. You can assist your fundraising staff through your cultivation and stewardship efforts.

- *Cultivation* is sharing information and educating *potential* donors or funders about the organization's mission before they're ever asked to give financially.

» *Stewardship* is maintaining connections with *current* donors and funders by sharing updates on the organization, thanking and recognizing their contributions, and sustaining personal relationships, among other things.

Partnering with fundraising team members

As a board director, you aren't expected to know everything about your organization's fundraising. Like managing programming and running the daily operations, fundraising is primarily a staff responsibility. Staff will work in partnership with the board to make sure you have the information and confidence you need to engage with your networks and bring new support to the organization as well as sustain your connections with current donors. The key word here is *partnership.*

REMEMBER

Boards can open doors to connections in ways that staff often can't. You bring to your board service all the relationships you've built over your entire lifetime and career. Think work colleagues, neighbors, college friends, and similar community relationships. Your warm introduction allows the organization to skip the cold call and rely on your reputation and the trust you've already built.

Here's an example: A staff member wants to apply for a grant from a local family foundation that you have a connection to. Rather than writing the grant, which is the staffer's job, you can personally introduce the staff member via email, connecting them with a contact at the foundation and sharing a bit about why you value the organization's mission and why you joined the board. Your introduction may increase the chances of the foundation approving the gift, based on your personal connection to the application.

TIP

Although board directors don't often solicit donations, you may find yourself invited by fundraising staff to attend a meeting with a donor or lend your voice to a fundraising campaign by sharing your connection to the mission. Staff should always accompany you on any meetings with donors or help you draft a letter or other communications that will go out to donors. As a bonus, sincerely sharing your insights and impact stories about the mission keeps you inspired to serve on your board. Relying on your director of fundraising.

If your organization is lucky enough to have a director of fundraising, lean on them and respect their expertise. Next to your executive leader, they will be your greatest resource when it comes to figuring out how to plug into fundraising. They will drive strategy, manage staff and volunteers, and oversee all aspects of the donor's journey, from their first gift to their legacy giving plan. Bring them your questions, introduce them to your connections, give advice when asked, and follow their lead.

REMEMBER

Be nice to your director of fundraising. They have a big job. They're often leading small teams, moving large sums of money, and juggling many different balls — from giving campaigns and event planning, to long-term strategy and day-to-day administrative tasks. Always ask how you can best support them and their team, engage thoughtfully during meetings, and remember that fundraising takes time. They need your patience, partnership, and grace.

Beyond the Dollars: Overseeing and Evaluating Fundraising as a Board

If your organization relies on fundraising, your board must figure out the right level of oversight and governance the staff needs from you. This looks different for every organization and will need to evolve as your fundraising program expands. If you're involved at a high level, your work may include:

- Setting or guiding overall fundraising strategy in partnership with staff.
- Writing policies for gift acceptance, conflicts of interest, confidentiality, and documentation to keep your practices legally sound (see Chapter 16).
- Recruiting, onboarding, and training board directors capable of supporting the mission.
- Monitoring fundraising performance, including reviewing progress toward monetary goals and event outcomes, and examining whether fundraising campaigns and programs are attracting and retaining a diverse group of donors.
- Maintaining compliance with government regulations and registration requirements.
- Supporting a culture of philanthropy by modeling generosity through your own giving and advocating for the mission in your community.

TIP

Establish regular reporting practices at meetings to keep the board informed about fundraising activities. Small organizations may need to dive deeply into fundraising issues only once a year, whereas larger nonprofits may have to form a committee to oversee fundraising on a quarterly or even a monthly basis. You won't always have meeting time available for fundraising discussions, especially if you're dealing with more pressing issues. Your primary responsibility is to ensure that someone is owning the work and you have a mechanism for ongoing monitoring.

Measuring success

Board directors typically look at fundraising from a black-and-white perspective: Are we raising money, yes or no? But fundraising is about building relationships over time, and donating is voluntary; therefore, it can be difficult to tell if you're making any headway. In addition, donor numbers and donation amounts can fluctuate with external circumstances such as a downturn in the economy or changes in donors' giving priorities.

You can measure the success of your organization's fundraising efforts in many ways. The following sections explain some key performance indicators and strategic metrics that may be useful in evaluating growth in your nonprofit's fundraising.

TIP

Pinpoint the fundraising tactics that can work well for your organization. Some fundraising tools, like direct mail campaigns, social media giving, and major gift donations, may work for organizations with big donor bases, but not necessarily for smaller grassroots nonprofits. Look to organizations with a budget and mission focus similar to yours to put your fundraising efforts in context and understand the quirks of your donor base.

Donor retention rate

Your *donor retention rate* is the percentage of donors who have renewed their annual gift year over year. A standard nonprofit's donor retention rate hovers around 50 percent. Recall that external factors such as an economic recession, political shifts during an election year, and changes in income or personal circumstances can affect a person's giving. If you see consistent growth or maintain stability in your retention rate, your fundraising is successful.

Here's an example of donor retention documentation for a nonprofit animal shelter.

	2021	**2022**	**2023**	**2024**
Total Donors	482	427	493	483
Renewed	204	197	223	219
Percentage	42%	46%	45%	45%

In this example, the donor retention rate has remained stable and consistent, even as the total donor and renewing donor numbers fluctuate. This consistency shows that the fundraising staff does a good job renewing donors year over year for this nonprofit.

Cost per dollar raised

Your *cost-per-dollar-raised* ratio shows how much money you need to spend in order to bring in $1 in donations. It can also indicate that you may be spending too much in one area of fundraising. You can refer to your cost-per-dollar-raised ratio when you analyze the success of fundraising events, such as an annual gala. In the following example, a zoo spent 70 cents for each dollar it raised at its 2025 gala, a positive sign that the organization isn't spending more money than it's bringing in:

Fundraising revenue: $125,000

Fundraising expenses: $87,645

Cost per dollar raised (expenses ÷ revenue): $0.70

Total revenue versus goals

The executive director or director of finance may present a financial report at a board meeting that helps you gauge the progress you've made toward the fundraising goals set out in the annual budget. Fundraising committees may see more detailed breakdowns of total revenue versus fundraising goals for line items such as annual events, grants, individual contributions, corporate giving, and endowment income. Here's a simple breakdown of a cat rescue organization's progress toward its annual goal during the second quarter of its fiscal year:

Fundraising goal (Jan–Dec): $50,000

Progress to date (May): $24,498

Progress toward goal (%): 49%

This nonprofit has been very successful, raising nearly half of its annual goal at the midpoint of the year (May). This is a good sign that its fundraising efforts are healthy and functional, and its board can collaborate with the fundraising director to find ways to build on this momentum.

TIP

Be careful when comparing your organization's fundraising numbers to other nonprofits' totals. A local youth orchestra with a donor base of parents and alumni likely won't raise as much as a community symphony that can attract more affluent donors. Different fundraising outcomes don't necessarily indicate that one organization is better at fundraising than another. Setting realistic fundraising goals informed by the demographics of *your* organization's donor base will help keep fundraising reports grounded in reality.

Annual donor growth

Calculating the growth of your donor base year over year gives you some perspective on your nonprofit's ability to attract and retain/renew donors. Here's what the percentage of annual donor growth may look like for a youth housing organization:

	2021	2022	2023	2024
Total donors	548	654	631	702
Donor growth (%)		19%	–3%	11%

WARNING

As a board director, you are not entitled to see a full list of individual donors, and it would be inappropriate to ask for one. Donor data is confidential; access should be limited to staff who need the information to do their work. When donor data is being shared with the board, it should be anonymized and presented in the aggregate — in totals, trends, and overall performance. Where possible, identifying information such as names should be left out. It *is* appropriate for the board to review strategy materials, financial data, compliance records, performance metrics, grant awards and amounts, fundraising policies, and major gifts that may affect financial planning.

Preparing the board for its oversight role

Most board directors aren't experts on fundraising, nor should they be. However, you need to understand how fundraising works if you're going to be effective governors and stewards. Your organization should be designing board training/continuing education programs and integrating them into your annual workplan (see Chapter 9). Ongoing board training should cover the following topics:

- How to talk about the organization and its impact and get comfortable telling donors why you personally donate to the cause.
- An overview of the types of revenue your organization receives, including cash, grants, and in-kind gifts, and the difference between restricted and unrestricted gifts.
- The different ways board directors can give and support giving (see the earlier section "Exploring the Four Ways Boards Give").
- Clarity around the board's fundraising roles and responsibilities, especially if you have fundraising staff.
- When and how to make monetary donations throughout the year, and how to maximize your gift (for example, giving during a matching campaign).

- Basic fundraising ethics and confidentiality, including conflicts of interest and donor privacy.
- What success looks like, from setting (and reaching) fundraising goals to monitoring the organization's fundraising performance.

If you have an executive director or fundraising staff, invite them to facilitate a discussion about fundraising during an upcoming board meeting. You can also invite a third-party consultant to teach a workshop or read a book together on fundraising. In addition to book-clubbing this chapter with your board and staff, we recommend *Fundraising For Dummies*, 4th Edition, by Beverly A. Browning (Wiley), or *Boards on Fire*, by Susan Howlett.

Encouraging full board engagement

As the governance leaders for a nonprofit, a board that's 100 percent engaged in giving their time, expertise, and resources throughout the year is succeeding in its fundraising role. By demonstrating your willingness to give, you're showing your community that you care. This is important for building public trust and donor confidence in your nonprofit. More support means greater access to the programs and services you provide.

Your oversight role requires you to understand how your nonprofit's fundraising efforts are unique: which strategies and tactics help you attract new donors and retain current ones, and how you can engage the community in supporting your mission. Helping your nonprofit build its resources fulfills your duty of care to the organization. Your fundraising stewardship, along with your personal giving, can create a strong culture of philanthropy in which all board directors see and feel the impact of their giving.

IN THIS CHAPTER

» Understanding the differences between advocacy and lobbying

» Meeting the legal requirements to participate in advocacy

» Keeping your advocacy in bounds

» Following important advocacy guidelines

Chapter 14 Advocacy and Lobbying

Advocacy is one of the most valuable, and most misunderstood, activities a nonprofit can undertake. At its core, it means speaking up: for the people you serve, for the issues your mission stands for, and for the broader public good that your part of the sector exists to advance. It isn't the same as lobbying or a form of partisan policies. Instead, it's the work of educating decision-makers and shaping public understanding.

Advocacy actions can be as big as helping shape state or federal policy or as small as writing a letter to your local legislator. A board can be an especially powerful advocate, capable of building durable relationships with community members and lawmakers that help advance the mission and demonstrate civic leadership. A healthy nonprofit sector depends on the public's understanding of your work, and that's where you come in.

In this chapter, we explain the critical difference between lobbying and advocacy and lead you through the legal guardrails every board director needs to understand. We also share creative ways to educate and engage your board in advocacy work, and we make the case for why every organization, regardless of size or mission, should be doing so.

Comparing Advocacy with Lobbying

Before engaging in any advocacy activities as a board or organization, you have to understand the line between advocacy and lobbying — and why that distinction matters legally. *Advocacy* is the broad act of expressing support for a cause, initiative, idea, or policy. It's an opportunity to educate, inform, and raise awareness about why an issue should be important to the community. The following activities are considered advocacy:

- » Sharing research, education, or analysis on a topic
- » Raising public awareness about a specific issue
- » Discussing broader social or economic challenges your community is facing as well as possible solutions
- » Encouraging elected officials to consider and include your issue in their budgeting priorities
- » Describing how a specific approach or solution to an issue may benefit your community

Lobbying is a narrow form of advocacy. It involves attempting to directly influence a lawmaker to vote a certain way on upcoming legislation. These actions fall into the lobbying category:

- » Asking legislators to vote for or against a piece of legislation
- » Asking the general public to contact their representatives to vote a certain way
- » Organizing a rally in support of your specific issue
- » Circulating or signing a petition on your organization's behalf

Here's an example: A nonprofit addressing homelessness may publish a report on the state of housing insecurity in its city, sharing data and stories to help the public and policymakers better understand the urgency of the issue and potential solutions. This approach is advocacy. If that organization then contacts a lawmaker and asks them to vote yes on a bill that would help fund housing in the city, it has crossed into lobbying.

And here's another: A nonprofit dedicated to reducing gun violence in schools may visit its legislators to speak about the impact that gun violence has on the local community. Board directors, staff, and community members can share their stories and the organization pass out materials to help educate lawmakers on this issue, and it's still considered just advocacy. If this education goes on to ask lawmakers to support a specific piece of legislation, it has now moved into lobbying for the bill to pass.

WARNING

Crossing over the line separating advocacy and lobbying comes with major consequences. You risk inviting IRS scrutiny that may lead to losing your tax-exempt status, incurring fines, and damaging the public trust you depend on to be successful.

Just as damaging, however, is that your organization self-censors and avoids all advocacy out of fear, leaving critical issues — and the communities they serve — without a voice.

Looking at the Limitations on Lobbying

Here's the good news: All nonprofit organizations are allowed to engage in both advocacy and lobbying. For example, during the COVID-19 pandemic, many nonprofit organizations advocated for assistance and lobbied lawmakers to pass relief funding legislation. This critical work ensured the sector endured through a time of serious challenge.

WARNING

That said, if you're a 501(c)(3) organization, the IRS has established that that you can't qualify for and maintain tax-exempt status if a "substantial part" of your activities as an organization focus on lobbying and influencing legislation.

But what does *substantial* actually mean? The IRS uses two tests to help nonprofits get it right: the substantial part test and the expenditure test. Understanding these guidelines can give your organization the confidence it needs to engage.

The *substantial part test* is the original, vague IRS rule for lobbying. Under this test, lobbying can't make up a substantial part of what your organization does year over year. Unfortunately, the IRS never defines what *substantial* actually means. It looks at a mix of factors, including how much time your staff spends on lobbying and how much money you spend, weighed against everything else your organization does. Because of this lack of specificity, most organizations find this test unhelpful and turn to the expenditure test in the following section instead.

The *expenditure test* is clearer than its counterpart in the preceding section. A one-page IRS form called the 501(h) Election allows your organization to formally opt into a system where your lobbying activity is measured in dollars, with a sliding scale based on your budget. This approach means the IRS isn't holding smaller organizations to the same standard as large ones. Table 14-1 has the specifics.

For example, as of this writing, if your budget is under $500,000 you can spend up to 20 percent of that amount (so $100,000) on lobbying every year. As your budget grows, the percentage decreases. However, the system does have a ceiling regardless of how big you get: You can never spend more than $1 million in total lobbying.

REMEMBER

One final thing worth knowing about the expenditure test is the distinction between direct lobbying and grassroots lobbying. *Direct lobbying* means communicating directly with legislators. *Grassroots lobbying* means encouraging the public to contact legislators on your behalf. Each has different limitations (grassroots lobbying has further restrictions), so tracking both separately is worthwhile.

TABLE 14-1 **IRS Expenditure Test**

Amount of Exempt Purpose Expenditures	Lobbying Nontaxable Amount
Less than or equal to $500,000	20 percent of the exempt purpose expenditures
Greater than $500,000 but less than or equal to $1 million	$100,000 plus 15 percent of the excess of exempt purpose expenditures over $500,000
Greater than $1 million but less than or equal to $1.5 million	$175,000 plus 10 percent of the excess of exempt purpose expenditures over $1 million
Greater than $1.5 million but less than or equal to $17 million	$225,000 plus 5 percent of the exempt purpose expenditures over $1.5 million
Greater than $17 million	$1 million

Data from IRS.

AFFILIATING WITH A 501(C)(4)

If a nonprofit anticipates doing more political activity than the 501(c)(3) status allows, it needs to form or affiliate with a 501(c)(4), which permits a much broader range of lobbying and political activity. This type of structured relationship enables one organization to focus on educational activities and pushes all lobbying and political advocacy work into another, all the while benefiting from a shared resource pool. The key here is ensuring clear legal separation and good systems for compliance and expense tracking clarity.

You can find many examples of 501(c)(3) organizations affiliated with 501(c)(4) organizations, including the ACLU and the ACLU Foundation or the Sierra Club and the Sierra Club Foundation. In each situation, one advances a political agenda and the other focuses on programming and education. If you're considering going this route, here are a few things you need to pay attention to:

- **Two separately incorporated entities:** Each organization has its own unique EIN and files taxes separately, with distinct bank accounts and financial records.
- **Independent boards:** Each organization requires separate and distinct bylaws, boards, and board meetings. Though some overlap between the two boards is fine, you need individuals that serve only one or the other to ensure independence.
- **A cost-sharing agreement:** If you plan to share employees, office space, or equipment, you need to carefully track this split and make sure each organization pays, in full, for the portion it uses. This move guarantees the 501(c)(3) isn't subsidizing the 501(c)(4).

Warning: Don't treat setting up a 501(c)(4) affiliated entity as a DIY side project. It's incredibly legally and financially complex and comes with real risks. Always consult a lawyer before deciding to go down this route to verify your organization and mission are protected.

Avoiding the Bright Red Line

A 501(c)(3) is absolutely prohibited from doing some things under any circumstance. Even a little bit. These infractions include the following:

- Expressing support or opposition of any candidate for public office, whether for president, the city council, or the local school board
- Raising and gifting money to specific candidates or campaigns on the organization's behalf
- Rating or ranking candidates based on their position on a specific issue
- Holding candidate forums, publishing voter guides, and conducting voter registration drives unless you include equal coverage of all candidates and points of view

WARNING

To be clear: This isn't a gray area. It's a bright red line, and if you're caught violating it, your organization risks losing tax-exempt status and potentially faces fines and other taxes. Advocacy and education can so easily accidentally slip into lobbying and political activity. Maybe you make a social media post or send a newsletter out to your list about your issue in order to raise awareness. That's all fine. But if you include just a single sentence asking people to contact their legislators or suggest how to vote on an upcoming ballot, that communication has tipped over the bright red line. One sentence is all it takes. Table 14-2 illustrates ways to ensure you stay on the right side of the line.

That's why training and preparing anyone who communicates on behalf of your organization with talking points is so important. Focus on the broader message surrounding your cause and mission, why supporting it is important, and facts and figures that support your case.

TABLE 14-2 **Staying on the Right Side of the Line**

Problematic Language	Why It's Problematic	Better Language
I think this bill is wrong.	Personal opinion language can imply the organization's position informally, which lacks credibility and professionalism.	Our organization opposes the proposed budget cuts to mental health funding.
Vote no on Proposition 12.	Telling people how to vote on a ballot measure is prohibited political activity. Even one sentence puts you over the line.	Proposition 12 would reduce funding for mental health services by 30 percent. Here's what that means for our community.
Candidate Marie supports our cause and is the right choice.	Rating, ranking, or expressing support for any candidate, at any level, puts your tax-exempt status at risk.	We shared our policy priorities with all candidates and invited them to respond. You can read their responses at [link].
Contact your legislator and tell them to vote yes.	A single sentence asking people to contact legislators or vote a specific way turns education into lobbying.	Your legislators are currently debating this issue. Here's what you should know.
Our opponents are wrong about this issue.	Oppositional language can veer into politics and undermine your credibility as an educator.	The evidence points in a different direction. Here's what the data shows.

TIP

If your organization is starts undertaking a larger volume of advocacy and lobbying work, consider hiring a lobbyist. These professionals are trained on how to compliantly navigate among advocacy, lobbying, and political activity in their work and communication. They can help your organization stay organized and avoid any risk or semblance of doubt from local, state, and federal entitles.

ENGAGING WITH POLITICAL ACTIVITIES AS A PRIVATE CITIZEN

You and your employees still have the First Amendment right to participate in political action and exercise free speech on your personal time. You just can't use any resources from your organization to do so. However, you must make a distinction between your personal and professional self.

Here are things you can do to make sure you're clearly acting as a private citizen when engaging in political activity:

- Don't wear any clothing branded by your organization. Leave badges, hats, bags, and even lanyards at home.
- Use your personal email and phone, never your organization's.
- On social media, use a disclaimer like "Views are my own and do not represent [organization name]." This information ideally appears both in your posts and in your bio.
- Never use your organization's letterhead, branded email footers, or mailing lists.
- Don't organize activities on your organization's time.
- Don't recruit volunteers, donors, staff, and so on through any organizational channels.
- If you speak to the press, introduce yourself by name only, not your organizational title. Go a step farther and indicate that you're there as a private citizen.
- If you're signing a petition, use your own home address.

Warning: Because nonprofits benefit from public funding, board directors and executives carry a higher degree of public visibility than they realize. If you're concerned that your personal participation in an advocacy effort may be mistaken for an organizational position, consult a lawyer before engaging.

The Do's and Don'ts of Advocacy

Advocacy and lobbying can shift resources and change lives — and you're more ready than you think. The key is knowing where the boundaries are so you can speak up with confidence. In the following sections, we provide a quick reference on the essential things you should and shouldn't do as you get started with engaging your board and organization in advocacy and lobbying efforts.

Do get educated

Before you do anything, your board directors need to become experts at understanding the differences among advocacy, lobbying, and political action. Have everyone read this chapter and talk through specific examples of situations so directors can ask questions. You should also bring them up to speed on advocacy and lobbying work already in motion at your organization, what you hope to achieve through this work, and just how much money you're willing to spend on it.

Do adopt a written policy

Having a policy on advocacy, lobbying, and political activity is a good idea, regardless of whether you're actively engaged in the work. A comprehensive policy outlines what is and isn't permissible behavior and provides compliance procedures so everyone knows how to stay on the right side of the law.

Even if your board doesn't plan to start anytime soon, the reality is that these situations have a way of finding *you*. A community partner may ask you to cosign a letter on a shared issue, a donor may invite your executive to a political fundraiser, a board director may way to speak up on a social issue, or a staff member may want to attend a protest. Having a policy in place means your team knows what to do, what to decline, and when to ask for more guidance. The Nonprofit Board Toolkit at `www.dummies/nonprofit` for a sample policy.

Do keep it organized

Without the right systems, even the most well-intentioned organizations end up in hot water. As a board, your job isn't to track every little detail yourself. It's to make sure you have the structure in place to ensure compliance. Consider the following:

- Track and report your lobbying expenditures consistently.
- Create a central file to hold all relevant documents, including filings, talking points, and reports.
- Know whether your organization has the 501(h) Election and keep a record of it. (As we explain earlier in the chapter, the 501(h) Election is what an organization uses to opt into the IRS expenditure test.)
- Build updates into your board meetings so it's normalized.

» Designate a compliance person or committee to lead and monitor the work. (See Chapter 11.)

» Orient new board directors and provide refreshers on an annual basis.

» Document any situations where you, your board directors, or staff members engaged in political activity.

Do make it easy

If you're going to win over hearts and minds to your cause, you need to come equipped with the stories and data to do so. Work with management to create talking points, one-pagers, and fact sheets directors can use in their calls and community conversations. Create templates for common emails. And when engaging with elected officials, have one person coordinate scheduling, brief the group before engaging, and debrief after so folks feel good about the work they've done.

Do wear a board badge or nametag

Wearing a nametag or board badge that identifies your affiliation signals to anyone engaged with you that you're advocating/lobbying as a board director and not a private citizen. The more clearly you can distinguish between your personal and professional advocacy efforts, the more easily you'll be able to engage with confidence! Flip to the nearby sidebar "Engaging with political activities as a private citizen" for details on participating on your own time.

Do engage with and thank your lawmakers

Lawmakers and elected officials can be valuable partners to your nonprofit. Sharing your nonprofit's impact with them or inviting them to events where they can participate in or observe your work in action can amplify your organization's ability to impact more people in your community. Remember, these folks are the same people responsible for setting budget priorities and making decisions that affect the place you live, work, and play — decisions that can help or hurt the communities you serve. Most importantly, say thank you. Just like you, lawmakers work in service of the public and seek to enrich the entire community. Building a relationship with your lawmaker is as easy as expressing gratitude.

Do share your story and educate the public

Your personal story matters, especially when you're educating and advocating. Advocacy relies on the stories of everyday citizens who are impacted by an issue or a need. So don't be shy in sharing your feelings about what your mission means to you, how you came to the organization, and why you became a board director. Citizens and lawmakers alike understand the significance of board governance and the part you, as a board director, play in ensuring the whole community's health and durability.

Do partner with coalitions

An African proverb says, "If you want to go fast, go alone. If you want to go far, go together." For nonprofits, this idea couldn't be more true. The majority of nonprofits lack the capacity to engage in advocacy or lobbying on their own. That's where coalitions come in.

Coalitions bring organizations together around a shared issue, pooling and amplifying their voices, resources, and relationships. They do the heavy lifting on monitoring local, state, and national legislation and take the lead on coordinating collective action and response work. Sometimes these coalitions are loose affiliations between leaders, but more often they're independently organized 501(c)(4)s with a membership process and are beholden to delivering resources to you, their organizational partners. Fortunately, many of these coalitions already exist, and a little research can likely reveal groups at the national and local level aligned with your organization's work. For instance, the nonprofit arts sector has medium-specific organizations such as Theatre Communications Group (for nonprofit theatre companies), the League of American Orchestras (for symphonies and orchestras), Opera America, and Dance/USA, among many more. Not every action or bill directly affects your nonprofit, but be aware of what's affecting the broader sector and country. Many social, economic, and cultural issues are deeply intertwined. Staying informed, even of things that feel a bit distant from your mission, keeps you ready to act and protect the communities you serve.

Don't endorse a candidate

Under no circumstances can your 501(c)(3) organization endorse a candidate for public office. This issue is important enough that we gave its own main section ("Recognizing the Bright Red Line"), and we're repeating it here because the stakes are so high. We know this ask can be hard in practice. Sometimes a candidate's platform is built around the issue your nonprofit is trying to address. Maybe they've even volunteered at your events or donated to your cause. Feeling excited for their leadership is natural, especially if you think they get what you do. But none of that changes this rule. The moment your organization endorses a candidate, you're putting your mission at risk. You can talk about the issues and provide education that enhances and lifts up this candidate's platform, but cheer for the cause, not the person. If you're going to preserve public trust, you need to demonstrate you're nonpartisan and that your organization is about the mission, not politics.

Don't coordinate with campaigns

Although we promote joining and participating in collective advocacy, you must draw a distinction between working alongside like-minded organizations and working alongside campaigns, because they're very different things. The IRS strictly prohibits nonprofits from participating in political campaigns, which includes giving donations to, volunteering for, or supporting a candidate's campaign. Meaning that, although you may share values with a campaign, you can't share resources, staff, or the megaphone. Your organization must remain neutral because the work of nonprofits is to help everyone in a community, not just the people who voted a certain way. The moment your organization is perceived as an arm of a campaign, you risk losing the trust of people you serve.

Do be hopeful

Challenging systems and trying to affect things over the long term can be slow, difficult work. As you undertake the work of advocating and lobbying on behalf of your mission, set small, achievable goals, lean on community, and remember why you got started in the first place: your connection to the mission and the impact it has on your community.

IN THIS CHAPTER

» Tackling the quirks of nonprofit finance

» Seeing the board's role in financial oversight

» Interpreting standard financial statements

» Breaking down the budgeting process

Chapter 15
Governing Organizational Finances

Have you ever sat through a finance presentation, nodding along while secretly having no idea what you were really looking at? Well, you're in good company. Many board directors come to the boardroom with various subject-matter expertise. But that doesn't always include experience overseeing finances, and it rarely crosses over into nonprofit finance, which comes with some quirks. That's okay.

REMEMBER

What's not okay is staying the dark about what your organization is doing with its money. As we explore in Chapter 3, directors carry a fundamental fiduciary responsibility to their organizations. Your duties of loyalty, obedience, and care now require you to get educated on your organization's finances and engage with financial reports with a strategic awareness. To be clear, your job isn't to *do* the finances (that's what staff is for). Your job is to lean in, learn new things, ask thoughtful questions, and speak up if you have concerns.

In this chapter, we show you how to analyze your nonprofit's financial performance, providing an accessible how-to on financial oversight. We explain basic concepts, common reports, and things to look out for. Don't worry; we've written this chapter for every board director, not just the financial wizards on the board.

Looking at How Nonprofit Finance Is Unique

Whether you've spent your career working in finance or have only managed your household budget, nonprofit finance will likely feel both familiar and odd in various ways. The core concepts are the same: Money comes in and money goes out. If you have some left over to invest or provide cover in case of a rainy day, fantastic! However, the rules, language, and expectations around nonprofit finance are meaningfully different. We don't cover them all in depth in this chapter, but the following sections outline a few key concepts you need to understand before you dive into board service.

Your nonprofit needs to make a profit

First and foremost, your nonprofit needs to make a profit. The idea that nonprofits can't make money is a pernicious myth that has created a financially fragile sector. A healthy organization is one that can sustain a profit year over year and leverage that money to build reserves, invest in programs that support the people inside and outside the nonprofit, and grow the mission's impact. We debunk this myth more thoroughly in Chapter 22.

Not all revenue is created equal

Like any business, nonprofits make money in different ways. The primary path is through contributions and earnings. *Contributed revenue* includes money from individual donors and private companies as well as grants from foundations and governmental agencies. *Earned revenue* comes from selling services and goods related to the mission. Organizations with savings and investments may also generate investment income.

But here's what matters most for the board to understand: Sometimes money comes with strings attached — and serious ones at that. Whenever your organization earns a dollar, whether from a ticket sale or a donation, it gets recorded in one of two ways: as unrestricted or restricted revenue. Understanding the difference between restricted and unrestricted funds is critical to understanding the risk and financial health of your nonprofit.

- **Unrestricted revenue:** *Unrestricted* is the most desirable form of revenue for nonprofits because your organization can use it however it wants: to pay staff salaries, cover overhead costs like rent, invest in a new program, or whatever. The only thing you're accountable to is the mission.

» **Restricted revenue:** On the other hand, the organization must use *restricted* revenue for a specific purpose or program as designated by the donor, grantor, or funder. These funds go toward general expenses and overhead, and they typically come with reporting requirements and time limits.

REMEMBER

Two organizations with the same budget may have very different financial positions, depending on how funds are designated. A nonprofit with $2 million in restricted grants likely has less flexibility than one with $2 million in unrestricted earned revenue.

Overhead isn't inherently bad

Overhead is a crucial part of running a healthy organization. It includes things like staff salaries, rent, technology, professional services, and other administrative costs. Starving an organization of essential infrastructure, skimping on competitive pay, and making do with outdated technology is a risk to your organization. You can read more about this myth in Chapter 22.

Your governance liability scales with the organization

Good governance and financial oversight in a small organization look very different than a large one, and best practices for one may not be for another. As an organization grows, so does the complexity of the financial ecosystem the board is responsible for overseeing. Restricted gifts, employees, facilities, investments, endowments . . . as the organization expands to take on each of these, so do your responsibilities. Joining a smaller nonprofit may be the right starting point if you're less familiar with finance and board governance.

REMEMBER

Not only do you need to add directors with relevant expertise as you scale, but the whole board also needs to grow its financial knowledge and governance capability. When looking at prospective directors, choosing people scaled to your level of experience is just as important.

Balancing the Three Essentials of Good Oversight

Even though the specific responsibilities of the board vary depending on the organization's size and complexity, you want to focus on three essentials to achieve excellence in financial oversight: culture, expertise, and time, which we cover in the following sections. Figure 15-1 shows the three essential elements of good oversight.

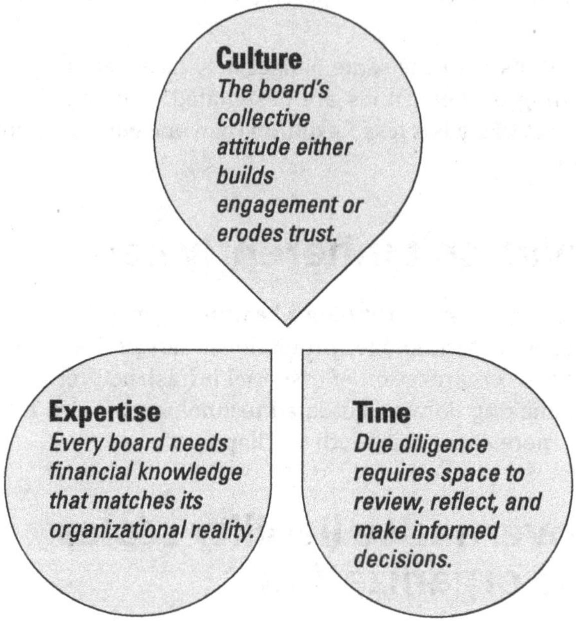

FIGURE 15-1: The three essentials of good governance.

Creating a healthy culture

Culture is the foundation of good governance. Beyond any policy or process at work, the boards' collective attitude in the boardroom will either amplify building engagement or erode trust. When that culture is healthy, you see it in how the board operates:

- **You encourage asking questions and don't assume comprehension.** No one is embarrassed to ask, "Why does this exist?" or "What is this?" Directors are comfortable expressing their doubts or gaps in knowledge, and people make a sincere effort to ensure everyone understands what they're looking at and what it means for the organization.
- **Education is a routine, ongoing practice.** New board directors go through an orientation. The treasurer or staff leader bridges reports with added context; a presentation comes before budget votes; periodic training sessions make their way into the boardroom.

» **Reports are delivered on a regular schedule and are accessible to a nonfinancial audience.** Directors can track trends and spot variances easily and don't need a bachelor's degree in accounting to make sense of the numbers.

» **Everyone understands their role.** The board president, the treasurer and finance committee, management, and individual directors are all clear on what they're responsible for, including when they need to weigh in and how to raise concerns.

Finding expertise

Every board needs to find expertise that meets the financial reality of its organization. A retired bookkeeper may be a perfect fit for a small community nonprofit, whereas an organization with complex investments, restricted funds, and real estate needs a much deeper bench of experts such as wealth advisors or CFOs. Directors with for-profit financial experience can be particularly valuable because they bring tend to bring a commercial attitude toward financial strategy management and forecasting that many nonprofits can benefit from. At the same time, individuals with nonprofit financial experience can ensure the board doesn't miss the nuances unique to the nonprofit sector, such as managing donor restricted gifts and strategizing overhead costs. (Flip to the earlier section "Not all revenue is created equal" for more on restricted revenue.) These directors also help inform their for-profit colleagues of the delicate balancing act between fulfilling the mission and achieving a healthy bottom line.

TIP

Having financial professionals on your board roster bolsters your organization's reputation, not to mention donor and funder trust. Publicly listing directors and their company affiliation on the organization's website is common and can signal credibility and inspire confidence in those interested in investing in your mission.

REMEMBER

A board doesn't need to be composed entirely of financial professionals to achieve excellence in financial oversight, but it does need to have access to the right knowledge at the right time. Staff, vendors, and consultants/firms can help provide support for strong financial practices in your nonprofit.

You don't need to be a financial wizard as a board director in your first six months or even your first year. However, you're expected to become an expert in your organization's finances over the course of your tenure. That means asking questions and engaging in education so you can understand the reports you receive, make informed decisions about strategy and programs, confidently vote on the budget, and weigh in on financial policies.

Managing time

Time is your most limited (and most valuable) resource, especially in managing your organization's money. You and the board need time on two fronts:

- **Conducting due diligence:** You need to distribute financial reports well in advance of board meetings so directors can review them properly. Board meetings need to carve out enough time for financial education, report walk-throughs, and follow-up questions. Some financial processes, like budgeting, can be time intensive, and rushing through them undermines oversight. Above all, sometimes you just need time as a board to sit with big questions — to not have to rush headlong into major decisions with financial implications.
- **Personally understanding your nonprofit's finances:** Good governance requires a commitment to spending time understanding the reality of the organization's financial picture. When reports arrive in advance, read them in advance. Come to the meeting with questions already written down. Follow up after meetings with anything that may have been unclear and seek out the information you need to feel like you truly understand what you're looking at.

WARNING

Board directors can face real legal exposure when financial problems go unaddressed. To turn a blind eye, even unintentionally, can open the door to public scrutiny or liability. Don't hesitate to ask for clarity when you need it.

Understanding Common Financial Reports

Nonprofit financial statements are reports that summarize your organization's financial activities and overall health. They may show information at a moment in time or over a period of time, and each conveys a different story.

One of the core duties of your role is to read and review any financial statements provided ahead of each board meeting and identify questions and comments that help you and the board better understand the financial picture of the organization.

You may rely on staff or external consultants (like auditors, CPAs, and bookkeepers) to summarize the finances, but doing so isn't a substitute for your understanding. This knowledge is a critical part of monitoring the organization's overall health and sustainability.

REMEMBER

Every organization approaches financial reporting differently. The following sections dig into the core concepts and explain frequent reports nonprofits use, but you still need to sit down with your treasurer, senior financial leaders, or finance committee to understand how your organization really works.

K.I.S.S: KEEP IT SHORT, SILLY!

Your board should work with management or your financial professionals to ensure that reports are clear, brief, and written in a way that a nonfinancial audience can access. This approach means everyone on your board can understand the money and make better decisions more easily. People are less likely to read a ten-page budget sheet with every single line item or a lengthy written narrative, and that's more likely to lead to misunderstanding. Don't be afraid to use colorful graphs and charts!

If you're looking at financial statements for the first time, it can be overwhelming. It's like learning an entirely new language! But stick with it. The more you look at the terminology and numbers, the more comfortable you get. It takes practice and patience.

TIP

To find out more about financial reports, check out *Reading Financial Reports For Dummies* by Lita Epstein (Wiley).

Statement of financial position (balance sheet)

The *statement of financial position* is the nonprofit equivalent of a balance sheet. This report is a snapshot of your financial situation at a single point in time, specifically looking at what you own *(assets)* and what you owe *(liabilities)*. It also shows the difference between the two *(net assets)*, usually broken down by whether funds are unrestricted, temporarily restricted, or permanently restricted.

Assets

You may see many types of assets on your balance sheet.

- *Liquid assets* include things like cash on hand and bank balances, prepaid expenses (for example, insurance paid in advance for the year), and short-term investments.
- *Long-term assets* include property and buildings, equipment, furniture, vehicles, and any long-term investments (such as an endowment or board reserve).
- Other asset classes may appear, such as "pledges receivable" (donations that have been pledged but not yet received).

A good report also ensures assets are classified as either restricted or unrestricted. (You can read more on those designations in the earlier section "Not all revenue is created equal.")

Liabilities

Liabilities include everything your organization owes and are split into two categories: current and long-term. *Current liabilities* include obligations due within the next year, such as accounts payable (for example, bills and invoices that are due), accrued expenses such as salaries and taxes that haven't been paid yet, and rent and credit card debt. On the other hand, *long-term liabilities* are obligations that extend beyond a year, like a mortgage or deferred revenue tied to multiyear grants.

Balance sheet questions to ask

Here are some key questions to ask when reviewing balance sheets:

- **How many months of operating expenses do we have in cash?** If all revenue suddenly stopped, how long could you continue to carry on operations before cash ran out? The general recommendation is to have between three and six months' worth of operating reserves on hand. Having less than two or three months is a red flag, but so is having too much, such as one to two years' worth. An excess signals you aren't in urgent need of funds and may lead to a decrease in donations and grants.
- **Do we have a line of credit (such as a credit card), and are we relying on it regularly to cover essential operations?** Having credit cards to cover routine operational expenses such as travel, online purchases, vendor payments, and so on is totally normal (and necessary). It not only is more convenient but also minimizes the need for staff reimbursements. However, regularly relying on credit cards for major operating expenses such as payroll or utilities may signify the organization is struggling with cash flow. It isn't an immediate red flag, but it's certainly worth probing more deeply.
- **Are we carrying significant credit card debt?** Many credit cards carry high interest rates, so every month you carry credit card debt, you must spend donor dollars to cover the cost. Nonprofits should aim to pay credit cards off every single month so they never carry a balance on a card.
- **How much of our money is actually unrestricted versus restricted?** Understanding how much money your organization actually has access to at any given time is critical. As we explain in the earlier section "Not all revenue is created equal," restricted assets offer a lot less spending flexibility than unrestricted assets do. If most of your assets are restricted, the organization has fewer options for covering operating costs and respond to unexpected needs. Having more unrestricted assets gives you real freedom to make

decisions about the mission and operations. Restricted money isn't bad, but it needs to be monitored against the larger picture.

» **Are unrestricted net assets growing or shrinking?** Your *net assets* are the value of what you have left over after you subtract your liabilities from your assets. These are also classified as restricted or unrestricted. Ideally, you want to see your unrestricted net assets sustaining at current levels or growing, which indicates a healthier financial position overall.

Statement of activities (income statement)

The *statement of activities*, otherwise known as an income statement or profit and loss statement, tells the story of your organization. It shows how you make money and where you're spending it over a given period. You typically review it quarter over quarter against your budget and prior year's performance. Think of it as your budget in motion.

A good income statement also flags *variances*, which occur when actual financial performance is different than budgeted performance or past performance. Anywhere you're off track is a flag that may warrant closer attention or action.

BALANCE SHEET RED FLAGS

The following are concerning items to see on your organization's balance sheet:

- **Negative net assets:** This situation means your organization owes more money than it has; it's a major indicator of financial distress.
- **Liabilities that are growing while assets stay flat or are shrinking:** If what you owe is growing faster than what you're making, you'll eventually run out of money to pay your bills.
- **Shrinking cash position:** You need cash to operate on a day-to-day basis. If your cash position is shrinking, your organization is headed in a dangerous direction that may impact your ability to pay vendors and staff.
- **More restricted assets than unrestricted assets:** This scenario limits your flexibility to cover administrative costs and unexpected needs.
- **No line of credit:** This one is more of a yellow flag. Credit cards offer organizations a critical safety net and cushion for managing inevitable cash flow gaps that come with grant funding and donor cycles. Without a line of credit, your organization carries a little more risk.

REMEMBER

Always read your statement of activities alongside your balance sheet (which we cover earlier in the chapter) for a complete picture of your organization's financial health.

Revenue

Your organization brings in revenue in a variety of ways, depending on your mission:

- *Earned revenue* is any money your organization receives from selling services and goods related to the mission. This category can be things like tickets for workshops, tuition for educational programs, gift shop merchandise, and fees associated with professional services. This type of revenue offers your organization more financial predictability and stability and reduces the reliance on grants and donations.
- *Contributed revenue* is any money people contribute to your organization (think individual donations, grants from governmental agencies and foundations, and sponsorship dollars for an event). It also includes in-kind gifts, such as donations of computers, clothing, food, furniture, and so on, as well as pro bono services a professional firm provides. Basically, contributed revenue occurs when someone gives something to the organization without anything in return. As we mention earlier in the chapter, these gifts sometimes come with restrictions or reporting requirements that can limit how your organization can spend those dollars.

Expenses

Your organization has to spend money to fulfill its mission, run daily operations, and raise more money. Expenses look different in every organization, but they often fall into some common categories:

- *General administration and management costs,* often referred to as overhead costs, cover anything required to maintain daily business operations outside of program and service delivery. This area may include rent and utilities, insurance, office supplies like printing and postage, IT and technology like computers, professional fees for consultants and accountants, travel and meeting expenses, and board meeting costs. It also should encompass any salaries, wages, and benefits of executive-level and management staff (executive director, finance team, human resources, and general admin staff).

REMEMBER

The board shouldn't shy away from funding general administrative and management needs because these items form the essential infrastructure that powers everything your mission work is built on. Without strong leadership, sound systems, and modern technology in place, your mission will stall out.

- *Program expenses* are any expenses directly related to delivering your mission programs and services. The specifics vary widely from organization to organization. A nonprofit running a farm may include things like fertilizer, seeds, and farmstand fees. One running an education program may need online classroom software, print out materials, or workshop supplies. It also should incorporate the salaries, wages, and benefits of any staff responsible for program delivery.
- *Fundraising expenses* are anything you spend on raising more money, such as running a gala, hiring a fundraising consultant, producing marketing materials for a campaign, or using a piece of software to manage your donor database. It also should include the salaries, wages, and benefits of any staff responsible for fundraising. You always want to be looking at how much you spend on fundraising in relation to how much you're raising to assess whether it's a good return on investment.
- In some cases, you may also incur *capital expenses,* which are funds used to buy, fix, or maintain physical long-term assets, such as a facility or expensive equipment.

Income statement questions to ask

Here are some important questions to pose as you review the statement of activities:

- **What are the biggest gaps between budget and actual performance (actuals), and why? Were these variances anticipated or a surprise?** Looking at where variances occur allows the board to understand where overspending or poor performance may be happening or corrective action is necessary. Furthermore, you need to analyze the reasons behind any variance that was unanticipated or surprising to make more accurate and realistic projections in the future.
- **Are we operating at a surplus or a deficit, and is that by choice?** A *surplus* is when your organization makes more money than it spends and thus has some leftover at the end of the year (a profit) that it can put into savings or other investments. This scenario is the ideal state; it allows your organization to build a stronger financial foundation and reinvest in its programs and people.

A *deficit,* on the other hand, is when you spend more than you make and end the year with a loss. Sometimes, organizations strategically plan to have a deficit, choosing to spend reserves to make targeted investments such as upgrading technology, launching new programs, or hiring more staff. However, unplanned deficits (whether because of rising costs, lower donations, or poor budgeting) are a major issue and a red flag that requires swift action and course correction.

- **How diverse is our revenue?** A huge portion of nonprofit organizations rely on a single source of revenue, which places them at huge risk for financial hardship. What happens if your primary source of revenue falls through? How will you make sure programming continues? For example, say funding from one donor makes up about 50 percent of your organization's revenue. If that donor decides to redirect or reduce their giving next year, your organization will be left in the lurch trying to find other resources — or worse, cancelling programs. Diversifying revenues creates a stronger financial safety net, ensuring your organization can provide its programming with minimal disruption regardless of whether one source falls through.
- **Is our spending reflective of our mission and strategy?** If your board has stated your priority is X, does your organization's revenue and spending actually show that? As a board, look at where expenses are distributed at a high level. For example, if youth workforce development is important this year, but you're only spending 5 percent of your budget on it, can you really say it's a priority? As the saying goes, "Your budget reveals what you value."
- **What percent of expenses are related to fundraising? Are these costs warranted relative to benefits received?** It costs money to raise money, and some of these costs are certainly warranted. A gala that costs $50,000 but raises $350,000 is a good deal, but one that raises only $100,000? Not so much. Remember, every dollar you spend on fundraising is a dollar you can't spend on programming, so you want to look for a good return on investment (ROI).

  A very strong ROI is a 5:1 return (meaning you raise $5 for every $1 spent). A return of 2:1 or less may indicate inefficiencies or poor performance. Ask the treasurer or management to provide this level of analysis with your reporting. For more metrics of fundraising success, see Chapter 13.
- **Are we paying staff enough?** Staff are the lifeblood of your organization, and nonprofits are serious businesses. Although setting salaries and wages for staff is the executive director's job, the board should be asking questions like "Are we offering competitive wages and benefits? What's our compensation policy, and is it equitable?" For example, are female employees paid for the same amount of work/level of position as their male counterparts? Does your compensation provide a cost-of-living adjustment for all full-time employees? Ask a similar set of questions about executive compensation as well.

INCOME STATEMENT WARNING SIGNS

The following are red flags on your income statement:

- Operating with a deficit year over year with no plan
- Repeated variances in the same category, suggesting a problem with forecasting
- Overdependence on one or two sources or revenue, posing a risk to operations if one was to disappear
- Expenses growing while revenues decline or stay flat
- High fundraising costs with lower return on investment
- Surprises that management should've seen coming

The Form 990

The most important financial report that the board is responsible for is the *Form 990*. This document is your organization's tax return, which is made available to the general public. As a board, your role is to ensure that the form is complete, accurate, and submitted on time to the IRS.

The 990 includes more than just your financial performance numbers; It reports on how you're delivering your mission's impact. It discloses the identities and compensation of board directors and executives while also showing where money comes from (grants, donations, and so on) and where it goes (programs, fundraising, administration). Altogether, it shares a complete story about your organization over the past year.

We aren't going to walk through every line of the Form 990. That level of detail is best left to your accountant or financial staff. Instead, in the following sections we share what due diligence looks like and what to keep in mind as you work the process.

Filling out your Form 990

Before you submit your 990, you need to jump through a few hoops:

1. **Finalize your financial statements and collect impact data,** making sure everything is accurately reconciled and your biggest accomplishments are captured.

2. **Figure out what version of the 990 you should be filing.**

   It comes in a few formats depending on the size of the organization:

   - Form 990-N (e-postcard): Gross receipts less than $50,000
   - Form 990-EZ: Gross receipts less than $200,000 and total assets less than $500,000
   - Form 990: Gross receipts more than $200,000 or total assets more than $500,000

3. **Fill out the 990.**

   We recommend engaging a financial professional that specializes in nonprofit accounting to either fill out or review your 990. This move ensures you're compliantly reporting your revenues and expenses.

4. **Have your finance committee review the 990 in depth.** Include the individual responsible for preparing it.

5. **Send a draft of the 990 to the full board at least two to three weeks before it's submitted.** Collect any questions and confirm answers go out to the full board as well. Individuals should be reviewing to confirm the numbers and program impact data align with what they've seen all year.

TIP

The IRS doesn't require the board to vote to approve the 990 for submittal. However, we recommend doing so because it guarantees space for people to ask questions and creates a record in the minutes that it was reviewed.

Considering other reports

As we mention earlier in the chapter, the complexity of your financial reporting grows as your organization does. Depending on how big you are or how complex your operation, you may encounter the following reports.

Statement of functional expenses

A *statement of functional expenses* is a standardized nonprofit financial report that breaks your organizational expenses into three categories: program, administrative, and fundraising. Organizations use it to fill out the Form 990 we discuss earlier in the chapter; it ensures all organizations are reporting similarly fashion, which makes reviewing and comparing against previous years and other nonprofits easier for the general public.

Statement of cash flows

A *statement of cash flows* shows where your cash comes from *(cash inflow)* and where it goes *(cash outflow)* during a specific period reveals whether you have enough cash to cover expenses. Nonprofits mostly use it internally to show whether the organization is maximizing its resources and find opportunities or areas of concern to be addressed.

If your organization is delivering its programs and raising funds effectively, it should have a positive cash flow. *Note:* Some nonprofits operate seasonally, and their cash flow fluctuates in response. A performing arts company that performs eight months out of the year may experience high cash flow from tickets around each show or during the season and a low cash flow during the offseason. Cash flow statements serve as a forecasting tool for future planning and for pacing out expenses.

Audit materials

As your organization grows and takes on larger grants, it may choose or be required to get an audit. An *audit* is an independent assessment of your organization's financial performance and internal controls. After the process is complete, a report is usually generated and issued to the board.

REMEMBER

The IRS requires nonprofits to undergo an audit only if they receive a federal grant of more than $1 million. State law, grant makers, and foundations may also require audits. Considering how costly and time-intensive these processes can be, your organization should consult with a financial professional to determine the best approach for your situation.

Investment performance report

If your organization has investments, this type of report shows you how your portfolio has performed over a specific period, including any losses or gains. The board needs to look at where money is invested to ensure that funds are being managed sustainably, ethically, and in alignment with organizational values.

Narratives

A *narrative* is a detailed written explanation that explains revenue and expenses, including any assumptions that have gone into estimates or an accounting of circumstances that may have led to variances. These items are as brief as a one-pager with bullet points summarizing the report's highlights, including key wins, grants/funding received, and heads-up flags for the board to be aware of.

Dashboards

As an organization gets larger, it may choose to use a *dashboard* approach to reporting. This element is a visual snapshot of an organization's financial health, including key performance indicators and metrics, charts and graphs, and other top-level numbers. This makes it easier to get to the big-picture conversations without having to browse through dozens of spreadsheets without your head spinning!

Tackling Budgeting and Planning

Every nonprofit needs a budget, but a budget is far more than a financial management tool. Where you spend your money is a direct expression of your mission and values. How much you invest in different programs, how well you're paying staff, how much you spend on administration and keep in your reserves . . . all these things say something about who you are and what you believe as an organization.

For this reason, budget oversight is one of your key responsibilities as a board director. It comes with three dimensions: contributing during the development of the budget, formally approving the budget, and actively monitoring performance against the budget throughout the year. In this section, we briefly discuss each.

REMEMBER

No two organizations approach budgeting the exact same way. The right structure depends on what your organization does and what its scale is. Some nonprofits budget by project and others by department or function. Some operate on a one-year (annual) budget cycle, but others plan across multiple years. What matters is that your budget is comprehensive, easy for your board to understand, and consistently developed year over year.

Determining who leads the process

Who owns the budget process depends on your organization's size and structure. If your organization doesn't have staff, responsibility for developing and overseeing the budget likely falls to the board treasurer or the finance committee. Make sure you select board directors who have real financial experience to own and lead the process.

If your organization does have employees, the most senior financial person on the team is the one who usually takes lead responsibility for budget development. In small organizations (fewer than 20 employees), that's probably the executive director. As an organization grows and brings on dedicated financial leadership (such as a director of finance, a controller, or a CFO), leadership may be assigned farther downline.

Regardless of who leads the process, the board's role remains the same: to provide input, ask questions, approve, and monitor the budget and its goals. Even if the staff does the building, the board still needs to do the governing.

WARNING

Staff or third-party contractors like bookkeepers can help organize your finances and the day-to-day building blocks that help start the budgeting process. However, they can't be responsible for developing it entirely.

Preparing and approving the budget

At a high level, the budgeting preparation process follows the same essential arc: Gather information, project costs and revenue, consolidate, review, and approve. In the following sections, we look at each a little bit more closely.

Gathering information

The process begins by collecting as much relevant information as possible about where your organization has been and where it's going. This step may include looking at things like:

- Past financial performance reports, sometimes spanning several years back in order to see trends over time
- Program plans showing what activities or services you're planning to deliver in the cycle ahead
- Grant requirements, including any funding restrictions or requirements on expenses and any known dates that grants will be paid out/received so that you can project when revenue will be accounted for
- Staffing plans, including any known or predicted changes to head count and/or compensation
- Current and previous investment plans, snapshots, and reports such as endowment performance and reinvestment plan
- Anything else that reflects how the organization functioned during the last budget cycle and how it expects to function in the next

TIP

Many organizations also use this moment to reflect on the larger political, economic, and social context and determine whether they need to factor any risks into their planning process. An upcoming election, a recent shift in the funding landscape, changes in the regulatory environment, and broader economic conditions can all affect revenue or costs.

Projecting revenue and costs

With the relevant information in hand (see the preceding section), you're ready to project revenues and costs. Accounting for year-over-year recurring costs and stable funding streams such as a multiyear grant is easy. New or variable costs projections require more work, including soliciting estimates, doing some research, or making some educated estimations. In larger organizations, individual departments typically prepare their own budget of revenues and expenses that then get rolled up into a single larger, organization-wide budget.

Sending to the finance committee for review

After the budget has been drafted, it typically goes to the finance committee for first review. The committee does a deeper dive, looking line by line, stress-testing assumptions, and requesting revisions where needed. This layer of scrutiny is important because it ensures that those with the deepest financial expertise have already rigorously examined the budget by the time it reaches the full board. After one or more rounds of revision, the final budget goes to the full board for approval.

Approving the budget as a board

Approving the budget is a responsibility that belongs to the whole board, not just those who serve on the finance committee. The person leading the budget development process should present it to the board by walking through the numbers at a high level; covering key assumptions underlying the numbers; and pointing out areas of notable investment, any risks the board will want to monitor, and what the organization is ultimately trying to achieve in the upcoming cycle. After the presentation, open the floor for questions before calling for a vote to approve.

REMEMBER

If you aren't on the finance committee, the budget approval meeting may be the first time you're seeing the budget in detail. This situation is perfectly normal. Your job is to show up, read the materials, and ask questions. Most importantly, don't be shy! No question is too basic, and you have a right to understand what you're approving — especially if something seems unclear or inconsistent with the organization's mission.

REMEMBER

Repeat after us: "Nose in, fingers out." This phrase is a reminder about where your role begins and ends. As a board director, your job is to understand the big picture and make sure the budget reflects the mission and strategic priorities. It's *not* to wade into the operational weeds, so to speak, and debate individual line items. How many staples to order, which vendor is being used for supplies, or whether a travel budget should be $4,500 or $5,000 are all too far down in the details. When reviewing the budget, keep your questions focused on strategy and impact. That's where your perspective as a board director is most valuable. Table 15-1 offers some tips.

TABLE 15-1 Asking better budget questions

Instead of Asking This	Ask This
Why are we spending $50 on staples and postage?	Are our administrative costs in line with other organizations of our size and type?
Why does the marketing budget look so high?	How are our investments in marketing improving our visibility and access to services?
Can we get cheaper caterers for the gala?	Is our events strategy generating a strong enough return to justify the investment?
Why are we paying so much for software?	Are we appropriately investing in the infrastructure and tools our staff needs to be effective?
Can we cut the training budget?	How are we investing in staff development, and what's the risk if we reduce the investment?

Monitoring the budget

Ongoing monitoring is arguably the most important part of the entire process, and it continues from the moment one budget is approved until the moment the next one is approved. You engage with the budget regularly through the financial reports we discuss earlier in the chapter. You compare actual financial performance against what was budgeted and look for variances. From there, you can ask questions and make adjustments as needed.

In an ideal world, actual performance would track perfectly against budget, but in practice it rarely does. And that's not necessarily cause for alarm. Budgets are built on assumptions, and assumptions change when they meet reality — new information emerges, programs evolve, people behave in unexpected ways, costs suddenly rise, or something happens externally. Deviation from budget is normal; what matters more is how you question and respond to it.

At minimum, we believe a healthy board is reviewing financial performance at least once a quarter. That means the full board receives a high-level set of reports, with the finance committee conducting a deeper, more detailed review as needed. The frequency of reporting and depth of engagement expected vary with the organization's size and complexity.

In larger institutions with professional financial staff, the board is most likely operating at a very high altitude, with a focus more on strategy, trends, and risks. In smaller or younger organizations, board directors may need to be a little more closely engaged with the specifics. Either way, the obligation is the same: Open up the reports, read through them, and speak up.

Changing course on the plan

The best laid plans are just that: plans! Sometimes, despite everyone's best efforts, circumstances demand that the plan changes. Nonprofits commonly reach the midpoint of the cycle and realize the budget doesn't reflect reality. Depending on how off course things have drifted, the response may be to *reforecast* (update the existing budget to reflect new assumptions and conditions) or, in more extreme cases, to abandon the budget and build a new one from scratch.

TIP

Not every variance warrants a reforecast, but some things do. We're talking things that fundamentally affect the organizations' ability to do business, like major, unexpected shifts to operations; unpredicted disasters or crises (think COVID-19); sudden or significant losses of funding; or shifts in public policy or conditions. What these situations share is that they fall outside the range of predictability and create a situation where the original plan is unworkable as a guide. In these cases, board and management need to work together quickly and in close coordination.

REMEMBER

Having to reforecast or rebuild your budget can feel like a failure. And sure, you'll certainly learn lessons and discover ways you can more effectively predict risk in the future. But it also is a sign of a board and management team that's paying attention and willing to make hard calls in service of the organization's long-term health.

IN THIS CHAPTER

» Discovering key policies to protect your organization

» Ensuring you enact necessary safeguards outside policymaking

» Creating an ethical foundation for board governance

» Building a culture of compliance

Chapter 16

Protecting Your Mission with Good Policies and Legal Practices

When it comes to governing a nonprofit, setting policy may be a bit tedious, but it's incredibly necessary. The policies you put in place protect your organization from serious legal or ethical risks. We're talking about how your nonprofit handles conflicts of interest, what happens if an employee raises a legal concern, how to protect confidential information, how the board and staff make decisions that align with the mission, and much more.

Your nonprofit operates on trust. Donors give you money; the IRS grants you tax-exempt status; your community shows up and volunteers. This is all possible because of the assumption that you're running an ethical and transparent operation. Your code of conduct, governance and operational policies, and legal practices are key to protecting all that goodwill.

But good policies aren't only about protecting your organization and its reputation. As we discuss in Chapter 3, board directors carry a legal and fiduciary responsibility to the organization they serve. When things go wrong, you and your fellow board directors are accountable for those outcomes too.

REMEMBER

Risk comes in many shapes and sizes, and as your nonprofit grows, you'll inevitably encounter some of them: financial risks, operational risks, governance and compliance risks, reputational risks, and so on. You can combat these risks in many ways, which we explore in Chapter 17, but one of the most impactful ways your board can help manage risk is by setting good policy.

Policies just make your life easier in the long run. Clearer guidelines create fewer awkward conversations down the road, help you ground your decision-making, and build confidence that the organization is fulfilling its mission. The good news is, you don't need to write all your policies at once.

In this chapter, we aim to give you working knowledge of where nonprofits tend to get in trouble, which policies your organization simply must have, where to start, and how to foster a culture of ethical leadership. This is about building an organization worth the trust people put in it.

TIP

Many nonprofits, especially small- to mid-size ones, take a reactive approach to risk management, creating policies only when issues arise. But by then, the damage is often already done. Don't wait for something to go wrong. The best time to get your policies in order is before you need them.

Understanding Governance and Operational Policies. During your time serving on your board, you'll deal with two types of policies, governance and operational.

- *Governance policies* are high-level, board-driven rules ensuring legal compliance and adherence to strategic direction. These help the board manage circumstances that present significant risk to the organization or come with serious consequences if mishandled.
- *Operational policies* are staff-driven, day-to-day rules and procedures detailing how work is done. They address things like remote work, health and safety, technology use, hiring and recruitment, and so forth. These policies are set and managed by your nonprofit's executive.

Determining the policies you need

Not every situation requires a formal policy. Keep in mind that every policy comes with the burden of more processes to follow. Having too many policies will end up slowing down decision-making and frustrating staff while also sending a signal of distrust. So, the real question is whether an issue is worth reviewing, documenting, and managing over time. You'll likely need a policy when:

- The stakes are high (in cost, risk, time, number of people affected, and so on).
- The consequences of getting something wrong are serious.
- The issue is ongoing, and everyone would benefit from a straightforward policy addressing it.
- Guidance is needed for others to act consistently across the organization.
- The issue impacts an entire department or multiple teams.

Long story short? Write a policy if the stakes are high and people need clear guidance on how to act consistently. If it's a one-off or low-risk situation, manage it in the moment.

Knowing when to engage a lawyer

When it comes to writing policies, you're not required to consult a lawyer. State nonprofit associations offer templates for all the policies covered in this chapter. That said, you should engage legal counsel if you operate in a highly regulated area (such as health care, housing, immigration, and the like), if you're facing a significant amount of exposure to risk, or if you're unsure how to adapt a policy to your organization's needs.

On the other hand, you may find yourself picking up the phone to call your lawyer when it comes to interpreting and applying your policies. A personnel dispute or termination, a formal complaint, and the threat of potential litigation are all situations that require you to interpret, document, and act on your policies. A legal consultation can help you navigate the situation and minimize and manage the risk.

Getting clear on the logistics

As you start thinking about creating policies for your organization, you'll want to make sure everyone is clear on who leads the process and who gets a say, how a policy gets approved, and what to do if someone veers off course. Here are five common logistical questions boards ask about policymaking:

- **Who drafts policy?** Typically, the governance committee writes the governance policies the board must follow. Operational policies, such as those found in an employee handbook, are more commonly drafted by the nonprofit's staff.

- **Who approves policy?** The board approves all governance policies and occasionally is responsible for approving operational policies.
- **How often should policies be updated?** You should review your governance policies every two or three years.
- **What happens if someone violates a policy?** You must investigate and respond to any violations. The specific procedures and consequences, including who investigates and decides on the possible responses, will vary depending on the nature of the violation and the requirements of the policy that was violated.
- **Do we need a policy for everything?** Please, don't go overboard. Policies should be broadly written and address areas of real risk. Start with issues that are critical to your organization and build from there.

Writing Essential Governance Policies

Governance policies are guidelines that tell your board and staff how to handle situations that present risk to your organization. Whether you're writing a new policy or updating an existing one, here are a few things to keep in mind:

- Assess your organization's specific needs and risks before starting.
- Involve key stakeholders in policy development.
- Clearly articulate each policy's purpose, procedures, and who is impacted.
- Review and update policies every 2-3 years to keep them relevant and effective.
- Ensure policies are written accessibly in plain terms that can be understood by anyone reading.
- Check that your policies comply with state and federal law.

If you are just beginning to compile a set of governance policies for your organization, start with some of the most important ones: conflicts of interest, whistle-blowing, grievances, and document retention, which we look at in this section.

TIP

From there, your board can expand its effort, adding policies that are relevant to your unique operation. In this case, try to tackle one policy a month or assign the policy-writing project to a committee to complete and maintain. Recognizing that this is a big undertaking, build your policy manual bit by bit instead of all in one go.

Conflict of interest policy

Does this scenario sound familiar? Your organization needs a caterer for its gala. A board director who runs a catering company offers a discount, and without looking any further, the board agrees to the deal. Or the board votes to appoint a new director who turns out to be related to an existing one. Or a fellow director asks you to donate to another organization they're involved with. Situations like these come up more often than you'd expect, and all are examples of a conflict of interest.

A *conflict of interest* occurs when a board director or employee is in a position to influence a decision that may result in personal, financial, or professional gain. It can also include circumstances that *appear* to be beneficial to someone affiliated with the nonprofit, even if there was no wrongdoing. Anyone working for your organization has a responsibility not to use their position, or the organization's name, property, or programs, for personal benefit.

A conflict of interest on its own isn't necessarily illegal, but it must be disclosed, recorded, and managed transparently. Failure to do so can result in reputational harm, loss of community trust, and legal penalties.

A well-written conflict of interest policy should be policy #1 in your board manual. It must (1) require individuals on the board and staff to disclose any known or suspected conflicts of interest, (2) prohibit directors from participating in discussions about or voting on any matter that may personally benefit them, and (3) outline a method to resolve conflicts and define consequences for violating the policy (including dismissal).

TIP

Conflicts of interest aren't always obvious. Here are some common scenarios to help you identify conflicts that may arise:

- A director accepts gifts, favors, gratuities, or anything of monetary value from contractors or vendors.
- A director participates in the decision to award a contract to a vendor that they or a member of their immediate family personally benefits from.
- A director recommends the hiring of a family member or close friend, and the board approves the recommendation without a competitive, transparent hiring process.
- A director is a close relative of the executive leader or a member of staff.
- A director serves on the board of a nonprofit with a similar mission and service area, and is expected to fundraise for both.
- A director is romantically involved with a member of staff or another director.

Enforcing your policy

You can prepare for and actively manage conflicts of interest in several ways, including taking these precautions:

- Issue an annual questionnaire requiring board directors to list their employers, businesses they own, family members and their business interests, and other boards they serve on.
- Conduct a formal review process of conflict disclosures via your governance or executive committee.
- Keep accurate records of any decisions that may involve a conflict by taking careful minutes at board meetings and maintaining good document-retention practices.
- Train your board to identify conflicts, using learning tools such as role-play.

Handling conflicts

Don't panic! A conflict of interest isn't automatically a crisis. What matters more is how you handle it. The moment you recognize a potential conflict, the right move is to act quickly and transparently.

- Disclose the conflict orally or in writing to another board officer or the designated committee. It's better to err on the safe side and report anything that seems to cross the line.
- Recuse yourself from any discussions or voting that pertains to the conflict.

If you're unsure if a situation presents an actual conflict, talk with a governance consultant, HR professional, or legal advisor and document what you discover.

REMEMBER

In some circumstances, a conflict is significant enough to require additional steps, up to and including removal from the board. For example, dismissal likely will be necessary when a board director has a financial stake in a major decision or is in a close personal relationship with a senior staff member. Obviously, whether a conflict constitutes a need for removal depends on the specifics of each situation.

WARNING

Ethical governance sometimes means going beyond right-or-wrong compliance. Failure to manage conflicts of interest can lead to damaged relationships, loss of public trust, regulatory scrutiny, and, in serious cases, personal liability for board directors.

Whistleblower policy

No one likes to think that something dishonest or illegal may be occurring inside their organization, but misconduct can happen anywhere. A whistleblower policy essentially says: *If you see something, say something*. It encourages people to come forward with credible concerns about wrongdoing without fear of retaliation. This includes concerns about fraud, theft, or misuse of funds, falsification of records, illegal activity, harassment and discrimination, or any conduct that goes against the organization's stated values and policies.

Your whistleblower policy signals to your community that you take ethical governance seriously. A well-written policy should:

- Identify who is expected to report concerns and under what circumstances.
- Clearly state that anyone who comes forward in good faith will be protected from retaliation of any kind.
- Define a path for raising concerns, including whom to contact and how.
- Name a compliance officer or ombudsperson responsible for receiving, investigating, and resolving complaints.
- Detail how complaints will be acknowledged, investigated, documented, and resolved.
- Acknowledge that reports must be made in good faith, with reasonable cause.
- Commit to protecting the identity of the whistleblower to the greatest extent possible.

Beyond the specifics, having a whistleblower policy in place contributes to an overall culture of transparency and accountability, and gives your organization the opportunity to address issues before they escalate into a greater risk.

Even without a policy in place, whistleblowers have many legal protections. U.S. law prohibits all corporations, including nonprofits, from retaliating against anyone who raises the alarm on possible financial mismanagement or misconduct. And more than 45 states have enacted further protections for whistleblowers.

TIP

Picking the right ombudsperson can be tricky, depending on your organization's size and resources. Ideally, you want to retain an independent third party, such as a lawyer or auditor who has no stake in the outcome and can investigate any complaints objectively. In practice, most nonprofits pick a board director. If you choose this path, designate at least two people to receive complaints so someone neutral is available to investigate if the complaint involves one of them.

Grievance/complaint policy

Every organization needs a way for people to raise concerns about how they're being treated. This may sound like whistleblowing, but the difference is a grievance is a complaint about something personal, whereas whistleblowing is a report about organizational wrongdoing. Anyone connected to your organization should be able to file a grievance, whether they are a staff member, volunteer, board director, or program participant. A few examples of grievances include:

- Concerns about unequal pay or problematic working conditions
- Feeling singled out, disciplined, or passed over in ways that seem unfair
- A belief that organizational policies are being applied unfairly
- A conflict with a colleague or supervisor that hasn't been resolved through normal channels
- Unwanted comments, jokes, or behavior related to race, gender, age, religion, disability, or other protected characteristics

A well-written grievance/complaint policy should detail who can report a grievance and how to do it. It also should identify who receives and investigates complaints, address how privacy will be protected, reaffirm that the person making the complaint will not be retaliated against, and explain what outcomes are possible for different circumstances, how updates on the investigation will be provided, and how documentation will be managed.

Anti-harassment and anti-discrimination

Harassment and discrimination deserve particular attention. Whether you choose to develop a standalone anti-harassment and anti-discrimination policy or include it in your grievance policy, you need to define what constitutes harassment and discrimination, explain how to report it, identify who investigates complaints, prohibit retaliation, and spell out the consequences for harassing or discriminatory behavior.

Importantly, many states *require* organizations to have a written anti-harassment and anti-discrimination policy, posters in the workplace, and paid training for employees. Make sure you or your nonprofit's management check what's required by local laws.

The board's role in grievance management

Grievance and anti-harassment/anti-discrimination policies are operational, because they pertain to how staff and volunteers are treated day-to-day, and the resolution process will involve the executive leader or other members of management.

That said, your board needs to be aware of these policies for one critical reason: What happens if someone accuses the executive of harassment or discrimination? Staff need to know how to vocalize their concerns, and your policy should explicitly identify an alternative path, through the board or an ombudsperson, for complaints involving senior leadership.

Document-retention policy

At some point, your organization will get a call that requires you to comb through your records: the IRS looking for financial documentation, a lawyer wanting a copy of a personnel file, a donor looking for a receipt from a gift they made several years ago. A document-retention policy ensures your organization is keeping important records for the right amount of time, in the right format (electronically or as hard copy), and disposing of them properly when the time comes. In the Online Appendix, you will find a Document-Retention Guidelines table that provides a list of documents you must retain, along with guidelines on how long to keep them.

In addition to identifying how to store critical documents and for how long, your policy should address how to destroy documents and who is responsible for maintaining compliance with the policy.

WARNING

The IRS requires tax-exempt organizations to keep books and records needed to show compliance with tax rules. These records must be available for inspection. If your organization doesn't keep tax-related records, you may be subject to severe penalties.

Confidentiality policy

As a board director, you may have access to a wide range of sensitive and confidential information, including:

- Financial records and internal financial discussions not yet public
- Legal matters, advice from counsel, and insight into pending litigation
- Business negotiations, contracts, and partnership discussions
- Information about program participants or beneficiaries
- Board deliberations, individual votes, and discussions from executive sessions

- Strategic plans and organizational decisions not yet public
- Donor information, including giving history and communications
- Personnel data, including information about hiring, performance, and compensation

Good governance runs on trust and is only possible when directors have *both* access to this type of sensitive information about the organization *and* the freedom to engage in candid discussions. A confidentiality policy plays a key role in making that trust possible. When board directors know that discussions stay in the room, they can speak freely, express unpopular opinions, and work through disagreements. That kind of open conversation is what good decision-making requires. A well-written confidentiality policy should cover the following topics:

- Why the policy exists and whom it applies to
- A list of what information is considered confidential, including examples where appropriate
- Explicit protection of individual votes, positions, and executive session discussions
- Guidelines on how sensitive information should be handled and stored
- Requirements for destroying or returning confidential materials when someone departs the organization
- Consequences for breaching confidentiality

Exceptions as required bylaws. A copy of the confidentiality policy should be given to every board director to review and sign when they join the board. A board officer or your governance committee should actively maintain these acknowledgments and ensure they are up-to-date.

Expanding Your Policy Manual

Once you've written up and approved the essential four policies from the previous section, you can begin to look at other policies your board might need, including those governing board and executive compensation, gift acceptance limitations, artificial intelligence usage, and more.

Board compensation policy

It's a common misconception that nonprofit board directors cannot be paid for their service. In fact, no federal law prohibits compensation for the board. The IRS simply requires that such compensation be reasonable, documented, and consistent with organizational policy.

That said, unpaid board service is the widely followed custom in the nonprofit sector, and many funders and donors view compensation of board directors with skepticism, because it raises questions about independence and conflicts of interest.

If your board decides to compensate its members, you will want to ensure you have a policy in place, the decision is documented and reviewed by legal counsel, compensation is benchmarked against peer organizations, and you're prepared to disclose board compensation publicly.

On the other hand, reimbursing board directors for out-of-pocket expenses is both common and appropriate. Costs of traveling to board meetings (especially far away), conference registrations, mileage, and similar expenses can add up, and asking volunteers to absorb those costs can create barriers to participation. Your board should codify which expenses can be reimbursed, what type of documentation is required, whether there are any spending limits, how reimbursements are processed, and who approves them.

Executive compensation policy

As we discuss in Chapter 4, the board is responsible for hiring, supporting, and evaluating the CEO/executive director, which also includes approving a salary and benefits package. However, this isn't as simple as it sounds. Not only has the IRS set out regulations governing executive compensation, but donors and funders factor executive pay into their assessment of an organization's overall credibility.

An executive compensation policy establishes the process for how your organization determines the salary and benefits for your chief executive. This should include an independent review and approval by the board or executive committee without any conflicts of interest, a comparison of salary and benefits data against similar organizations (size, location, mission), and documentation of all deliberations and the final decision.

Additionally, your organization will have to disclose on your IRS Form 990 how you review top management compensation and the amounts your executives and senior leaders are paid. We talk more about setting executive compensation in Chapter 19.

Gift acceptance policy

Not all gifts to nonprofits are created equal, and not all donations are good for your organization. A gift acceptance policy defines what types of donations your organization will accept and outlines procedures for receiving and acknowledging them, ensuring that you maintain legal compliance, donor accountability, and stakeholder trust. It also protects the organization from accepting gifts that are misaligned with your mission, ethically complicated, or potentially risky.

REMEMBER

Your policy doesn't need to cover every possible type of gift . . . at least not right away; it's impossible to anticipate every donation that may come through the door. Start with what you know you're going to receive, such as cash, checks, and grants, and create a review process for new or unusual gifts above a certain threshold or with specific restrictions. When evaluating a gift, your organization should be asking three critical questions:

- Does this gift align with our mission?
- Are we factoring in any costs to receive, manage, maintain, or liquidate this gift, and what are we *actually* getting (the net value)?
- Is there a risk to our reputation, our relationships, or our operations?

WARNING

Not every gift is worth saying yes to. The clearer you can be up front about the types of donations you'll accept, the easier it is for donors to support you. Some common situations where you may consider saying thanks, but no thanks, include:

- Donations or grants that come with too many restrictions or would push your organization into activity outside the mission (that is, into mission drift)
- Gifts of real estate that are too costly to manage, maintain, or sell
- Outdated technology, equipment, or secondhand materials
- Personal property that is difficult to liquidate (jewelry, vehicles)
- Gifts from corporations whose values conflict with your mission
- Certain types of risky investments, such as cryptocurrency, NFTs, and stock in companies that are highly volatile

AI usage policy

Staff and board directors may use artificial intelligence (AI) tools to create content, analyze data, provide customer support, automate fundraising outreach, take meeting minutes, and more. For resource-strapped organizations, the efficiency gains of using this technology can be significant, but AI also introduces risks to data privacy, confidentiality, and organizational integrity that boards need to take seriously.

An AI usage policy is a relatively new but essential addition to your governance policy tool kit. At minimum, your policy should set expectations about which AI tools and platforms can be used, by whom, and for what purposes, and what data can be entered into an AI platform. Never assume everyone is comfortable with AI in the boardroom, especially automatic notetakers that record the details of your conversation. If you're unsure where to start, NTEN, formerly known as the Nonprofit Technology Enterprise Network (`https://www.nten.org/`), offers free training, guidance, and model policy language for nonprofits navigating the AI space.

Additional policies

Beyond these, your board may also consider the following policies:

- **Crisis communication:** A crisis communication policy identifies who is authorized to speak on behalf of the organization, what information can be shared with the public, and logistics for convening an emergency board meeting or communication tree.
- **Social media:** A social media policy outlines confidentiality standards for social media use, who has authority to post on behalf of the organization, expected behavior and content guidelines, protocol for handling negative remarks, and consequences for misuse.
- **Investment:** Organizations that consistently run a surplus have a responsibility to manage those funds wisely. One approach is to invest the money until it is needed in the future. An investment policy outlines how an organization's money is invested, who has authority to make decisions, what level of risk is acceptable, how to monitor performance, and ethical guardrails. While boards may choose to adopt many other financial policies, an investment policy is most common.

Protecting Your Mission beyond Policy

Beyond policymaking, the board can do other things to protect your organization. From ensuring you have the right insurance, to putting protections in place for staff, to navigating major contracts, there's a lot to consider and oversee.

Requiring insurance and indemnification

REMEMBER

Here's something that surprises a lot of people: Serving on a nonprofit board comes with real personal liability. You can be named in a lawsuit or be held responsible for decisions made in the boardroom. We don't say this to scare you, but to make sure you understand the importance of insurance and indemnification.

Your organization should carry a mix of insurance policies, which we dig into in Chapter 17, including general liability and directors and officers insurance. You can also have a policy requiring these types of insurance to be in place.

Protecting intellectual property

When you're starting a nonprofit organization, intellectual property (IP) is rarely top of mind. However, as your organization grows, your name gains recognition, and your programs grow in impact, IP becomes a governance question. As always, you don't need to be an expert in IP to ask good questions and know which issues to bring to legal counsel. Here are some things to consider:

- Your name and logo can and should be trademarked if you haven't done it already. This protects your brand and gives you legal standing if someone misrepresents your organization.
- Content your staff creates belongs to your organization automatically. Content created by contractors, however, belongs to *them* . . . unless your contract explicitly says otherwise. This is an easy thing to get wrong and a common source of dispute. As more and more organizations rely on contracted/outsourced support, it's an important issue to keep an eye on.
- If you share your program materials with others or use someone else's materials, you may encounter licensing agreements. Having someone who understands the terms of these contracts and how they may expand or limit your ability to deliver on your mission is important.

REMEMBER

It's time to tag in legal counsel if you're entering into a relationship under a contract generated by someone else (for more about contracts, see the upcoming "Contracts" section); another organization is using your name, logo, or materials without permission; your programs are being replicated by another organization;

you're expanding into new states; or someone accuses *you* of using their materials without permission.

Creating an HR handbook

Whether you are a volunteer-run nonprofit or have hundreds of employees, your organization needs to establish policies and procedures for employment, HR compliance, and volunteer management. An HR handbook outlines your core values, sets expectations, and reduces legal exposure. Key things that need to be covered in your handbook include:

- A code of conduct
- Your compensation model, including benefits, performance review, bonuses, and pay schedule
- Performance management and grievance resolution processes
- Classification of employees versus independent contractors
- General workplace policies like technology usage, safety, remote work, and anti-discrimination and anti-harassment policies
- Background check requirements, especially if your organization works with vulnerable populations
- Youth training requirements, especially if your organization works with minors

What ends up in your handbook is highly dependent on your organization's mission, programs, and operations.

REMEMBER

Though the responsibility for drafting employee and volunteer management handbooks is usually delegated to the executive leader, the board needs to confirm that it's being done. In the absence of staff, the duty to set HR policy falls directly to the board. In that case, we recommend assigning the task to one or two people and bringing in outside counsel to ensure you have all your bases covered and legal obligations met.

Submitting regulatory filings

Ensuring your organization is making all the necessary regulatory filings is part of fulfilling your duty of obedience (see Chapter 3) as a board director. If you're at a large organization with employees, staff will handle this, but the board bears ultimate responsibility for knowing what's required and confirming it gets done.

Key filing obligations include your IRS Form 990 (for reporting financial data), state charitable solicitation registration (often required in every state where you fundraise), annual state filings to maintain good standing, and donor reporting requirements.

Overseeing contracts

No matter what kind of mission your nonprofit is advancing, the odds are good that you'll need a contract at some point. Before signing on the dotted line, your organization must do its due diligence. Expectations and controls, including the criteria for when a contract needs board review and formal approval, can be set through policy. You may need to review the following types of contracts:

- Lease agreements for real estate or equipment
- Executive employment agreements, as well as transition/separation agreements
- Contracts with large vendors for buying or renting goods or services
- Grant contracts with donors, private foundations, or government grant makers
- Loan agreements
- Affiliate, member, or volunteer contracts
- Contracts with other nonprofits to provide services, such as memoranda of understanding and partnership agreements

If your board is asked to review a contract, it's important to exercise sound fiduciary oversight by:

- Fully reading through all clauses of the contract before signing anything, reviewing what's included in the terms, what the cancellation/termination clauses require, and what happens if something goes wrong.
- Voicing any concerns over potential risks or the organization's ability to fulfill the contract terms.
- Proactively managing and addressing any conflicts of interest.
- Keeping documentation and meeting minutes pertaining to the review, discussion, and approval of the contract.
- Ensuring signatories are approved and authorized by your bylaws.

TIP

When in doubt, consult with a lawyer before signing any high-stakes or complex contracts. This will ensure that your organization's interests are protected and you have all the necessary safeguards in place to navigate disputes and ensure compliance.

Setting financial policies

As your organization grows, so will the complexity of its financial needs. You may find that your board or staff needs to adopt a more comprehensive set of financial policies to answer certain questions. For example, who handles cash and what types of controls are required? Who makes deposits? Who can spend money, sign checks, and use a credit card? Can the same person write checks and reconcile the books?

Can funds be spent without preapproval from the board or a committee? How much can the executive deviate from the budget before requiring board approval? Work with your board treasurer and the organization's staff to ensure you are compliant with all legal requirements and operating with sound controls and accounting practices.

Laying Your Ethical Foundation

It's critical that nonprofit leaders and directors maintain the highest ethical standards in all their actions. The first step every organization should take to lay an ethical foundation is to draft and adopt a code of ethics. This guiding document outlines your core values; sets the expectations for everyone who leads, governs, or represents the organization; and underpins every subsequent policy written for the organization. If your policies tell people *how* to act in specific situations, your code of ethics tells them *why* their behavior matters.

REMEMBER

Your code of ethics is *not* a rulebook detailing what to do in every single situation. That would be impossible to write. Rather, it's a broad statement of what your organization stands for and the values that guide day-to-day decisions. For this reason, every organization's code of conduct will look a little different but will generally contain the following elements:

- A statement that all decisions should, first and foremost, serve the organization's mission
- An explanation of your core values and why they matter

» An outline of the broad expectations for ethical conduct, including affirming the board's three legal duties (See Chapter 3 for more on that.)

» A shared responsibility clause, making clear that the core values apply to everyone in your organization, from board directors to volunteers

» A process for raising concerns, so that people feel safe calling out behavior that appears inconsistent with the code

Writing a code of ethics is only the first step. From there, you must bring it to life by sharing it with your board, staff, volunteers, and vendors; referencing it during meetings and onboarding; and reviewing it every few years to keep it up-to-date.

Creating a Culture of Compliance

If you want to be part of an organization that defaults to doing the right thing, you need to create a culture of compliance. This means everyone across the organization knows what policies exist and why they matter, and follows them because they genuinely care about upholding standards of ethics and integrity. In motion, this may look like staff and board directors raising concerns without fear of retaliation or having regular conversations about compliance (not just when things go wrong).

TIP

When setting your policies, you need to be clear and keep things accessible. Write your policies in concise, plain language. Engage multiple stakeholders in the policy-writing process. Store policies in a centralized location with shared access. Train both the board and staff on new policies, answering any questions that arise. Develop processes and systems that make it easy for people to stick to the policy, and create a feedback loop that monitors whether policies are working as intended.

Performing regular policy reviews

We recognize it's not usually feasible to review every single one of your policies each year. That's okay. What matters is that you have a *plan* to perform regular reviews and you adhere to it. A simple tracking sheet can go a long way here. You don't need anything fancy — just a running list of your critical policies, the date of the last update, who performed the review, and a link to where the policy is stored.

If your board has one, your governance committee would be a natural home for this type of ongoing policy review. If you don't, the responsibility for reviewing policy falls to the full board. We recommend assigning it to the board secretary.

Accessing helpful resources

An abundance of professional service organizations provide templates and model language for all the policies covered in this chapter. These institutions engage lawyers to create these policy templates and then make them available at a low cost or free. Here's a short list of some resources you may find helpful:

- National Council of Nonprofits: www.councilofnonprofits.org
- Nonprofit Risk Management Center: www.nonprofitrisk.org
- Alliance for Nonprofit Resources: www.anrinfo.org
- Blue Avocado: www.blueavocado.org
- BoardSource: www.boardsource.org
- NTEN: www.nten.org (for policies pertaining to technology and AI)

Accessing help resources

IN THIS CHAPTER

- » Recognizing the different types of risks that nonprofits face
- » Building a plan for monitoring and handling risks
- » Tackling decline and dissolution

Chapter 17

Managing Risk and Dealing with Crisis

Nobody wants to think about what could go wrong when things are going right. But as a board, that's one of your responsibilities. The nonprofit that survives hard times, such as budget shortfalls, leadership transitions, pandemics, or reputational hits, has more than luck. It does the thinking and planning ahead of time to ensure it's resilient.

In this chapter, we dive headfirst into risk management, starting with an overview of the most common risks organizations face before walking you through how to respond to and mitigate those risks, how to build a plan your organization can rely on, and what tools that make it all easier. We also address the hardest scenario a nonprofit may ever face: dissolution. It's a long road to get to that point, so we outline the signs so that you know before it's too late.

Navigating the Six Categories of Risk

Every nonprofit faces risks. You're running a complex business, with limited resources, in a world that's constantly changing. Some risks come from within a governance blind spot, an error in a financial projection, or a key person who holds too much institutional knowledge. Others come from the outside, such as a shift in the economic or funding landscape, a change in program or employment regulations, or a natural disaster. Unfortunately, you can't eliminate risk entirely. What you *can* do is understand where you're exposed and prepare your organization to weather the worst.

Ferreting out financial risks

Financial risks are among the most consequential threats your organization can face and the most within your control. With a clear understanding and good safeguards in place, you can significantly reduce the risk of missteps that threaten your reputation and your legal standing.

Fraud

Fraud is the intentional diversion of charitable assets for personal gain, and anyone inside *or* outside the organization can commit it. An employee may embezzle funds, steal office supplies, or create a fictitious vendor that bills the organization for services never rendered. A volunteer may pocket donated goods. A contractor may overbill for services. A board director may vote on a decision they have a financial stake in.

REMEMBER

No organization is immune to fraud, and the common perpetrators of this crime are often trusted insiders. To protect against fraud, you should create and maintain key financial policies, conduct background checks on anyone handling money, put spending limits in place, conduct regular audits and reviews, and train staff on what fraud looks like. Read more about financial oversight in Chapter 15.

Misuse of funds

Misuse of funds occurs when money is spent in ways that don't align with its designated purpose. This designation is important with *restricted funds,* where the funder gives legally binding directions on how that money is used. (More on this topic in Chapter 15.)

Like the fraud we discuss in the preceding section, misuse of funds is considered criminal conduct and comes with severe consequences. A funder may withdraw any current funding or close the door for future support. Your reputation can be damaged, and you could lose public trust. More seriously, the IRS can levy fines or revoke your tax-exempt status, even leading to federal charges or jail time for leadership.

To minimize this risk, track restricted funds separately from unrestricted funds and keep documentation for every gift and grant. Your treasurer and finance staff should understand the restrictions attached to every dollar, reviewing grant contracts and confirming donor intentions in writing when gifts are received.

Revenue concentration

Revenue concentration risk exists when a single source (a donor, a grant, or earned revenue line) makes up more than 30 percent of your budget. At that level, losing that source would create a crisis. For example, say a major grant unexpectedly ends, a long-time donor shifts priorities without notice, or your gala underperforms. Suddenly the organization is scrambling, forced into hard decisions like cutting staff and cancelling programs.

TIP

Boards should treat revenue diversification as a core sustainability strategy, with a goal that no single source exceed 20 to 25 percent of total income. Staff should monitor the funding mix and maintain open communication with donors around their long-term priorities. As a further backstop, aim to have three to six months' worth of expenses in reserves to give you a cushion to respond without having to take drastic action in the case of a sudden turn of events.

Looking at legal and regulatory

Nonprofits face a wide range of legal and regulatory risks. Some are universal to all, while others are specific to your sector or service area. Running afoul of these regulations can range from something as simple as forgetting to file an annual report to as grave as violating employment law. Failing to stay compliant with legal and regulatory requirements can result in loss of tax-exempt status or serious legal action.

REMEMBER

Your nonprofit status is a privilege. Rules govern almost every aspect of how your organization operates, from where you collect money to how you work with employees and volunteers to how you engage the public. Failing to follow the rules can dearly cost your mission. The following sections describe rules you should pay particular attention to.

Registrations and charitable solicitation

In most states, you can't start legally fundraising and operating until you've also registered to solicit donations there. After you've registered, you must submit ongoing filings and reports to stay in good standing, and the board is ultimately responsible for ensuring that gets done. (That's part of the duty of obedience we cover in Chapter 3.) Stay on top of this responsibility by registering in every state where you solicit donations (before you solicit) and maintaining a calendar of deadlines so nothing slips through the cracks.

WARNING

Soliciting even a single donation from an out-of-state resident or by using online platforms and social media can trigger multistate registration requirements. Consult a nonprofit attorney before you begin.

Private inurement

Private inurement occurs when an organization insider personally benefits from the organization's work or donations of the community. Unlike fraud, it doesn't have to happen intentionally or secretly; it may just be sloppy governance.

Examples include the CEO receiving an excessive salary or a volunteer using donated equipment for personal reasons. The IRS strictly prohibits these types of behaviors, and consequences range from being personally fined to losing the organization's tax exempt status. You have several defenses against this risk, including adopting a strong conflict of interest policy with required annual disclosures, benchmarking executive compensation, and competitively fielding contracts.

Political activity and lobbying

Nonprofits must tread very carefully when participating in any type of advocacy and lobbying. The IRS has drawn a bright red line between what it considers acceptable advocacy for your mission and inappropriate or illegal political activity. Crossing that line, even unintentionally, can subject your organization to intense scrutiny. We cover this issue in depth in Chapter 14.

Contracts and legal agreements

Every organization interacts with contracts, from office leases to vendor service contracts to grant agreements and program partnership arrangements. These relationships are part of doing business, but every agreement carries legal obligations. And with those obligations come risks: financial exposure, unfavorable terms, multiyear commitments, difficult termination clauses. If left unchecked or unmanaged, you can end up in muddy water. See Chapter 16 to find out more about managing contracts.

Employment and labor law

The law holds nonprofit organizations to the same standards as their for-profit counterparts in terms of employment and labor law, and lawsuits in this domain are among the most common and draining legal actions a nonprofit can face. The risk is compounded by the fact that many organizations operate with informal policies, a heavy reliance on volunteers and contractors, and little to no professional HR support. Even if intentions are good, the exposure can be crippling. Things to watch out for include the following:

- Incorrect classification of employees as independent contractors or non-exempt staff as exempt
- Improper use of volunteers or interns in roles that require compensation or employment
- Wage and hour violations, including unpaid overtime and missed breaks
- Gaps in harassment, discrimination, and other critical HR policies
- Recurring staff complaints or low satisfaction scores
- Failure to provide required accommodations under the American Disabilities Act (ADA) and/or Family Medical Leave Act (FMLA)
- A nonexistent, outdated, or noncompliant employee HR handbook

As a board, your role in managing this risk is mixed. Day-to-day HR operations fall to executive management, but you're responsible for ensuring the organization has policies in place to stay compliant. In practice, this task means maintaining an up-to-date handbook, ensuring access to HR expertise (staffed or contracted), and confirming that complaints and staff concerns are being addressed. Your annual executive performance review can provide valuable insight on that last point.

Governance violations

As we explain in Chapter 3, every board has three core legal obligations: the duties of care, obedience, and loyalty. Governance violations occur when the board or an individual director fails to meet any one of them. These failures can expose both the individual to personal liability and the organization to serious legal and financial trouble.

Keeping an eye out for operational risk

Operational risk touches nearly every aspect of how the organization functions, and falls into three broad areas: people and culture, program and service delivery, and infrastructure.

People and culture risks

Your mission is only possible because of people. Staff and volunteers are the heart of everything you do, and a strong team with a healthy culture is what allows your organization to deliver at the highest level. But people are also unpredictable. They struggle. They leave. Sometimes they create conflict or toxicity in unseen ways. That's what makes this category of risk difficult to manage. You can do all the right things and still find yourself blindsided or in crisis.

TIP

The warning signs are worth knowing:

- Concentration of critical knowledge or expertise with a single person and nowhere else
- Burnout and chronic understaffing
- Overreliance on volunteers for essential functions
- Unresolved conflict between board and staff
- Compensation that can't compete locally

Left unaddressed, all these issues can lead to an organization that can't deliver on its mission.

Program and service delivery

Programs can struggle or fail for many reasons, from disruptions due to staff departure to growing faster than your capacity. Boards should stay close to program performance data and ask, "Are our programs sustainable? Do we have contingency plans if a partner or vendor falls through? Are we growing responsibly?" These issues can be hard to spot from the boardroom, but staying curious and asking good questions is the most effective way to do your due diligence and manage this risk without overstepping.

Infrastructure risks

This category includes the following:

- **Facility and capital needs:** Buildings ages and equipment wears out. Think of pipes bursting, HVAC systems breaking down, or accessibility upgrades getting pushed off year over year until someone finally complains.
- **Technology and equipment breakdowns:** Almost every nonprofit needs technology to function: CRM/donor databases, financial and accounting systems, project management tools, email, document storage, and communications systems. The organization faces major risks if those systems fail, go out of date, or are compromised by a cyberattack.
- **Supply chain disruptions:** Some organizations depend on suppliers or vendors to help deliver their programs and services. That may be food, medical supplies, printed materials, or facilities support. When one of these groups suddenly raises prices, fails to deliver, or closes, it can cause interruptions that prevent you from serving your community.

Infrastructure risks are easy to put off or overlook until something finally breaks. These types of issues can quickly escalate into costly emergencies, forcing program closures and creating liability exposure.

TIP

The greater you scale, the more you need a capital improvement plan in place. The organization needs to keep up with and invest in technology, manage single-vendor dependencies, and account for what can be substantial costs.

Surveying strategic risk

Strategic risks are enterprise-level threats to your organization's long-term direction, relevance, or sustainability. Unlike operational problems, a policy or a new hire can't easily fix them. Addressing them requires a shift in strategy and a significant investment of time and resources. They also tend to develop slowly, making them hard to identify early. Examples include these:

- **The strategic plan runs off course.** It may have looked right when you adopted it but become misaligned as circumstances changed, such as unexpected leadership transitions or new information emerging.
- **The organization drifts away from its mission, often through well intentioned decisions.** But the more you say yes to things outside your core work, the more you dilute your impact and confuse donors and the communities you serve. Consider a disaster relief organization offered a six-figure grant to deliver literacy education to refugees. Accepting may seem like an opportunity, but doing so pulls resources in a new direction and risks alienating donors who gave specifically to support disaster relief.
- **The community your organization was built to serve has changed, and your programs haven't responded or adapted.** Examples include a food pantry designed around a low-income neighborhood that has since been gentrified or a mental health organization that was focused on in-person services that hasn't adapted to offer telehealth options.
- **The executive leader resigns and momentum stalls.** The organization is left without clear direction during the gap.
- **The organization attempts to pivot or grow but hasn't adequately planned or accounted for the necessary resources to support the transition.**
- **The funding model no longer covers the cost of delivering your services.** The price point is off, the economy has shifted, or you no longer can deliver at the scale you have historically.

Repelling reputational risk

Your reputation is one of your nonprofit's most valuable assets. It takes years to build and can be destroyed in a matter of hours with one bad news story. Executive or board misconduct, a public call-out letter from staff, harassment complaints, high turnover, program failures, and poorly worded social media posts are just a few things that can put you at risk.

Boards can take practical steps to safeguard their reputation. First, model ethical leadership and adopt a code of conduct you actually enforce. Create internal channels for staff and community members to raise concerns. Have a crisis communications plan that identifies who speaks for the organization if something goes wrong. Periodically review your online presence, and be mindful of who you're associated with or uplifting.

REMEMBER

How you handle a public relations crisis often matters more than the crisis itself. Transparency, accountability, and proactive communication can preserve trust even in the most difficult moments.

Evading economic, environmental, and political risk

This category includes all those risks that exist beyond your control: the environment, the economy, and the sociopolitical landscape.

The environment

Floods, fires, earthquakes, and other natural disasters can destroy facilities and equipment, displace staff and volunteers, and shut down your organization overnight. Get to know the environmental risks common to your area and seek out emergency response and business continuity resources from agencies like FEMA, local emergency management offices, your insurance provider, and fellow nonprofits like the Center for Disaster Philanthropy or the Red Cross.

REMEMBER

Even if the chances seem slim, having a plan in place to protect your people and assets is far better than facing a crisis unprepared. If you rent a facility, ensure your landlord or storage facility also addresses these plans.

Economic shifts

An economic downturn affects everyone, though the impact looks different depending on your mission and subsector. Human services organizations often see a surge in demand, while arts and culture organizations see participation and support decline as audiences cut discretionary spending. Individual giving and corporate sponsorships may drop, and foundations may grow more cautious. Organizations without reserves or diversified revenue are especially vulnerable when economic tides turn.

Policy shifts

A shift in federal or state funding priorities, usually around election season, can result in a major grant or public funding disappearing with little warning. Changes in regulations or public controversy around your issue can also affect your funding and your ability to operate. This risk is hard to plan for, but staying informed and building relationships across the political landscape can help buffer the impact.

Managing and Responding to Risks

The risks facing organizations today are more complex and consequential than they were even a decade ago. From cybersecurity threats to regulatory shifts to climate change, boards can't control everything, but they can ready their organizations.

Overseeing risk as a board

The board should operate at 10,000 feet — looking across the full landscape of risk, setting the organization's attitude toward it, putting policy in place, and monitoring things long-term. Executive leadership operates closer to the ground, owning the day-to-day work of identifying and responding to risk. Here are three simplified examples of how the line gets drawn:

- **Donor data is leaked.** Executive leadership coordinates with IT, notifies affected parties, and works with legal to contain the damage. The board evaluates whether the right controls were in place and holds leadership accountable for the response.
- **A flood damages your facility.** Executive leadership is responsible for communicating with staff, coordinating repairs, managing insurance claims, and keeping operations running. The board allocates additional resources for the response, assesses whether the organization was adequately prepared for the risk, and improves policy for next time.

- **The CFO is discovered to have committed fraud.** Executive leadership removes access and terminates the employee, secures records, and manages the fallout on the staff side. The board forms a task force to conduct an independent investigation, takes responsibility for communicating with stakeholders and the public, and critically examines how its governance practices may have allowed the situation to happen.

Managing risk well looks like this:

- **Setting clear roles and responsibilities:** Everyone, from the boardroom to the management team to the staff on the ground, understands their role in assessing, mitigating, and monitoring risk.
- **Setting the appetite for risk:** The level of risk your organization is comfortable with is defined and revisited over time. As strategy evolves, the board looks at what can go wrong as much as what can be achieved.
- **Conducting regular risk assessments:** The board periodically looks at what can go wrong, how likely it is, and what the impact would be.
- **Maintaining a risk register:** You have a living list of potential risks your organization faces, each assigned to an owner. Escalation paths are clear so that when problems surface, no one is asking who handles it. We cover the risk register more in the later section "Mitigate."
- **Putting controls into place:** Policies and systems exist to detect, escalate, and respond to key risks.
- **Monitoring the landscape:** The board pays attention to the external environment, including regulatory shifts, emerging technologies, and competing organizations. The risk management plan is updated and reflects what's happening in the world.
- **Building a diverse board:** The board has the collective expertise to assess all major risk categories objectively. Different backgrounds, sectors, and lived experience help surface risks that a more homogenous group may miss.
- **Engaging outside experts:** Specialists are brought in when a category of risk falls outside the board's existing knowledge.

Understanding liability

REMEMBER

You're most protected when you act in good faith, with due diligence, and in the organization's best interest. Board and personal liability usually arise not from mistakes but from neglect, concealment, or self-interest. Situations that can create liability for you and the board include things like the following:

» Approving misleading or fraudulent financial statements

» Ignoring evidence of misappropriation or accounting irregularities

» Failing to file required government reports or disclosures

» Overlooking or failing to disclose a conflict of interest

» Ignoring a whistleblower claim or internal report of wrongdoing

» Receiving personal benefits or perks not disclosed to the board

» Making decisions outside the board's scope of authority

» Mishandling volunteer or donor data

The common thread here is that each of these things is a choice: You can choose to look away, stay silent, or act badly, or you can choose to fulfill your legal duties. Liability always follows a pattern of red flags that were ignored. Here's a scenario: A regional nonprofit runs after-school programs for at-risk teens. A volunteer is later accused of misconduct, and it's discovered that background checks weren't completed for six months due to budget cuts. The board had received a report noting this gap but took no formal action.

Here are some questions to ask in this situation:

» **What could you do if you were on this board?**
  - Demand immediate suspension of unscreened volunteers.
  - Require written policy enforcement and a tracking system.
  - Ensure insurance covers abuse claims.
  - Document all actions to show due diligence.

» **Is the board or organization liable?**
  - **Organization:** Yes, for negligence in supervision and failure to protect minors.
  - **Board:** Potentially, if evidence shows directors knew of risks and failed to act (that's a breach of the duty of care from Chapter 3). If board minutes show they ignored the report, personal liability could be attached.

» **What can the board do to reduce liability?**
  - Implement and enforce a written child safety and screening policy.
  - Ensure background checks are conducted for all staff/volunteers before engagement.
  - Review risk reports promptly and document corrective action.
  - Consider liability insurance with molestation/abuse coverage.

Tracing the risk management cycle

How do you identify what risks your organization is vulnerable to and plan for them? The risk management cycle, shown in Figure 17-1, is a well-known framework businesses and nonprofits use to identify, assess, mitigate, and monitor risk. It's a continuous process that keeps the board and management on the same page and prepares for the worst.

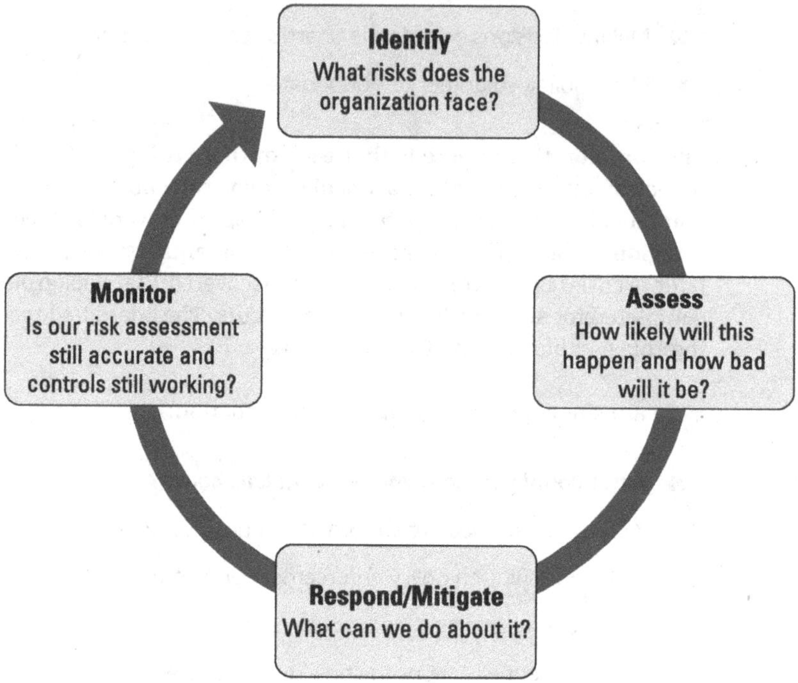

FIGURE 17-1: The risk management cycle.

Identify

What risks does your organization face? Start by creating an inventory in partnership with executive leadership, staff, and other key stakeholders. ***Remember:*** The people closest to the work often see things you'd never even consider.

Assess

What's the probability this risk will happen, and how serious would the impact be? After you've identified what risks your organization is exposed to, you need to evaluate and prioritize which risks demand immediate attention and planning and which you can watch over time or deal with later.

Mitigate

How will the organization respond to and mitigate each risk? Organizations commonly consider four approaches:

- **Treat/control:** Reduce the likelihood of this risk by putting policies, procedures, and other types of controls into place.
- **Transfer/share:** Shift the risk to another party by using insurance or contracts.
- **Tolerate/accept:** Acknowledge and accept the risk and choose to live with it, usually because the cost of addressing it outweighs the exposure.
- **Terminate/avoid:** Stop the activity or remove the organization from the situation that created the risk all together.

When choosing the best approach, many organizations use a combination of methods to provide complete and through coverage of the risk. From here, both the board and executive leadership create a *risk register*, which lists every category of risk along with the strategies for managing and mitigating that risk. This tool should be reviewed quarterly or annually, depending on the nature and scale of your operation. Table 17-1 shows examples of mitigation strategies.

TABLE 17-1 Examples of Risk Mitigation Strategies

Situation	Defined
A community center offers after-school and summer programs for school-aged children. Child safety is a key consideration, with potential risk for harm to a child in the organization's care, legal consequences, and reputational damage.	**Treat/control:** The center implements mandatory background checks for all staff and volunteers before they begin working. **Transfer/share:** The center takes out liability insurance to cover the organization in the event of a claim. **Tolerate/accept:** The center accepts it can't control all risks and that children will interact with adults across many settings. Exposure to risk is inevitable. **Terminate/avoid:** The center shuts down the program if the risk is perceived as too great.
A performing arts center operates out of a historic building with aging infrastructure and hosts events for hundreds of audience members in its theatre every year. Fire is identified as a significant risk.	**Treat/control:** The theatre installs a sprinkler system. **Transfer/share:** The theatre takes out property insurance to cover cost of damage to the building or claims arising from injury to audience or staff members. **Tolerate/accept:** The theatre accepts some level of risk is inherent to operating in an older building and current levels of fire mitigation, including extinguishers, are enough. **Terminate/avoid:** If an inspection reveals the building is unsafe and/or costs to install sprinklers are too great, the board may decide to suspend performances until the building is made safe or to relocate entirely.

Monitor

The fourth step in the cycle is to assign each identified risk on your risk register (see the preceding section) to a board director, committee, staff, or a third party to monitor year-round. The person assigned should have the expertise to understand it and the authority to act. Establish thresholds for when a risk needs to be escalated to the full board; once a year, jump back to the start of the process (in the earlier section "Identify") and keep the picture up to date. Keeping an eye on key insurance coverages.

Insurance is an essential risk management tool and safety net that protects your organization in the event the unexpected occurs. No matter how careful and well run your nonprofit is, accidents happen, disputes arise, disaster strikes, and legal action is taken.

The two nonnegotiables

REMEMBER

Without question, every nonprofit should carry the following two types of insurance, regardless of their mission or scale:

- **General liability:** This option is the primary form of insurance, covering bodily injury, property damage, and personal injury. If someone is hurt at your event or a visitor trips in your office, general liability is your first line of defense. Most landlords and venues require proof of this coverage to even work with you.
- **Directors and officers (D&O):** This form of insurance protects board directors, officers, and senior staff against claims of wrongful acts in governance. That may include things like mismanagement, errors in judgment, failure to follow the bylaws, or breaches in fiduciary duty. Without D&O in place, board directors can be held liable and their personal assets put at risk. Having this policy in place is critical for recruiting and retaining quality leadership, and you should never serve on a board without it!

Additional coverages to consider

Beyond the essential policies we outline in the preceding section, your organization may choose to add on coverage to manage risks that are specialized to your operation, such as the following:

- **Workers compensation:** It provides coverage for medical costs and lost wages for employees who are injured or become ill as a direct result of their job. It's required by law in most states.

- **Business auto and property insurance:** This insurance covers your organization's physical assets, including office spaces and buildings, vehicles, and equipment your organization uses for operations. Protection typically covers damage, theft, or liability arising from use.
- **Umbrella policy:** Think of this option as your backup plan for your backup plan. If something really bad happens and the bill ends up being more than what your regular insurance covers, an *umbrella policy* kicks in to cover the rest.

Recognizing Decline and Crisis

Many nonprofits have accepted crisis as a way of life, and given recent pressures, that's understandable. But the hard reality is that organizations can trace most crises requiring turnaround or leading to closure back to things well within their own control. It's a matter spotting the signs early, identifying root causes, and being brave enough to act.

Watching for the red flags

Here are some warning signs to recognize before it's too late:

- **The mission or market has shifted.** Fewer people use your services, donors start pulling back, programs get cancelled — these are all signs that what you're doing may no longer fit what your community needs.
- **You're on financial thin ice.** You've been running deficits for several years, and reserves are dwindling. Payroll is a struggle, debt is climbing, and essential needs get deferred. Reports come late and are marked with inaccuracies. You're running out of money . . . and time.
- **Your business model needs a rebuild.** The way you raise money or run your programs isn't covering costs or creating the impact you hoped for, and you don't have the staff capacity or skills to close the gap. The problem lies with structure and strategy, not lack of effort.
- **People problems are taking their toll.** Leadership, board, and staff are burned out, turnover is high, and dysfunction goes unchecked. Performance suffers, and no one seems to rally the organization forward.

Getting to the root causes

So how does an organization end up in crisis? In most cases, the answer goes back to executive leadership, the board, or (usually) both. Executive leadership and the board's governance are two sides of the same equation, and when either one is struggling, the warning signs we talk about in the preceding section are rarely behind.

Poor leadership

The chief executive is responsible for leading strategy, programs, and people. When they're unskilled, inattentive, or mismatched to the challenge at hand, a crisis is right around the corner. We cover in depth what to do when this happens in Chapter 20.

Poor governance

Boards that allow organizations to slide into crisis are typically guilty of a few common missteps:

- **Failing to act in a timely manner:** Year over year, financial performance declines, program enrollments drop, reports start running late, and yet the board keeps waiting and hoping things will turn around. This delay is sometimes willful, but the board may also not be getting the full picture because executive leaders are withholding or spinning information.
- **Failing to hold leadership accountable:** People make excuses for poor performance, staff friction, reporting errors, and recurring risk exposures to reputation and tolerate the issues without consequence.
- **Setting unrealistic expectations without providing the resources leadership needs to meet them:** The bar is high, but the budget and staffing levels aren't, and leadership gets blamed for falling short.
- **Lacking necessary financial, legal, or operational expertise:** Boards can't see problems in the first place, and they miss warning signs entirely.
- **Failing to manage the board itself:** Directors tolerate bad actors and ignore conflicts of interest, and at some point the board itself becomes the problem. We cover board dysfunction at length in Chapter 25.

Finding a path forward in crisis

If the board does manage to agree that the organization is facing a crisis, several paths are open to it, as we explain in the following sections.

WARNING

Whichever path you choose, the board needs to have a candid conversation about whether the current executive leader is the right person to lead the organization through it. If the crisis emerged on their watch, especially if the causes are internally driven, then they probably aren't. Turnarounds, mergers, and dissolutions require specialized expertise that most leaders don't have. This area is where interim executives and turnaround professionals shine.

Turnaround

A *turnaround* is the process of stabilizing a struggling business and making changes that lead to sustained improvements and growth. It requires someone to come in and take a hard look at people, processes, programs, and even the very purpose of the organization and plot a course toward stability. Scope can vary from a full-scale rethink of the strategy and mission to a focused fix of one or two aspects of the operation. But it's always a deliberate, intensely paced, concentrated effort toward improvement, not a gradual drift.

TIP

If you're interested in reading more about how to navigate a nonprofit turnaround scenario, we recommend the book *Nonprofit Turnaround: A Guide for Nonprofit Leaders, Consultants & Funders* by Jan Glick (Jan Glick & Associates) or the wealth of online resources at `www.glickdavis.com`.

Alliance or merger

An *alliance* or *merger* occurs when you find a partner to share or transfer the risk you're currently carrying. You have a whole spectrum of options here, from *joint operating agreements* (where you partner with another nonprofit to split costs and resources needed for doing business) all the way up to a full legal merger (where two organizations become one). In every case, the goal is to ensure the mission survives, even if it has a different look or name.

Dissolution

Sometimes the right — or only — decision is to close down. *Dissolution* is the planned sunset of your operation and organization, where you wrap up or hand off programs and services, lay off employees, distribute charitable assets, and put the mission to rest. We talk more about this option in the later section "Dealing with Dissolution."

Identifying what can make things worse

Even when the board agrees a crisis exists and has committed to a course of action, a few mistakes can create more trouble:

- **Moving too slowly:** When you're in crisis, every delay costs money, morale, or credibility with people who matter most. The board needs a different way of working together during this time. Recognize that getting consensus before acting may not be possible, and leverage tools like *provisional decision-making* (where you make the best call you can with the information you have right now) to get the organization stepping forward.
- **Avoiding tough personnel decisions:** You need confident, expert leadership at the helm if you're going to make it through the storm. Keeping the wrong people in place can be costly. Let go of executive leadership and directors on the board if they aren't skilled and ready to meet the moment.
- **Underestimating culture:** A famous phrase says that culture eats strategy for breakfast. If internal dynamics are broken and culture is toxic, no fix to programs, operations, or the mission will make much of a difference long-term. Board and staff must clean house and align behind a shared set of values and vision before pushing too hard into change.
- **Trying to do too much at once:** When in a crisis, everyone has their own opinion on what should be done first. But these situations require a sharp and triaged response. If you spread your resources and focus across too many priorities or try to take on too much change all at once, you risk exhausting an already stretched team. Look to the executive committee of the board and appointed executive leadership to point the way.
- **Failing to communicate with stakeholders:** People fill the silence with their own stories . . . which are usually the worst versions! Staff, donors, volunteers, community partners, and the public all need proactive management and communication. Getting ahead of the narrative and being transparent about what you're doing is key to bringing people along.

Dealing with Dissolution

Not every mission lasts forever. Dissolution is one of the hardest decisions a board ever faces and comes with a wide array of emotions: grief, guilt, and a sense of failure. But closing an organization isn't always a bad thing. Sometimes it's an act of stewardship. Maybe the mission has been fulfilled, the landscape changed, or the community better served by stepping aside. Organizations dissolve for many reasons:

- **The mission has been fulfilled.** You've accomplished what you set out to do; the scholarship fund has deployed all its resources or a disaster organization is winding down now that recovery is complete. Because you have little to continue doing, the board decides it's time to sunset.
- **You're facing a persistent or unresolvable crisis.** You're dealing with a major challenge that has no reasonable solution. You've lost major funding or failed a capital campaign, or the business model has been running years of deficit without any hope of rebuilding in time.
- **Leadership has transitioned or failed.** You don't have the necessary people to continue. A founder departs without a succession plan, or key staff leaves and recruitment is too tall of a task or has repeatedly failed. Flip to Chapter 20 to check that you have a succession plan in place to minimize this risk.
- **You've consolidated.** You've joined forces with another organization through alliance or merger. You consolidate assets and hand over programs, whether to another entity or to an entirely new one you've formed together. You can read more about these consolidation options in the earlier section "Alliance or merger."
- **External forces have come into play.** You're closing because of things beyond your control. Maybe a pandemic has hit and your programs can no longer run, flooding has destroyed your building and equipment, or a recession has caused donors to pull funding.

Figuring out whether it's time to close down

People who start and run nonprofits aren't wired to quit. They see problems as things to be solved and a bad year as something to be weathered. That spirit is what keeps the organization alive through hard stretches — and can keep it alive longer than it should be.

REMEMBER

Knowing when to call it quits is one of the hardest judgment calls in leadership. The difficult part usually isn't about recognizing whether things are bad. It's figuring out whether you should be doubling down and fighting harder or accepting the moment and letting go.

The following are signs that it may be time to close down. No single item on this list means it's over, but if several are true at the same time, or have been for a while, the conversation is worth having.

- You've had multiple years of running deficit budgets with no realistic path toward stability.
- Key funders are reducing their gift size or not renewing.
- Programs have already been discontinued or are continuing to drop in participation numbers.
- The issue your organization was created to address is no longer relevant or is being better met by other organizations.
- You can't recruit or retain good leadership on staff or on the board.
- You have chronic staff turnover and collapsed morale, with no plan for stabilization.

REMEMBER

The board directors won't always agree on this course of action. Some will be ready to cut their losses. Some will see a turnaround. Many will be in denial. Everyone needs space to be heard, and someone needs to find a way to move forward.

Managing the dissolution process

Dissolution is a legal process that comes with obligations to the state, the IRS, your employees, and the community you served. It's a final chance to act with integrity, demonstrate the values your organization stood for, and wind down with the same care and dignity you brought to the work. Here are the steps:

1. **Develop a dissolution plan.** Map the dissolution process, interim leadership, timeline, distribution of assets and liabilities, and how stakeholders will be informed.
2. **Vote to dissolve.** Check your bylaws for the required threshold. In the minutes, note the reason behind the dissolution decision and, if anyone dissents, offer to document that on the record.
3. **Settle debts and obligations.** Pay all remaining staff first, including final paychecks, accrued leave, contractual commitments, and so on. Then settle all outstanding vendor contracts. You need to pay everyone you owe before you can start distributing what's left.

4. **Distribute remaining assets.** After you've settled your debts, you can transfer any remaining assets to another qualified nonprofit with a similar charitable purpose. In many states, this distribution process requires the attorney general's approval. ***Remember:*** You can't make any distributions to directors, staff, or private individuals.
5. **File the final paperwork.** Submit dissolution documents to Submit dissolution documents to your state filing office, notify the IRS, and file your Form 990. Requirements vary by state, so check what's required of you.
6. **Archive critical records.** The board should designate someone responsible for storing and maintaining records after the organization closes until the statute of limitations is met. This party may be a board officer or legal counsel.

Selecting someone to lead dissolution

Closing an organization comes with uncertainty and administratively grueling work and has a way of dragging on. Asking a permanent leader to absorb that burden while also trying to figure out their next chapter isn't fair, so hire a professional interim leader to see the process through. Doing so allows everyone to move on with dignity.

Honoring the human side

Be respectful of the fact that people will respond differently to the news. Give staff and board as much time as is reasonable to process the situation, offer input, and weigh in on the path forward *before* the vote to dissolve. Don't shy away from hard questions, and accept that looking for creative ways to adapt or hold on is human nature. Recognize it for what it is: grief.

After a decision is reached, be timely with communications. Reach out to funders and donors and thank them for their support. Get a press release out and ensure everyone has talking points so the board and staff are speaking with one voice.

Speaking of staff, do absolutely everything you can to provide a safety net through the transition, including offering severance, references, outplacement services, extended benefits, and professional connections. Anticipate unexpected costs and a longer runway. Dissolution almost always takes more time than you think and costs more than budgeted, and surprises have a way of showing up even there at the end.

REMEMBER

And, when all is said and done, find a way to celebrate and honor the work the organization did, the lives it touched, and the people who made everything possible. A good ending is its own form of leadership.

IN THIS CHAPTER

» Seeing how measuring board performance leads to good governance

» Looking at the scope of whole-board assessment

» Preparing for and running the assessment process

» Looking ahead to board transformation

Chapter 18

Measuring Board Performance

The board is responsible for overseeing its organization, including the impact and financial performance of programs and the effectiveness of executive leadership. It's a key part of public accountability and good governance. However, how an organization figures out whether the board is doing a good job may surprise you: It's the board itself!

Getting caught up in strategic planning, fundraising, and the business of committee work is so easy that you can forget to check in. But a healthy board is a board that regularly turns inward and reflects: How are *we* doing? Are we governing or just meeting? Is the board diverse and sustainable? Do people speak up or sit silently? Are we adding value, or are we bottlenecking the work? An annual board assessment is one of the best ways the board can engage with those questions and grow. In this chapter, we explain the four domains of board health and common signs of both functional and dysfunctional behaviors. We then get practical and walk you through how to run an assessment and act on what you find.

Understanding Why Board Assessment Matters

Boards spend considerable time identifying and recruiting directors with skills and expertise that best serve the mission. But as any good leader knows, hiring is only the first step; a room full of talented people doesn't automatically create an effective governing team. It takes ongoing work to build and sustain excellence . . . and that's where regular assessment comes in.

REMEMBER

Every assessment surface *something*. Don't be discouraged; that's the point. Boards are constantly evolving: Directors cycle on and off, new challenges emerge, and there will be things that will pop up that you never saw coming. What matters is that you commit to improving year over year.

Deciding how often to assess your board

Imagine you're driving and you hear a faint buzzing noise. Nothing crazy, so you ignore it. But over time, it gets louder until you can't ignore it. By the time a mechanic gets under the hood, it's no longer a loose screw; you need a new engine. This is a lesson for boards: Small problems don't stay small.

While we can't prescribe a one-size-fits-all approach to board assessment, we have a few recommendations:

TIP

- **Build board assessment into your annual calendar.** Whether you're assessing annually or biannually, it's more likely to happen if you plan for it, and consistency is what makes assessments valuable.

  When scheduling your board assessment, consider your entire board year. Pick a time when organizational activity is slower. People are more likely to engage thoughtfully when they aren't stretched thin.
- **Assign ownership.** If everyone on the board is responsible for assessment, then no one is. Pick a specific committee to lead the process (either your governance or executive committee) so someone has accountability for making it happen.
- **Find time to check in.** Don't wait until the next assessment cycle to revisit results and hear how people are feeling. A check-in — during a board meeting or by the assigned committee — is an opportunity to review progress on goals set from your assessment, address blind spots, and get ahead of issues that have emerged.

- **Let the findings drive board education.** Use what comes up to shape learning moments throughout the year. During check-in meetings, find out what directors need to learn and where they want to grow.

REMEMBER

If you're running the assessment, don't take feedback personally. Stay open, curious, and grounded in your duty to the board and mission. Remember that fellow directors are volunteers with very different experiences of the organization; they may miss pieces of the puzzle or see things you can't from your own vantage point. Negative feedback, though hard to process, can reveal real opportunities to improve culture, communication, and cohesion.

Looking at two levels of assessment

An assessment looks different for every board. Some boards may choose to have an informal, candid conversation over dinner, while others may administer a structured process with an outside facilitator. No way is truly "wrong."

That said, most boards that conduct assessments use surveying with rated questions and space for open ended observations, with the goal of giving the board a high-level picture of where they're thriving and where they have room to grow. To get the most complete picture, you want to assess at two levels:

- **The whole-board assessment:** A whole-board assessment invites every director to evaluate board culture, dynamics, governance practices, and effectiveness. Ideally, it's administered anonymously, with findings shared with the full board. The final result provides a bird's-eye view of how the board feels it's functioning as a team, and those findings can then drive decisions around education and activity across the board year.
- **Self-assessment:** A self-assessment asks each individual director to evaluate their own contributions and engagement level. It provides an opportunity for personal reflection and is where the best growth opportunities live. Ideally, the results are collected by the Board Secretary and shared with the board president or governance chair and serve as a launchpad for conversations around individual learning and better support.

TIP

Administer both types of assessments hand in hand. The whole-board assessment gives you an overarching picture of the boardroom, and the self-assessment goes a bit deeper, revealing where individuals are feeling uncertain and where they may need personal support or growth.

Detailing the Four Dimensions of Whole-Board Performance

To measure your board's performance, you need to know what questions to ask and what to look for. We like to look at four domains:

- » The people serving on the board
- » The culture they create together
- » The work they're responsible for
- » The impact they ultimately make

REMEMBER

No single area tells the whole story. A board can have impressive people serving but culture that stifles good conversation or make sure their governance duties are met and then realize their impact wasn't very great. These four areas ensure you're looking across the full scope of board performance and serve as a sound framework for building your assessment.

Assessing the people

Who is sitting around your board representing your mission and community matters more than almost anything else. A strong board is one that reflects the community it serves, with directors bringing the needed skills, backgrounds, and perspectives the organization needs to achieve its strategic goals and mission. These boards don't wait for a seat to open up before thinking about who should fill it. They're always asking who is missing and cultivating the next generation of leaders. Questions you may ask when assessing for the people category include the following:

- » Do board directors reflect the community we serve?
- » Do we have board directors reflecting the skills we need to meet our strategic priorities?
- » Do any major gaps in representation, lived experience, or background exist?
- » Is recruitment ongoing?
- » Are we reaching out to new communities and networks?
- » **Self:** Am I personally adding to the value in the room?

Considering the culture

A board's culture is defined by how directors show up, engage with one another, and commit to doing the work. A healthy board is one where directors feel welcomed and genuinely motivated to do the work. Leadership sets a positive tone, new directors are properly brought into the fold, and the board's values show in how the boardroom runs and the decisions are made. Here are some questions you may ask in a culture assessment:

- » Do board directors feel engaged and included? Do people speak up?
- » Is the dynamic between board and staff healthy?
- » Is the onboarding process thoughtfully designed and delivered?
- » Does board leadership model the culture?
- » **Self:** Am I individually contributing to an inclusive, open culture?

Scrutinizing the work

Every board has a core set of legal and fiduciary responsibilities, which we cover explicitly in Chapters 3 and 4. A board that's doing this work well understands the line between governance and management, actively oversees finances, evaluates the CEO, monitors progress against a strategic plan, and ensures the organization remains compliant and accountable to those it serves. When you're assessing the work domain, consider asking these questions:

- » Is the board fulfilling and meeting its legal duties and responsibilities?
- » Is the board regularly reviewing financial reports?
- » Do we have a fair, consistent process for evaluating the CEO?
- » Is the board monitoring the progress on the strategic plan?
- » **Self:** Do I personally understand and fulfill my responsibilities?

Investigating your impact

Ultimately, having the right people, fostering an amazing culture, and checking off the boxes of governance don't matter if they aren't also producing results. A high-impact board can point to tangible progress on the mission, a strong reputation, and a trusting relationship with staff. This domain is where you honestly

step back and ask, "Has our time, talent, and treasure really made a difference?" Question that help you evaluate the impact category include the following:

- » Is the board actually helping the organization achieve its mission?
- » Can the board point to specific ways it supports the organization?
- » Is the organization credible in the community?
- » Are board directors proud of and energized by their contributions?
- » **Self:** Have I personally done anything to advance our mission this year?

Starting the Assessment Process

Jumping from a casual "how are we doing?" at the end of a board meeting into a process that creates something useful can seem daunting if you've never done it before. But it's simpler than you think, and it gets easier every year. In this section, we break down everything you need to run a smooth assessment: what to communicate to the board, who does what, and key logistics to consider.

Communicating expectations and assuaging fears

WARNING

Don't send a survey without explaining what it's for or how you're going to use it. Without buy-in across the board, even the best designed assessment falls flat. Directors may rush through responses, answer defensively, or choose not to respond at all. Taking the time upfront to explain the value and answer questions can help build trust and ensure you get what you need. Here are talking points your board president or committee chair should use when talking about the upcoming assessment:

- » **Assessment is a key part of good governance and a way the board demonstrates accountability.** Every board director has an opportunity to weigh in anonymously and see the results in aggregate.
- » **Results will drive improvement.** We'll get to see trends and opinions on how we work together, how we think we're doing, and where we need to improve. This information will help us design educational opportunities and prioritize governance improvements.

» **Individual assessments support individual growth.** It's a chance to reflect and identify ways to engage more meaningfully in your service.

» **The process will be intentional and well designed.** We're committed to creating an assessment process that's fair and focused and that serves both the board as a whole and you individually.

» **Everyone is expected to participate.** For your assessment to be successful *and* thorough, all stakeholders should be expected to participate. Yes, everyone. This ensures that everyone's voice is included and that the assessment truly reflects *all* opinions, viewpoints, and feedback of the board. Be sure to tell everyone that their responses will be 100% anonymous and will remain confidential throughout the process.

» **Honest feedback is the foundation.** Candid and thorough responses, even when uncomfortable, will allow us to grow. Please hold us to our own standard of transparency by sharing how you truly feel.

The more clearly board leadership can articulate the assessment's value to the board, the more likely directors will be to lean in and participate candidly.

REMEMBER

Directors may feel nervous about the assessment process, especially if it includes a self-assessment component. If you're leading the process, don't dismiss concerns. How you respond in this early stage — whether that's with understanding or with defensiveness — sets the tone for everything that follows. If you're participating, push through that discomfort. Assessment will only make you a better director.

Squaring away the logistics

REMEMBER

Board assessment is a team effort. It follows, then, that the clearer you can be about who owns what, the smoother the process will run.

Here are common groups and individuals that participate in the process:

» **Project leadership:** Typically, the governance committee leads the annual assessment. If you don't have this committee, the executive committee, a one-off task force, or an objective individual (such as a consultant) can.

» **Individual directors:** Remind everyone that *all* board members participate in the assessment, including answering truthfully on surveys and in interviews as well as thoroughly reading and responding to results with thoughtful questions or clarification.

- **The board president:** The president sets the tone from the beginning. They need to model participation, foster the psychological safety needed for honest feedback, serve as a backup point of contact on the project, and be prepared to facilitate any needed conversations that emerge from assessment. The president is also responsible for ensuring that the process does not step into managing the work of staff and remains within strictly governing the process for the board rather than managing staff and assigning extra work for them. The board owns this process and the president ensures that they are supported in seeing this through form start to finish.
- **The executive leader:** Often, the board may invite the chief executive to provide their insights on board interactions with staff, observations of board engagement levels, and experience with boardroom behaviors.

TIP

Though you may ask for executive leadership to participate, the whole staff shouldn't be part of the process. Instead, share key takeaways with your executive leader related to the board-staff relationship because they're your best partner when addressing these types of concerns.

TIP

If your board is short on time and capacity, or simply wants to get an outside perspective, bring in a third party to facilitate. As project managers of the process, they can keep things on track and on time, interpret results more objectively, prioritize the areas that need the most attention, and can even deliver education to close gaps. Bonus: Many third-party options are surprisingly budget friendly as well!

Finally, if you hope to run a process that's realistically achievable, that respects people's time, and that ultimately creates a valuable resource, you need to figure out a few things before you dive into the planning.

These little logistical items can cause big headaches if you skip them:

- **Frequency/scale:** Board assessments can result in workplans that span multiple years. At minimum, we recommend conducting a self-assessment annually and then a whole-board assessment every two or three years.
- **Timeline:** Share the entire timeline with the board at the start of the process so everyone knows the expectations around participation and can factor it into their schedules. Give people two to three weeks when requesting responses to surveys, interviews, and questionnaires.
- **Confidentiality:** Confidentiality is an important consideration when conducting board assessments. For assessments focused on the overall function and health of the full board, we recommend presenting anonymous feedback in aggregate to encourage candor and honesty.

Running the Assessment Process

A board assessment follows a natural arc: planning, administration, and action. You start by designing and preparing the assessment, move into distributing surveys and processing the results, and culminate in a board discussion that produces a concrete workplan. The following sections give you a closer look.

Phase 1: Planning and preparing

Planning is everything! The first stage of conducting a board assessment is the preparation. It's a lot of work the first time you do it, but it gets easier and more efficient each time because you have the previous assessment to build on.

Collecting critical materials

To prepare your board assessment, you need to gather all the essential materials that explain directors' roles and responsibilities. Directors — and your board — can only be evaluated against the expectations they were given. These materials give you a clear baseline. You may want to look at things like the job description, code of ethics, workplans for the board and committees, and results from past surveys.

Creating or updating your assessment survey

The second step is to either create your assessment from scratch or revisit and update the one you used in prior years. We provide a simple set of assessment questions in the appendix to get you started, and you can find an abundance of free examples online with a simple search.

TIP

To maximize participation, aim to keep the total time required to complete the survey to about 10 to 15 minutes. Try to also have the majority of your questions be Likert-scale questions, where directors rate their level of agreement on a numeric scale (say, 1 to 5), rather than just answering yes or no. This makes results easier to compare and lend well to tracking trends over time. Though open-ended questions can provide valuable insight, use them sparingly; they're time-intensive to complete and generate lots of unstructured data.

Don't reinvent the wheel if your board already has an assessment. Having a consistent approach year over year is valuable because you can compare results and see more clearly where you're growing and where you may be stalled out.

TIP

Free templates for board assessments are easy to find online — and can be a good starting point if you're doing your first assessment. But make them your own. Mix and match what you find, add questions relevant to your mission and operations, and improve it year over year.

Picking the right technology

Consider tools that allow for anonymous submissions and are easy for directors to access and complete. You just need to be able to easily view and download results. Finally, test your survey with a small group before launching to ensure it doesn't have any bugs.

Orienting the board

Before you launch introduce the assessment, ideally during a board meeting. Talk about what you're surveying, the confidentiality of it, how results will be reported back, and the logistics. You may even want to preview questions to get directors more comfortable with accessing and using the technology. Don't forget to remind folks to stay grounded in the organization's values and their legal duties. You can read more about getting the board onboard in the earlier section "Communicating expectations and assuaging fears."

Launching the survey

Email the whole board. Outline the expected deadline and where to send questions and then issue a reminder every week as well as a final reminder the day before it closes. If you realize you have only 25 percent of people responding, you may need to call in board leadership to push people along.

Phase 2: Reviewing results

After the assessment survey/period closes, you need ample time to gather, review, and organize the results. The more questions you asked, especially open-ended ones, the longer this process takes. You will want to organize results into two major categories: what the board is doing well and where it may need to make adjustments.

For the whole-board assessment (see the earlier section "Looking at two levels of assessment"), always process results into a report that shows data anonymously and in aggregate. Focus on grouping feedback through common themes and trends rather than singling out people.

WARNING

If specific staff members or board directors are named (especially if they're named frequently), flag these cases for separate conversation. Keep the group debrief focused on how to make the board better as a whole. You can address and monitor issues with individuals in a separate, more appropriate setting.

A draft of the whole-board assessment report should be reviewed by executive committee first, with a focus on trends and areas of concern, identifying any areas of the report that are unclear, talking through actionable next steps, and figuring out how to facilitate the conversation at the whole-board level. This piece is the basis for the next phase, which we cover in the following section.

Phase 3: Acting on the results

After meeting in a small group (see the preceding section), you're ready to present the findings to the whole board. Issue the final report at least a week ahead of time so people have the opportunity to ask questions before gathering. You can include use a regular board meeting or set aside time in a special session or board retreat to more deeply dive into the conversation.

Focus the results presentation on the high-level points, summarizing the key trends and themes as well as possible next steps. We recommend leveraging breakout groups and other facilitation techniques to give people more time and opportunity to explore together.

After a thorough debrief, the whole board should have a shared foundation and understanding about the board's performance level. Board leadership can then review and adjust existing plans in response to the findings. Committees need to examine results relevant to their specific work and adjust accordingly. Across the board, you want members to translate results into real action, whether that's creating new educational activities to address gaps in knowledge, adjusting engagement opportunities, changing board recruitment, making broader improvements to governance, or improving board culture.

Finally, if your board conducted self-assessments, you need a way for individuals to debrief and take action on those results. We recommend board leadership or committee chairs carve out time to sit down with individuals who have concerns or questions or offer more direct support. Remember, assessment is a process about learning and growing, not punishing a gap in knowledge.

Reaping the Rewards: Board Transformation

If your board commits to assessment year over year, takes the process seriously, reflects, and works together to improve, the results can be transformative. Here are outcomes you can expect:

- **Smarter board directors:** The assessment process is a chance for individuals to reflect on their own knowledge of the organization, including its mission, finances, and programs, and identify where they still have questions. From there, they can find answers through education and better communication. Check out our ideas on board engagement in Chapter 7 and think about assigning people chapters in this book to read connected to gaps in their knowledge.
- **Engaged board directors:** When you ask directors to reflect honestly on their participation, including their attendance, their support of fundraising efforts, and how actively they're showing up in their role, they're more likely to take accountability. If you do it in a supportive way, your assessment can drive deeper commitment and giving.
- **Productive board meetings:** Your assessment should reveal how people *actually* feel about how board meetings are being run. With that insight, boards can make concrete changes to meeting preparation practices, facilitation approaches, and decision making, leading to a better use of time together. Chapter 10 has tips on running board meetings.
- **Productive committees:** Similarly, assessment gives committees insights that they can leverage to improve their meetings and focus their workplans. Chapter 11 has common practices you may want to consider.
- **Effective recruitment and onboarding:** Your assessment can also reveal the board's perception of its own diversity and ability to meet the organization's needs, including whether the board has the skills, experiences, and connections it needs to be successful. That clarity helps make recruitment more intentional. We share a bit more about how to find great board directors in Chapter 6.
- **Strong relationships with management:** The better the board understands their role in governance, the more likely they are to respect the line separating board oversight from day-to-day management. This balance leads to a healthier relationship and deeper respect and trust between management and staff.

5 Partnering with Staff

IN THIS PART . . .

Develop a strong partnership with the executive leader that will supercharge your organization. Assess their effectiveness and provide feedback they can use for their professional growth. Recognize the red flags in executive performance and get tools to navigate terminations with dignity.

Formulate a plan for what your board will do when your executive leader eventually moves on.

Look at how to build a healthy working relationship with staff members, including navigating the power dynamic, communicating respectfully, and appreciating their work.

IN THIS CHAPTER

» Selecting and onboarding an executive leader

» Creating a strong working relationship with your executive

Chapter 19

Navigating the Board-Executive Partnership

Without question, the most important relationship in your organization is the one between the executive leader and the board. When it's healthy, you feel it: The boardroom is dynamic, strategic discussions go deep, debate is both welcome and collegial, communication flows between meetings, and problems get shared early. In its best form, the relationship isn't the executive simply reporting to the board; it's the two partnering together to achieve something great.

But the reverse is equally true. When the trust and respect essential to this partnership break down, bad behaviors follow: micromanagement, withheld information, misalignment on priorities, and more. And when that happens, your mission is at risk.

In this chapter, we give you the building blocks for forming a strong relationship with your executive leader. We define the clear line between governance and management, explain how to hire and onboard your executive, and offer advice for communicating with that person. Finally, we provide a guide for managing performance. Throughout we include special considerations for dealing with founders and first-time executives.

TIP

In this book we use *executive leader* to refer to the individual at the head of your organization, whether that's the CEO, executive director, or, in some cases, a managing director. These titles are often used interchangeably, but they reflect different scales of work. Executive director is typically the right fit in earlier stages, when the top leader is hands-on and close to daily operations. As an organization grows past the $5-million/50-plus-employee mark, the role shifts from execution to strategy, and the CEO title is more appropriate, signaling to partners and donors the organization is operating at a professional level.

Hiring Your Executive Leader

Hiring a leader is the single most consequential thing your board does. This section is where we look at the full arc of executive search: ironing out the logistics, attracting good candidates, structuring a fair interview process, navigating staff dynamics, and onboarding.

WARNING

Direct everyone involved in the search to maintain confidentiality until the final candidate is publicly announced. Set this expectation with anyone who gets access to candidate information. A breach in confidentiality risks candidates withdrawing out of concern for their current jobs or reputations, along with internal disruption and damage to the organizations' credibility.

Starting the process

Before you dive into the deep end, here's a quick reality check regarding the time, budget, and division of duties involved in running a search.

- **How long will it take?** A typical executive search process takes three to six months. The larger your organization is, the more stakeholders are involved, which adds to the timeline. In particularly complex situations, the process can extend up to a year.
- **Who leads it?** The board can self-manage the search or retain a search firm to lead the process. If you choose the latter, look for a firm that can demonstrate a track record of successful placements in organizations that are comparable in scale, subsector, and geographic location. In both cases, the board needs to form an executive search task force to leading the process on the board's behalf. The task force works with the search firm (if you use one) to develop the profile, conduct and coordinate interviews, and make the final recommendation.

TIP

Serving on this task force can be exciting to many directors, but we strongly recommend limiting the size to three to five directors. If too few people are involved, the search is more susceptible to bias and limits the candidates' ability to get diverse insight into the organization. On the other hand, having too many people involved can be overwhelming and unnecessary. Maintain clear roles for each stage of the process while having a core group of decision-makers.

- **How much will it cost?** If you decide to hire a search firm, budget approximately 30 percent of the position's total compensation to pay the firm's fees. For example, if a CEO's compensation is set at $150,000, expect roughly $50,000 for the fee. If you self-manage the search, budget up to 5 percent of the executive's compensation to cover the fees associated with posting jobs on sites like LinkedIn and industry-specific job boards and to account for staff admin time. If you're open to non-local candidates, you need additional budget for fringe costs to bring the candidate in for interviews, such as travel, housing, and meals. You also need to decide whether and how much your board will offer for relocation assistance.

Writing the position profile

A traditional job description lists responsibilities and qualifications, which is appropriate for less senior positions. However, when you're searching for an executive leader, you're recruiting someone to bring vision, direction, and leadership to your organization at a specific moment in its history. That calls for something different: a *position profile.*

Great leaders aren't just looking for any job; they're seeking the right challenge for their strengths and abilities — something that excites their ambition and feels worth their time. A position profile tells the story of your organization, why the moment is significant, and the potential impact the right leader can have. It's a sales pitch and an opportunity description. Here's what you want to include:

- **About the organization:** That includes who you are, your mission, and your size.
- **The leadership moment:** Explain where the organization is right now and what the leader will inherit. Are you entering a growth phase? Navigating restructure? Sustaining success? Be upfront so the right leaders find you.

TIP

- **Strategic priorities as responsibilities:** Resist the urge to list the obvious. Every executive leader manages a budget, oversees programs, and supports fundraising. Candidates at this level know that. What they want to understand is what strategic initiatives they'll drive. This area is where the candidate can determine whether the challenge is the right one for them.
- **Qualities and competencies you're looking for:** Degrees and software proficiencies aren't helpful here. Focus on the experiences and qualities someone needs to be successful. Has this person led an organization of this scale before? Do they bring sector knowledge? Alongside experience, name values and ways of working that define your culture.

Setting compensation

If you want top talent leading your organization, you have to pay top dollar. Benchmark salaries at market rate, compared against similar organizations in your subsector and geographic region. This amount is your starting place. Then account for the complexity of the work as well as the strategic challenges and the level of risk the executive has to take on. Compensation should account for this totality, not just an average of other positions.

REMEMBER

Compensation is more than salary. It includes benefits like health and dental insurance, retirement, paid leave, and performance incentives. You also can offer relocation stipends, starting bonuses, housing allowances, professional development, flexible working arrangements, and more. Build and leverage the complete package to attract top talent.

Interviewing candidates

The meat and potatoes of looking for your next executive leader comes in the interview stage! Many factors and decisions set the board up for a successful interview process.

Right-sizing the process

In an executive search, top candidates are often actively engaged in multiple searches, and a drawn-out process can cost you the ideal hire. Three or four interview rounds should be more than enough to determine the candidate you want for the role. Anything more can fatigue the candidate and interviewers, blur judgment, and cause confusion down the line. How you run your search sends signals. Taking 15 rounds to decide says something about how your organization operates.

Choosing an interview format

You can effectively hold interviews in person or virtually. The most important thing is that all candidates get the same experience. Offering either as an option may feel like you're being flexible, but it can introduce a hard-to-qualify variable in the process because one candidate may have the advantage of making an in-person impression while the other doesn't. Keep the playing field level and protect the integrity of the process.

TIP

If your nonprofit has an office space, have at least one round where candidates can get a tour. This round is also the perfect opportunity to set up a meet-and-greet for staff so they can get a feel for their potential future leader in person.

Using a rubric

Boards get swept up by compelling candidates all the time. Maybe they're fantastic storytellers or have such a passion for the mission that everyone overlooks red flags. But passion can't close the competency gap. If a capital campaign is on the horizon, you need someone who has secured major gifts before. If you're in turnaround mode, you need a seasoned executive who's previously navigated one. If you're launching a new program, domain expertise may be nonnegotiable. Although enthusiasm is an asset, no amount can substitute for the hard skills needed for success.

The best way to distinguish between charisma and competency is to use a rubric, like the one in Table 19-1. List out the criteria for evaluating candidates, highlighting specific skills you're looking for and what qualifies as strong versus weak. Building a rubric together also surfaces disagreements early and gives everyone the same definition of "good" before you start the interview. Table 19-1 gives you a sample that the board of a $5 million STEM education nonprofit may use.

Standardizing questions

Use a fixed set of interview questions each round to ensure candidates get the same experience and you get comparable information to evaluate across the pool. It also reduces the risk of someone asking illegal or awkward questions in the interview, such as anything touching on age, race, religion, marital status, or anything unrelated to a candidate's ability to do a job.

TIP

Consider sending questions to candidates in advance. Real leadership rarely requires answers on the spot, and giving candidates time to prepare reflects the kind of thoughtful, structured communication you want in the boardroom. This approach allows you to evaluate their quality of thinking, not just their ability to perform under pressure. Check out the Nonprofit Board Toolkit online for some sample questions.

TABLE 19-1 Competency Rubric

Criteria	Weak	Mid	Strong
Leadership experience	Little to no experience leading an organization or senior team of similar scale.	At least eight to ten years of experience leading a large team or department or has served as executive in a smaller-scale organization.	Demonstrated track record of leading an organization through growth and change, at a similar or greater scale. At least 20 years in leadership.
Financial acumen	Little or no experience owning a budget or overseeing financial health.	Has managed a significant department or program budget and demonstrates an understanding of nonprofit financial principles.	Has owned a full organizational budget of comparable scale; can speak to navigating deficits and making tradeoffs, handling audits, or financial strategy.
Fundraising ability	No meaningful fundraising experience.	Some prior leadership experience with donor relationships, events, campaign support, and making asks. Experience may come from similar or smaller-scale situations.	Has personally led major gift asks or major fundraising initiatives. Can speak to specific achievements of comparable scale to our organization's needs.
Sector knowledge	No familiarity with the nonprofit sector or STEM education.	Demonstrates depth in either nonprofit management or STEM education but not both; can speak to challenges trending in one domain.	Deep knowledge of both the nonprofit sector and STEM education, including key players, funding opportunities, policy, and emerging challenges.
Executive communication	Interview responses are unclear, unfocused, or hard to follow.	Communicates adequately but can be long-winded, vague, or lacking enthusiasm.	Answers are clear, concise, and compelling; listens well, asks good questions, stays on point, inspiring storyteller.

Avoiding assigning presentations and projects

Asking candidates to complete projects or give presentations as part of their interview process is a practice we discourage. A well-run search process that includes looking at a candidate's track record, interviewing with strategic questions, and speaking to references should uncover everything you need to make the right call. Furthermore, having candidates do these types of projects disproportionally disadvantages those who are currently employed and don't have the bandwidth to complete an assignment on top of their existing responsibilities. If your board is insisting on assigning a project, then you need to insist on compensating candidates for their time at the hourly rate equivalent to the top of the posted salary.

Involving staff in the search

Wanting to include staff when searching for a new executive leader is very common. Staff involvement can be a great way to build buy-in, check candidates against the culture, bring functional expertise, and offer a perspective that the board may be lacking. However, without careful management and good communication, this good intention can create serious problems.

Productive ways to involve staff include soliciting input for the position profile early in the process through surveys or by informally consulting with mission-specific senior leadership. As you get farther along, host a structured candidate meet and greet, where the candidate can meet their potential future team in a lower-pressure setting. Be mindful of how this experience is set up so it doesn't end up with employees formally interviewing their future boss.

WARNING

Staff shouldn't sit on the search committee. This group needs to have sensitive, confidential discussions about candidate qualifications and compensation as well as about organizational needs. These conversations can be harder to have honestly with staff in the room and can put them in an uncomfortable position.

Considering internal candidates

The advice to treat your internal and external candidates the same is both right and incomplete. Internal candidates should move through the same process, but they require a more thoughtful touch. Unlike external candidates, they're people actively working in the organization while interviewing and bring deeper operational knowledge. Plus, the board likely knows them personally, which introduces bias in both directions that your task force needs to account for.

Furthermore, if your internal candidate doesn't get the position, they may end up as a direct report to whoever does. Set expectations early, be thoughtful about information you share with external candidates to balance things out, and keep communication more frequent. If they don't advance, offer candid feedback on why and be prepared for the reality that they may choose to soon move on. This situation is common but not always an indicator that something went wrong with the process. It simply happens when someone is ready for a role beyond the one they're in.

TIP

If you choose an external candidate over an internal one, make sure the incoming executive knows that before they start. They'll be walking into a dynamic that may include disappointment or divided loyalties that, if unknown or ignored, can lead to an unnecessary power struggle from day one.

TIP

If an internal candidate isn't qualified to advance, we recommend a courtesy interview using the same questions as any other first-round candidate. Even when you know you won't move them forward, the process reveals specific gaps, gives you the foundation for meaningful developmental feedback, and ensures they feel treated fairly. Pass your feedback to the executive leader, who can continue to develop and elevate them in other ways.

Checking references

Reference checks are a key risk-management step in the process, designed to validate the executive's achievements and their character. Request at least four quality references from your top one or two candidates. Ideally, these folks are the board president or directors of their current or former position. Direct reports, industry peers familiar with their work professionally, and community partners who've worked alongside them can help round out the picture, but they shouldn't be the main source. ***Warning:*** If a candidate can't provide a single board reference, that's a major red flag.

Approving the candidate

Before you can make an offer, the full board needs to approve the candidate. The search task force presents its recommended candidate at a board meeting and provides a high-level overview of the feedback collected throughout the process, as well as a copy of the candidate's resume and cover letter. The force makes the case for the candidate and holds discussion before seeking formal sign-off from the entire board. If people dissent, work through any concerns before you extend an offer. Ideally, the incoming executive has the confidence and mandate of the whole board, not just the search task force.

Making the offer and negotiating

With the vote secured (see the preceding section), it's time to make an offer. The board needs to align on what is and isn't negotiable and then give the task force the latitude to close the deal. Negotiating with the full board involved is slow and risks derailing the process. Loop everyone back in only if something material changes.

REMEMBER

Most executive candidates are already employed elsewhere and won't be able to start right away. A transition can take anywhere from several weeks to several months. Be flexible and remember that the care and respect a candidate shows the organization they're leaving reflects the care and respect they'll show yours.

Onboarding your executive

The most important part of the executive search process is onboarding. All the time, energy, and resources that just went into finding the right leader can be wasted if the organization mishandles this step. What happens in the first 90 days sets the tone for your executive's entire tenure, and the board can make a big difference, for better or worse.

Plan carefully for an impactful onboarding experience. Here are some guidelines:

- **Clearly define what success looks like in the first 12 to 24 months.** Set specific financial targets, operational benchmarks, and strategic milestones you expect your executive to hit.
- **Write up a 90-day onboarding plan.** A lot of people and priorities will be competing for your executive leader's attention. Prioritize their time by being explicit about what can and can't wait.
- **Establish a communication rhythm.** Identify how often the board president and executive will connect, sync calendars, clarify communication norms, and so on. Don't just assume your new executive will know what to do or where to be.
- **Make warm introductions to stakeholders.** The board needs to take an active role in facilitating connections instead of leaving them to chance. Host a dinner, have directors personally introduce the leader to staff, send out public announcements, schedule introductory meetings, or organize a community reception.
- **Plan for a 90-day reset.** A structured check-in with your incoming executive gives you an opportunity to revisit the position profile and strategic priorities together to make sure expectations are aligned with reality.

Working with Your Executive Leader

Building a healthy partnership with your executive leader requires intention. Put in systems for communication, respect the line between governance and management, calibrate the boardroom, and be proactive in delivering feedback. We offer tips from our time in the top seat in the following sections.

Understanding the four dimensions of your leader

When thinking about how your board supports your executive leader, consider their professional background and relationship to the organization. Are they a first-time executive or a seasoned leader? Did they found the organization, or are they stepping into a legacy? Are they from the nonprofit sector, or has most of their experience been corporate? The following sections break down the factors that shape how they show up as leaders and what they likely need from you.

Leadership maturity: First-timer versus seasoned pro

REMEMBER

No matter how many times someone has interacted with a board as a senior leader, nothing can prepare them for the first time they're accountable to one.

Although first-time executives are likely to be highly motivated and eager when they arrive, they're also still developing the skills to effectively manage pressure, pace the work sustainably, and advocate for themselves. In this case, the board needs to offer more structured check-ins and support early on as well as access to executive coaching and guidance on how to navigate board politics.

In contrast, seasoned executives ramp up far more quickly and come with a stronger point of view. They advocate for their needs, push back when expectations are unclear, and hold the board to a high standard of performance — a true peer in every right. The board must welcome the candor that comes with this type of leader and be flexible in its approach.

Organizational context: Founding versus inheriting

A founder is building the organization from a blank slate. They need room to experiment and iterate; they're operating in an environment defined by ambiguity. Here, the board needs to resist the urge to introduce too much structure too fast because doing so may slow the discovery the organization needs.

An inherited leader steps into something that has a history, an identity, and an established way of doing things. Making change and growing are slower and more complex, and the leader has to navigate a wide range of cultural and social dynamics that a founder simply doesn't. The board's job in this case is to be explicit about what must be preserved and what's open for change and then help them move the organization in that direction.

Organizational relationship: Insider versus outsider

Insiders come in many forms: an internal staff candidate, a board director who wants to step down and take the helm, a donor, or a dedicated volunteer who knows the organization intimately. What they share is a depth of knowledge about the organization and its programs, funders, and people.

WARNING

However, that familiarity may present a risk in the form of resistance to change and adherence to status quo. An insider is more likely to be guilty of the "We've always done it this way" mantra of stagnation, and boards need to be attentive to whether this leader has the appetite and vision to lead the organization forward.

Outsiders bring the opposite mindset, arriving with fresh eyes, no loyalties, and (usually) a desire to drive change. It's exactly what an organization may need to break old patterns and accelerate. But that's precisely where friction can emerge. If an outsider moves too fast without earning the necessary cultural capital and trust, they can create damage that's hard to repair. The board needs to help introduce and integrate an outsider and ensure change is paced so that it doesn't come at the cost of the goodwill the mission is built on.

Sector fluency: Nonprofit native versus cross-sector transplant

As we talk about in Chapter 22, nonprofits are as much a business as for-profits, and that's why leaders from both backgrounds can be highly successful at the helm.

Nonprofit natives arrive ready to navigate all the dynamics unique to working in the sector. They've led mission-driven teams and dealt with having to do more with less. In this case, their growth comes on the other side: being pushed to challenge sector assumptions, think outside the box, and innovate.

The cross-sector transplant often brings fresh thinking around earned revenue lines and an entrepreneurial instinct that can help an organization financially thrive. The gap lies in fluency about fundraising and nonprofit financial management, including grants, fundraising, and donor management. That learning takes time (and humility).

REMEMBER

Neither profile has an inherent advantage, and these are generalizations more than rules. You certainly may find a nonprofit native who's an exceptional strategist in earned revenue or a transplant who knows their way around fundraising thanks to time volunteering or serving on a board. In all cases, assess candidates for where their gaps are and build board support around what you discover.

Toeing the line between governance and management

In a nonprofit organization, you need to recognize a critical distinction between governance and management. The board is responsible for *governance*, including setting the mission, vision, values, and strategic direction. They must hire the executive, approve the budget, manage risk at a high level, and monitor organization performance. Meanwhile, the executive takes care of *management*, including implementing strategy, hiring and developing staff, operating within the approved budget, running day-to-day programs, flagging and mitigating risks, and being accountable for results.

REMEMBER

The board must understand and respect the boundary between governance and management and stay in its lane (see Table 19-2). Doing so protects both parties and the organization as a whole. A board that consistently crosses the line breeds a culture of resentment and second-guessing that inevitably leads to failure. Three things to keep in mind when thinking about good governance include:

- Executives can only be held accountable for results if they had the authority to make decisions and execute. A board that micromanages the executive compromises this authority. You want the right people at the right level making decisions in the organization.
- A board that gets too deep into the weeds of operations loses sight of the big picture, not to mention its objectivity, and is less effective in overseeing the executive.
- A board that gets distracted by the details is in a worse position to spot strategic and fiduciary risks early than one that stays in its lane.

TABLE 19-2 Respecting versus overstepping the line

Situation	Respecting	Overstepping
Hiring a senior leader	Board recruits the CEO; CEO and executive team make all other hiring decisions without board involvement unless invited	Board inserts itself in downline hiring or gets involved in staff performance management
Strategic planning	Board approves a three-year strategic plan and key priorities; CEO team develops the implementation plan and brings it back for informational purposes, not approval	Directors redline the operational plan and insist on specific tactics or require approval at each major milestone beyond what policy may require
Addressing an underperforming program	Board shares its concerns about the program, asks CEO for a plan, and reviews progress based on a timeline	Board goes directly to program staff to ask what's wrong or to give direction
Approving the annual budget	Board reviews and approves the overall budget, providing targeted feedback at a high level about overall revenue, expenses, and the surplus/deficit strategy	Board digs into items line by line, questioning specific costs or asking to adjust individual lines

Setting boardroom expectations

Anytime you bring on a new executive leader, expect a period of calibration as both parties learn how to communicate and work together effectively. First-time executives need more coaching on how to show up in the boardroom: what to present, how to frame it, and what level of detail is appropriate. The board should plan to offer feedback early and often throughout the person's first year. Seasoned executives require less handholding but may be set in their ways, making the adjustment more a matter of negotiation and flexibility on both sides.

Work with your executive leader to clarify the following:

- » What they should bring to the board on a monthly or quarterly basis in terms of written reports, financials, dashboards, program information, and data
- » How far in advance they need to send materials
- » What the board expects in the way of presentation for major deliverables like the budget and progress on the strategic plan, whether that's slides, verbal explanations, written reports, or something else
- » What the board needs to give the executive in terms of context, input, or decision-making support
- » What does and doesn't belong in the boardroom (because the board doesn't consider all information equally valuable or important)
- » Who does and doesn't belong in the boardroom (don't assume that senior leaders are in/out)

Designing the president-executive relationship

The relationship between the executive leader and board president is one of the most critical in your organization. It requires structure to function well, including clear escalation protocols and a commitment to eliminating surprises on either side.

The board president and executive should establish one-on-one meetings every other week (if the executive is early in their tenure or going through a crisis) or monthly (for more seasoned executives and steadier organizational states). This regular touch point ensures the organization's top two leaders stay in lockstep. The agenda may include things like critical updates or concerns that need board attention soon, work on strategic priorities, informal feedback on performance, discussion of board dynamics or concerns, and preparation for the upcoming board meeting.

REMEMBER

The board president isn't a coach, mentor, or direct manager, and the relationship isn't supervisory. The president's role is to govern and manage the board, not provide professional development or advice (unless the executive directly solicits it). Blurring the line into coaching can create dependency and undermine the executive's authority and trust.

REMEMBER

Navigate disagreements between the president and the executive with care and discretion. Work through things privately in a professional setting or with another board officer before it spills into the broader board dynamic. The executive has the right to push back on directives from the board; that's a part of the job. But after the board has listened and made its decision, the executive must either implement in good faith or accept that the role is no longer a good fit. What's not acceptable is either side going around the other to undermine or lobby individual board directors.

Understanding your relationship to the executive

As an individual board director, you have zero authority to personally direct or evaluate the executive on your own. That power belongs to the entire board alone. As they say, the board speaks with one voice. In practice, that means that if you have ideas about programs, concerns about the executive's performance, or opinions about a certain approach they're taking, you need to take them to the full board first. You exercise your power as a director through the deliberation in the boardroom, not directly over the executive.

Assessing performance and giving feedback

Many executives never receive formal feedback on their performance — only passing notes or concerns when something breaks. That's a failure of your duty of care, both to the organization and to the person you hired. Effective performance management requires a year-round commitment: setting clear goals, checking in as the year progresses, correcting small issues before they grow, recognizing good work, and conducting a formal annual assessment.

Setting clear goals in writing

The board and executive leader need to agree on operational and strategic goals that are specific, measurable, and set them through a strategic plan or an annual check-in. Examples include the following:

- Achieve a balanced budget.
- Launch a new program by a set date.
- Complete a major strategic priority.
- Improve staff retention.
- Increase community partnership by X percent.
- Build a plan to eliminate debt or pay off loan in X years/months.

Include a set of behavior expectations alongside these specific operational and strategic outcomes. These are harder to measure but just as important to include. Here are some examples:

- Provide the board with timely transparent updates.
- Build a strong senior leadership team.
- Model organizational values.
- Engage authentically with donors and other members of the community.
- Make decisions collaboratively.
- Represent the nonprofit in the community through speaking events.

REMEMBER

You must assess performance against both organizational goals and behavior expectations. An executive who hits record revenue is doing something right, but if they're also creating a toxic culture or keeping the board in the dark, the organization is at risk. Numbers can mask a lot. Having both sets of criteria gives a fuller picture of the leader's abilities and success.

Conducting an annual executive performance review

An annual executive performance review is a formal, structured process where the board assesses the executive's performance against set goals, expectations, and responsibilities of the role. It isn't a casual conversation or a platform for airing grievances. Instead, it should be a source of clear, honest feedback that can help the executive grow. Here are a few tips for running an effective executive performance review:

- **Structure the assessment around the goals** you set in the previous section and create a survey that has both Likert-styled questions for spotting trends and open-ended questions for capturing specific context.

- **Invite all directors to participate.** Everyone on the board interacts with the organization and executive in different ways. This approach brings a diversity of perspective and ensure the review is broad-based and less biased.
- **Solicit anonymous input from senior staff and direct reports.** Doing so adds important context around organization culture, but take the information with a grain of salt. Above all, these contributions must be kept strictly confidential.
- **Have the executive participate in the same assessment survey as the whole board.** Self-assessment exposes blind spots and misalignments, sets a more collaborative tone, and likely reveals things the board either forgot or overlooked.
- **Keep the debrief guest list small.** Only one person — the board president — should deliver the feedback, with a second person there to take notes. A full-group sit-down can feel like an ambush.
- **Make the debrief a dialogue.** This meeting is a two-way conversation about where the executive stands, what's working, and what needs to change. You want to partner on solutions and be open to added context on negative feedback.
- **Record what you discuss and any next steps you agree on.** This documentation protects the organization and keeps everyone accountable. Plus, you then have a nice baseline to start with next year. Both the board and the executive retain a copy of the final assessment.

TIP

Though you can self-manage the assessment process, we recommend using a third party because they bring structure, reduce bias, take the workload burden off board directors, and are more trusted when collecting data from parties with negative feedback. Cost varies but is usually modest, especially when compared to the cost of a poorly run assessment and damaged relationship.

Checking in throughout the year

Regular, informal check-ins keep the board-executive relationship healthy and feedback timely. A lot can change in 12 months; programs shift, external challenges emerge, staff resign, funding falls through, and small problems can quickly become big crises. Your executive shouldn't have to wait until the annual review to find out where they stand. A quick conversation can lead to quick corrections; waiting months to raise flags helps no one.

Celebrating success

REMEMBER

Executives rarely hear that they're doing a good job. Most people just jump straight to business and assume they know they're valued. However, a word of recognition can go a long way when you're under a lot of pressure. So next time your executive leader lands a major gift, gets through a hard season, or recruits a new senior leader, say something. Being kind costs nothing and plays a huge part in retaining great people at the top.

Managing underperformance

If your leader begins to struggle beyond simply making small missteps, the board needs to act. That means issuing written warnings and taking corrective action. For a deeper look at the warning signs and info on what to do if the situation reaches a boiling point, turn to Chapter 20.

Giving your executive a break

Sustainable leadership requires rest. Boards need to ensure their leaders get vacation every single year and enforce real disconnection while the executive is away. Check in after a time of significant work, such as a fundraising event or major initiative launch, and build it into regular dialogue.

If you're worried your leader may be showing signs of burnout, the board needs to have a candid conversation and take proactive steps to make sure the organization stays on track. Signs of burnout include the following:

- Slower response times and missed deadlines
- Shift from strategic to more operational/reactive focus
- Uncharacteristic mistakes
- Disengagement in meetings
- Shorter or less-thoughtful communication with the board and staff
- Increased irritability, especially about the mission or board
- Expressed hopelessness about challenges at hand

In these cases, time off or away from work can make a meaningful difference and restore the lost energy. In others, the only action may be to make a change at the top. Proceed with care and caution.

Investing in your executive

Professional development looks different for every executive, but some common investments include these:

- Executive coaching
- Leadership programs and certificates at universities
- Peer networks or CEO roundtables
- Sector-specific conferences
- Mentorship in professional associations
- Speaking opportunities

Use information from the executive assessment as well as input from your executive to determine the right approach. (You can read more on the executive assessment in the earlier section "Conducting an annual executive performance review.")

TIP

At this level, education and advisory support cost serious money, reflecting the complexity of the role. A reasonable annual budget sits somewhere between $5,000 and $15,000, depending on organizational size, with larger organizations investing more. If that number feels high, consider the cost of a burned-out or underskilled leader.

Planning for inevitable succession

A board can be absolutely certain about one thing: Your executive leader will eventually leave your organization. And yet most organizations are still caught unprepared. Do your due diligence today while the skies are still blue. Turn to Chapter 20 and begin putting in place your plans for succession.

IN THIS CHAPTER

» Getting ahead of executive absence and succession

» Clocking red flags in executive performance

» Taking steps to improve problematic leadership

» Terminating your executive leader

» Working with interim leadership

Chapter 20
Dealing with Trouble at the Top and Transition

Nothing good lasts forever. All executives, even great ones, eventually move on. Some of these transitions are planned and celebrated, and others are sudden, painful, or the result of a hard decision by the board. You can't always see this situation coming or fully control the outcome, but you can prepare.

In this chapter, we talk through preparing for various kinds of succession and absence. We dive into how to address yellow flags in executive performance before they become red flags and what to do if something is truly wrong. We also help you recognize what a legal and dignified termination looks like and what to do in the aftermath of such a situation.

Planning for Succession and Absence

Every organization eventually has to replace its executive leader, whether because of retirement, resignation, termination, or some other cause. It a matter of when, not if. Yet many boards are unprepared when the moment arrives and scramble to appoint a new leader as quickly as possible. Those hasty choices often turn out to be poor (and expensive) ones.

Succession planning is the process of identifying and developing the people, policies, and protocols needed to keep things stable through a leadership transition. Without a plan, a transition of this magnitude generates confusion, stalls programming, demoralizes staff, and erodes donor and funder confidence. Failure to plan for such a seismic risk is not only a disservice to your mission but also a neglect of your duty of care (see Chapter 3).

TIP

Talking about succession can feel disloyal or even threatening to your current executive leader, but waiting until transition is on the horizon is the worst time to have to pull a plan together from scratch. Don't avoid the hard conversation because it feels a little uncomfortable. If you normalize the topic early and integrate it into your annual performance review process, it becomes less jarring.

Looking at three succession scenarios

Though transitions occur for a variety of reasons, most scenarios fall into three broad categories: planned, forced/negotiated or unplanned. Each calls for a different approach by the board, so we look more closely at all three in the following sections.

Planned departure

A *planned departure* is where the organization gets enough advance notice to prepare for the transition. This transition scenario is the most ideal because the board is gifted something that the other scenarios don't offer: time.

For example, say a CEO announces they'll retire in 12 months. The board maps out a transition timeline, identifies potential internal candidates, documents knowledge, hands off key relationships, and coordinates with the incoming leader, who gets a chance to shadow the current executive for a month. In this case, an interim leader wasn't necessary because the board was able to run a search and place a new executive all before the current one departed.

Here's how to best handle a planned succession:

- **Start planning immediately.** Establish a timeline and identify critical relationships that need to be handed off. Document institutional knowledge and agree on a knowledge transfer process.

REMEMBER

- **Control the narrative!** Other stakeholders don't need to hear about a departure at the same time the board does. Be intentional about sequencing those conversations in a thoughtful way. Hold confidentiality until the time is right.
- **Talk strategy.** Decide what priorities will continue to advance and what should wait for new leadership. We know tying up all the loose ends is tempting, but sometimes that's not in the best interest of the organization. During a transition, the worst thing you can do is commit the organization to a direction the next leader may not be interested in pursuing.
- **Don't wait until the 11th hour to launch the search.** Start a search committee after your current executive has informed you of their intention to depart. The earlier you start, the more options you have, and the less pressure you'll feel to make a decision.
- **Revisit the job description before starting your search.** The board needs to reflect and ask itself whether the organization has changed since the outgoing leader was originally hired. The job today may not be the same as it was five years ago.
- **Celebrate the departing leader.** You can easily get so consumed by the logistics of the transition that you forget the *person* leaving. Meaningful goodbyes and gestures from the board matter to leaders as well as to staff and the community.
- **Plan for the overlap.** If a chance exists that the incoming and outcoming leaders will overlap, define the timeline of how the switch between leadership will work and when the outgoing leader's hard end-date will be. Unstructured time can create confusion about who is in charge and make succeeding hard for your new leader.
- **Ready yourself for change.** New leadership means new ways of working together. Even with an exceptionally smooth handoff, you may encounter friction. Recognize that as part of the process, give everyone grace, and try to stay flexible.

Forced or negotiated exit

A *forced exit* or *negotiated exit* occurs when the board and executive agree that it's time to part ways. Sometimes the leader sees the writing on the wall and agrees to step down. Sometimes the board initiates a performance conversation that leads to a departure conversation. And sometimes both parties realize it's no longer a good fit.

REMEMBER

The transition arrangement may include a long departure time frame and involve negotiating terms, timing, messaging, and communication about the departure. That's what distinguishes it from an unplanned exit (see the following section); in one way or another, both parties know that it needs to occur.

For example, say a CEO has been in the role for five years, during which time the organization grew significantly. Unfortunately, the leadership skills that got the organization there aren't the ones needed to take it to the next level. Both the leader and the board agree it's time for a change. They negotiate a separation agreement, with the CEO agreeing to stay six additional months, and the board releases a public statement.

Here are some tips for navigating this scenario:

- **Get legal and HR involved early in the process.** These types of negotiations need to be handled carefully. Don't wing it. Draw on the expertise of professionals who have seen and done this work before and can guide you through.
- **Agree on the public story — and stick to it.** A unified narrative protects both the executive's and the organization's reputations.
- **Move quickly after the decision is made.** Although giving your outgoing executive a long runway may be tempting, a prolonged timeline in this scenario will likely just breed uncertainty and instability.
- **Assume you'll need an interim leader.** Interim leadership understands how to drop in quickly and steer a ship to safety during times of transition. You may even exit your leader more quickly to get an interim leader in place because doing so gives you more time to figure out what you need next and reduces the risk of having a disgruntled leader in place.
- **Pay close attention to your outgoing leader.** Even with a signed agreement, a leader may disengage or undermine the transition, especially if they feel forced or shut out. Be prepared to accelerate the timeline or limit their access.
- **Treat the departure with dignity.** Even if the exit is uncomfortable, how the board handles it reflects the organization's integrity. Honor what the exiting leader built. Maintain confidentiality and respect the terms of the agreement.

Unplanned departure

This one is the worst-case scenario: the *unplanned* or *emergency* departure. In these situations, the executive leader suddenly vacates their position with little or no notice. The executive leader may initiate it because of a personal health issue, a family emergency, or a no-notice resignation. In the case of termination for conduct or performance, the board may be behind it.

The following sections describe how best to handle an unplanned departure.

THE FIRST 24 TO 72 HOURS

In an unplanned succession, the immediate priority is to stabilize operations and secure the organization for this period of transition.

- Whoever received the notice of resignation or incapacitation should inform the full board by email.
- Convene an emergency board meeting to discuss interim leadership and short-term messaging.
- Notify critical senior staff and request confidentiality. Make sure to let them know when you plan to speak with them next.
- Have the board president assume interim decision-making authority until the board can meet, working alongside senior staff.
- Take steps to revoke the departing executive's access to systems and facilities.
- Identify and place an interim executive leader within the first week. Flip to "Bridging the gap: Interim leadership and continuity planning" later in this chapter for our recommendations on finding and working with one.

REMEMBER

The goal in the first 72 hours is to ensure that your nonprofit has authorized leadership, that assets and access are protected, and that you have a clear internal message about what comes next. Everything else you can figure out after.

AFTER THE FIRST 72 HOURS

After the immediate crisis has been calmed, the work shifts from emergency response to steadying the greater transition. Work with interim leadership to keep the organization on track, communicate regularly with staff, and launch your search (which we talk about in Chapter 19).

THE BOARD PRESIDENT'S ROLE IN AN UNPLANNED EXIT

An unplanned exit is one of the hardest moments a board president may ever face. They're likely to be the one to receive the resignation — or be the person who has to deliver the termination.

TIP

The president should never deliver the news alone; they should bring along legal counsel, their vice president, or both.

Either way, it's an enormous responsibility and a very heavy task. In any sudden departure, the president needs to assume decision-making authority until the board convenes to outline a plan for interim leadership. They must use their best judgment and limit the scope of their decisions during this immediate moment. Don't forget that this departure is the board directors' problem to solve together, not the president's alone.

REMEMBER

If you're the board president in the case of a termination, remember that the board made the decision and that you are simply the messenger. This will be a heavy moment and you will carry a disproportionate share of the weight, both in the immediate crisis and in the months of navigating transition, search, and onboarding. Be kind to yourself: Build in rest, ask for help, and give yourself grace.

If you're a non-officer board director going through this, don't forget to thank your board leaders for the added hours they're putting in!

Sketching out what's in a succession plan

Not all succession plans are created the same, and they shouldn't be. The "right" plan is customized to your organization, factoring in its operations' scale and complexity, the senior leadership team's strength and capacity, the organization's maturity, and the nature of the departure. (You can read more about departure types in the earlier section "Looking at three succession scenarios.")

Though the details may vary, every plan should include a few universal factors:

- **Action plans for both planned and unplanned succession scenarios:** Include a clear outline of who has authority in these situations and what steps the board takes in the first 24 to 72 hours.
- **Options for interim leadership:** Outline the criteria you use to identify an interim leader and what that person is and isn't authorized to do.
- **The plan for running an executive search:** Detail who leads the search, what stakeholders are involved, the timeline, and a general framework for the process of finding a new leader.
- **An executive job description:** Review the job description for the executive director. Don't forget to update it annually alongside your executive performance review.
- **A communication plan:** Identify what stakeholders receive, through what channel, and on what timeline. This group includes both internal and external stakeholders covering senior staff, staff, donors, and the public.

» **Key contact information for all essential financial, legal, and operational relationships:** That means financial account managers and payroll providers, legal, insurance agents, and facility owners.

» **Access information for critical systems and facilities:** Get the details for items such as email and file storage systems.

REMEMBER

As your organization grows in complexity, you also may create succession plans for key senior leadership roles, such as the CFO, as well as key board leadership roles, like your board president or treasurer. Essentially, anywhere you have a role whose vacancy presents a serious risk to the organization, you need a plan for coverage and replacement.

Considering short-term absences and sabbaticals

If few boards plan for succession, even fewer plan for temporary absence. That's a huge oversight; the organization's work doesn't pause just because the leader takes time away. Staff still needs leadership, funders need communication and reporting, and the work marches forward.

Be aware of and plan for two common forms of absence: long-term leave and sabbatical. A *long-term leave of absence* is a break from work due to a personal circumstance such as a personal or family illness or parental leave. A *sabbatical* is an extended, intentional break (typically one to six months) that allows someone to step away from their day-to-day responsibilities. Unlike a vacation, a sabbatical is usually designed to allow leaders to reflect, pursue creative or academic interests, or just recover from the chronic stress of leadership.

In both cases, the board needs to identify temporary leadership coverage (read more about that later in this chapter in the "Bridging gap: Interim leadership and continuity planning" section).

Establishing boundaries with founders

When the leader who built the organization from the ground up finally departs the organization, they aren't simply leaving a job. They're separating from something that's deeply tied to their identity and sense of purpose. This phenomenon, called *Founder's syndrome*, can make letting go and moving on difficult for a departing founder to, even when there are the best of intentions.

WARNING

Boards are often inclined to ease the founder's transition by finding a way to keep them involved, such as staying on as a "consultant" or "strategic advisor." Some nonprofits even elect their founder to the board itself. Doing so may seem like a way to honor their contributions and retain institutional knowledge, but we strongly advise against it. A new leader needs a clean slate to work from and the freedom to make changes and lead the organization in their own way. That becomes difficult (quite frankly, impossible) if a founder remains present and empowered to weigh in on leadership decisions.

REMEMBER

The most generous thing a board can do for both the founder and the organization is to celebrate the founder's legacy publicly, acknowledge what they built, and then gracefully separate to create space for the nonprofit to grow under new leadership.

Taking in a few quick reminders for succession planning

Here are some points to keep in mind when thinking about succession planning:

- **Partner with your executive leader — early — to develop your plan.** They're best positioned to highlight risks to strategy and operations and hopefully will be honest about where they see themselves in five years.
- **Don't overlook internal talent.** Have your executive identify those with leadership potential within the organization and find opportunities to develop those strengths through stretch assignments and mentorship. You never know whether your next executive will come from within!
- **Appoint a single board leader or committee to maintain and update the succession plan on a regular basis.** Unlike a strategic plan, this item needs to stay fresh year-over-year.
- **Review and update the plan after every leadership change, including board officers and key senior leaders.** Each transition will likely reveal lessons.
- **Keep the plan confidential to board officers.** But ensure that the whole board and senior staff are aware of its existence.
- **Don't forget the financials.** Interim support and executive searches cost money. Consider this cost when planning for organizational reserves.
- **Engage a consultant, HR, or legal counsel to help develop the plan.** These professionals see this thing all the time and can help you avoid common traps.

» **Treat succession planning with the same urgency and attention you would any other major strategic initiative.** A bad transition can undo years of progress, so remember to plan for tomorrow instead of putting it off today.

Recognizing Signs of Trouble at the Top

Warning signs about your executive leader rarely arrive in a perfectly wrapped package or a loud-sounding alarm. More often, they're slowly unearthed through a variety of channels: annual performance reviews, audit findings, concerns raised by senior staff, whistleblower complaints, secondhand information from community partners, declining performance indicators, missed strategic milestones, negative media coverage . . . the list goes on.

After the signals are there, it's just a matter of whether the board is paying attention and is mature enough to act on what they see. In this section, we dive into the five common signs of trouble at the top, including underperformance, misconduct and integrity violations, breakdowns in relationship with the board, culture and people challenges, and general misalignment.

General underperformance

Underperformance is when your executive fails to meet established expectations and targets or is unable to fulfill the needs of the role. Sometimes it's obvious. Other times, it emerges as the organization evolves. Ultimately it boils down to a simple question: Is the executive able to do their job and do it well? Here are two broad situations where you may be seeing underperformance:

» **Your executive just isn't getting the job done.** They miss impact or financial targets. They set high goals for the annual gala and it falls flat, costing the organization money and the trust of donors. Budgets are delivered late or are inaccurate; core responsibilities are unfulfilled or are poorly managed.

For example, say an executive has been struggling for several years. Fundraising goals are consistently missed, and the development staff has turned over several times. Program participation has also been declining, and the reports the board asks for are frequently late, incomplete, or vague. The board has given feedback that the executive needs to provide more transparent updates and seek to strengthen the staff retention. The executive assures the board that change is happening, but change has been slow, if at all.

- **The organization has grown or changed in a way that has outpaced the executive's current abilities.** This situation isn't always a reflection of poor performance in a traditional sense; your leader may have done everything right up until this point. But the gap between what the role now requires and what the executive is capable of may just not be a match anymore.

  Maybe an executive has led a tiny grassroots organization for years, managing a modest budget and team. Then one day they secure a major financial partnership that dramatically expands the organization's resources and program delivery requirements overnight. Suddenly, the executive role shifts from being a very roll-your-sleeves-up doer to high-level strategic thinker. The role is now demanding more sophisticated financial management, oversight of a far larger staff, and new operational complexity that the current leader has never faced. In this situation, if the current executive struggles to manage the organization's new reality (and jeopardizes its stability or the partnership itself), change at the top may be unavoidable.

Here are some other examples of potential red flags. Not all of these will be present at once, and not all carry equal weight. Yes, a single significant failure can be serious enough on its own to warrant action, but the board shouldn't be tallying red flags against the executive leader. They should regularly assess the scale and impact of an issue as it arises, using best judgment and working toward a solution together.

- Being unwilling or uncomfortable with setting strategy or having a point of view on major strategic initiatives
- Requiring high levels of board input and involvement in operational decisions, which shows insecurity and lack of confidence in leading
- Consistently missing targets, deadlines, deliverables
- Avoiding or ignoring fundraising responsibilities entirely, especially if your organization is very dependent on fundraising
- Exhibiting poor financial management or budget oversight, with targets regularly exceeding or falling short of projections
- Receiving negative feedback from staff members or communities you serve
- Displaying avoidant or defensive behavior in board meetings
- Visibly struggling when the organization faces new complexity or scale

Underperformance cases often generate a lot of debate in the boardroom. Unlike clear ethical violations, where issues are more black and white, people have differing opinions on how to handle underperformance.

REMEMBER

Popularity and perceived effort can distort your judgment of an executive. People can easily confuse likeability and hard work with effective leadership. Make sure you have written performance expectations, an up-to-date executive job description, and a candid annual review. If gaps exist, don't let your personal feelings get in the way of fulfilling your professional responsibilities.

Poor culture and people leadership

A common leadership philosophy is that the tone is set at the top, meaning that the executive leader's behaviors, including their values and the way they treat people around them, ripple out through the entire organization. Strong leaders lift up those around them and foster an environment of safety, trust, and accountability that drives performance.

Problematic leaders create a poor environment for the team, marked by high turnover, gossip culture, and fear. As a board, figuring out what type of culture your leader is championing and whether/how that's affecting the organization's overall performance is difficult.

WARNING

Getting insight into the culture and people of your organization can be tricky. Executives are unlikely to tell you things aren't going well with staff. Their job security, reputation, and relationship with the board are all tied to the perception that things are running smoothly. More concerningly, they may be minimizing legitimate problems in hopes that issues will resolve themselves. As we like to say, trust that what your leader is saying is true, but verify.

You can get insights directly from staff members in a few different ways, some of them more appropriate than others depending on the circumstances:

- **Collect feedback from senior leadership.** You can do it as part of your annual executive performance assessment process (see Chapter 19). Always gather it anonymously because staff need to feel safe to be honest.
- **Request HR data as part of the executive dashboard.** That information includes voluntary turnover rate and employee satisfaction ratings, which can serve as early warning signs that things may be veering off course.
- **Ask the executive to conduct a staff climate survey and share the results with the board.** Unless you have a dedicated HR professional, limit this request to once every few years. The board should see the unfiltered results.
- **Ensure staff members are trained on reporting channels.** They should know where to go if they have a concern, especially if the concern is about the executive.

- **Request exit interview data.** When staff members leave, they're more likely to be candid, and patterns across these interviews can reveal a lot about the health of the culture. The board president or a designated director (not the full board) should review this information to protect the confidentiality of departing staff.

As you process feedback and review reports, here are a few things that may signal a major problem:

- Staff members report that they feel like they can't speak up or raise concerns without fear of retaliation.
- Turnover is high or increasing, and good people are leaving. The leader may be failing to build and retain a functional team, and the organization may have vacancies for long periods of time or a tolerance of poor performance from senior staff.
- Morale is low, with the pattern pointing back toward leadership.
- You hear reports of the executive taking credit for others' work, deflecting blame when things go wrong, dismissing people's ideas, and devaluating others in meetings and one-on-one.

WARNING

Not every perceived difficult personality type is a red flag. Leaders can be demanding, direct, and even unconventional in the way they lead but produce thriving teams and high results. It crosses a line when behaviors begin pushing out good people, turnover creeps up, and staff complaints start rolling in.

Strained relationship with the board

As we discuss in Chapter 19, the board-executive partnership is the single most important relationship to your mission, and both parties need to be on the same page. When things break down, or when the executive is unwilling to take direction, everything becomes harder. A few things that may indicate your relationship with the executive is under strain include the following:

- They're consistently late to board meetings, are unprepared, or present information that's vague or difficult to follow.
- They rarely share bad news with the board; that news makes its way to the boardroom from other sources instead.
- They meet feedback is met with defensiveness or justification rather than reflection.

- They treat board input as a formality and then do what they were going to do anyway.
- They make decisions that should require board approval, informing the board after the fact. Asking forgiveness rather than permission isn't encouraged in board-executive relationships.
- Their behavior means board directors dread meetings, disengage, or privately express frustration with the relationship.
- They push back on any attempt to set boundaries or establish oversight or accountability mechanisms.

REMEMBER

Healthy boards and executives push back on one another, and that's part of what makes good governance great. You want an executive who challenges you as a board and vice versa. The problem is when the executive consistently moves in a direction the board hasn't agreed to, when they respond to feedback defensively, or when honest communication is no longer possible. At that point, it's time to start talking about breaking up with your executive.

Strategic misalignment

If the executive and board aren't on the same page about the organization's strategic priorities, you're headed for trouble. When a board hires an executive leader, it recruits either someone to help set the vision or someone who is aligned with the existing vision. However, if the board and executive have different interests, resources will end up misspent; staff will receive mixed signals, frustration will set in, and the mission will pay the price.

For example, consider an education nonprofit where the board believes the organization's greatest impact comes from training teachers and helping them build capacity to serve more students. Meanwhile, the executive is passionate about directly serving students in classroom-based programs. Neither vision is wrong, but each represents a different reality. In this case, if the board and executive can't come to an agreed upon direction, the executive may need to move on.

REMEMBER

Strategic misalignment isn't always obvious and can stem from a number of places. Sometimes the strategy itself isn't clearly defined in the first place, leaving room for the executive to fill in the gaps with their own vision. These cases can usually be corrected. Sometimes the board and exec were aligned at one point, but the organization evolved, and the conversation never caught up. A facilitated discussion with a strategic consultant or even a workshop may help realign. But sometimes, a moment comes where the two parties have a fundamental difference in values or philosophy about what the organization should be and who it should serve and not enough common ground. The only thing to do in that scenario is to part ways.

Misconduct and integrity violations

Of all the types of trouble you may run into with your executive leader, this one is the hardest: The executive has done something wrong. We're talking about things like fraud, theft, harassment, retaliation, withholding critical information from the board, financial misconduct, and policy violations. The following is just a sampling of situations that fall under this category:

- An executive director falsifies financial reports to make the organization look like it's more successful or stable than it actually is.
- An employee raises concerns, and the executive subsequently excludes them from meetings and eventually terminates them.
- Multiple staff members repeatedly accuse a senior of leader harassment, but the executive fails to take any investigative or corrective action.
- An executive misrepresents their professional credentials in the hiring process, adding in an extra degree they didn't earn and inflating the details of their past roles.
- The executive shares confidential information, such as donor data, with unauthorized individuals.
- A board director discovers the executive has been running a side business on organization time, using staff hours and organizational resources to operate.
- The executive has been steering contracts to a company their spouse owns without disclosing the relationship, and they've financially benefited from every contract the organization awarded.
- The executive is actively talking negatively about the organization to community members, funders, donors, and the press.
- The executive threatens to share confidential information with the press unless their demands are met.

In each of these cases, the organization's finances, reputation, people, and mission are at risk. That's why swift action is critical.

TIP

When allegations of this nature come to light, take the claim seriously, investigate thoroughly, document everything, and show that the organization isn't looking the other way. Start with legal counsel. They're your best source of direction on how to navigate this situation. You also need to gather and preserve any relevant documentation. If the allegation involves harassment or discrimination, a proper investigation is necessary. Don't run this yourself. Bring in an HR consultant who knows how to handle these things and follow their process so that you're protected.

WARNING

The board must do its due diligence on any claim brought to it, out of respect to the person who came forward, who is (hopefully) acting in good faith; for your executive; and for the integrity of the organization. Ignoring a credible report or minimizing it is where real liability and reputational damage can occur. *Remember:* Inaction is its own form of misconduct, and even though the board isn't as public-facing as the executive may be, it'll be center stage in the spotlight if something bad happens. Even if nothing comes of the investigation, you've shown your community that no concern gets dismissed.

Responding to Trouble before It Becomes a Crisis

Not all signs of trouble mean a crisis. Sometimes they're just yellow flags that are calling for clearer expectations, minor course corrections, or external coaching. In this section, we discuss the various tools your board has for dealing with performance deficiencies and how to distinguish whether what's going on is just a rough patch or something severe enough that it may call for a change in leadership.

Using performance management tools

Performance management at the executive level looks different than any other employment relationship you've likely seen or been inside. We've included common tools boards use for giving feedback and dealing with trouble in the following sections.

Performance improvement plans

If you've ever managed employees before, you may be familiar with *performance improvement plans* (PIPs). This HR tool is designed for a supervisor-subordinate relationship where the supervisor can observe daily work, give feedback in real time, and enforce accountability.

WARNING

In the case of executive leaders, a PIP isn't an appropriate tool for performance management for multiple reasons:

» **The board doesn't have the day-to-day operational relationship with the executive that a supervisor has with their employee.** A board meets periodically, isn't embedded in operations, and can't provide daily oversight of progress against goals. Even if the board president meets with the executive somewhat regularly, their relationship isn't a supervisor-employee or coaching one; it's one of high-level governance and accountability.

- **A PIP risks overstepping the board's role.** The board's job is to set direction and hold the executive accountable for broader organizational outcomes, not to manage the methods they use to achieve them.
- **An executive's effectiveness depends heavily on the confidence of board directors, staff, donors and the public.** A PIP, even a confidential one, signals uncertainty about leadership and, if leaked, can trigger great instability.

Informal feedback and direct, private conversations

In an ideal situation, the board and executive have an open and ongoing channel for informal feedback, both positive and constructive. This setup helps build trust and eliminates surprises during more formal reviews as well as makes room for correcting mistakes more quickly, before they become bigger problems.

TIP

Feedback can become overwhelming if several directors are all independently providing input. As a rule of thumb, informal feedback should be channeled through the board president. Occasionally, committee chairs may collect feedback focused on their area of expertise and provide that to the executive, ensuring the board president is also aware. The key thing to remember is that feedback always comes from the whole board; if you have individual concerns you want to raise, you need to bring them into the boardroom first.

Sometimes an outside coach can help an executive develop the necessary self-awareness and leadership skills needed for navigating the challenges at hand. This approach can be valuable, but it has its limits. Coaching works best when the skill gap is specific, the individual is coachable, and the goals of the coaching are achievable within a fixed time frame. Ideally, the coach should be in touch with both the board and the executive to provide the most effective support for both parties.

WARNING

Having board directors step in to coach or cover for the executive leader isn't appropriate. Beyond being an unsustainable arrangement, it blurs the line between governance and management and sets up an inappropriate relationship between the board and executive. The organization also shouldn't absorb significant costs to compensate for leadership gaps that shouldn't exist in the first place.

Formal performance reviews

Alongside the regular informal feedback from the preceding section, your executive should also have a formal performance review. Through this assessment, the board can provide broad feedback across a variety of domains, including strategic achievements; fundraising outcomes; program impact; public relations; and organizational operations, culture, and more. Read more about executive performance assessment in Chapter 19.

Formal written warnings or board resolutions

When an issue has become a standing pattern without improvement, or when a serious concern arises, the board can issue a formal written warning or a board resolution. This documentation restates the expectations of the position and define what appropriate behavior or success looks like. It also should lay out a timeline for improvement and a structure for checking in on progress.

TIP

Include in any written warning that without sufficient course-correction, the board may need to take further action, up to and including termination. That may seem harsh, but it ensures the grave and escalated nature of the warning is unmistakably clear.

REMEMBER

Performance feedback can't be a group project. The best approach is to delegate the drafting to the board president or another trusted board leader who has sufficient insight into the issues at hand. To be clear, the board needs to have a conversation about the substance of the warning and define the key parameters, but leave the wordsmithing to one person or the executive committee.

Termination

If you've provided informal and formal feedback and performance hasn't improved, or if the issue is so serious that it requires action without warning (such as in the case of fraud), then termination is the last tool at your disposal. This move requires approval from the board and should involve a conversation with a lawyer before advancing. We talk more about how to make that decision in the following section and what to do after you make it in the later section "Firing Your Executive Leader."

Determining whether it's a temporary struggle or time to move on

Sometimes performance issues are a temporary bump in the road that you can work through with support, communication, and a little focused effort. Other times, the time, resources, or goodwill available can't make the necessary difference. The hard part is knowing which one you're dealing with.

It may be a rough patch if:

- The organization misses its goals, but the executive owns the errors, adapts, and comes back with a revised plan that regains the board's confidence.
- The executive is early in their tenure, is still finding their footing, and responds positively to feedback.
- The organization grows beyond your leader's experience, but they're coachable, willing to grow and take steps to strengthen the team around them.
- The executive is deficient in one area, such as HR or fundraising strategy, but leads effectively overall and you have a cost- and time-effective way to either coach or cover the skill gap.
- The struggles are clearly situational rather than a reflection of leadership behavior, such as a funding shift, policy change, or community crisis.
- Personal circumstances have temporarily affected performance, and the executive is transparent about next steps and any support they need.

REMEMBER

In all these cases, the executive takes full accountability, maintains transparent communication, expresses the intention to improve, and comes with a plan. Equally important is that a foundation of trust is still in place, and the board truly believes that change is possible and that the executive can deliver it.

But it may be time to make a change if:

- A mismatch exists between the leader's skillset and the organization's needs. In rapidly growing organizations, this type of mismatch is one of the most common reasons for leadership transition. For example, if your organization needs to raise money for a major capital campaign and your executive director admits they aren't a good fundraiser, training them up by the time the campaign commences will be difficult if not impossible.
- There has been a breach of values related to standards of conduct, transparency, or accountability, putting the board's credibility, reputation, and fiduciary responsibilities on the line.
- The leader made a failure of judgment or significant mistake that caused harm or changed how the board, staff, or community view them.
- Senior staff, donors, or board directors have lost confidence to the extent where recovery becomes harder than replacement.
- The leader shows a pattern of repeating the same negative behavior or mistakes (even minor ones) with no meaningful adjustment despite clear feedback.

» The executive has mentally checked out, meeting only baseline performance metrics and not investing in the organization's growth. Instead, they're letting it run stale or drift to the point where it's stagnant.

WARNING

As a board, you have to remember the duty of care and duty of loyalty we discuss in Chapter 3. Allowing these types of situations to continue unchecked or offering up one too many chances can create significant risk to the organization's reputation, financial health, staff, and mission.

Talking it out in the boardroom

REMEMBER

Ultimately, whether the problem is insurmountable is a board decision. The full board needs to come together, discuss what's happening, and figure out the path forward. Here are a few questions that may help guide that conversation toward clarity:

» Would we hire this person today for the organization we have now?

» Have we clearly documented what had to change? Did it change?

» Is the leader taking accountability, or are we seeing deflection and excuses?

» Is there a plan for improvement, driven by the executive, or are we hoping things just get better?

» Are we protecting the organization or protecting ourselves from the discomfort of replacing the leader?

» Is the struggle something we think is short term?

» Have we seen growth and improvement, or is a pattern repeating itself?

» Has trust with donors, staff, or the board itself been damaged beyond reasonable repair?

Taking the board vote

Check your bylaws to see whether any provision govern removing your executive and take note of any other required notice period or procedures.

TIP

If the vote passes and you agree with the decision, you can move to the following section and begin preparing for termination.

If the vote passes, but you disagree, then you're at an impasse. The core principle of governing as a group is that after a legitimate vote passes, directors are expected

to support the outcome. (This tenet is called *disagree and commit.*) If you're caught in this position, here's what you can do:

- **You disagreed but are able to commit to the board decision and can fully support the transition.** You didn't have a legal or ethical objection, just a difference of opinion. Maybe you felt that the timing was wrong, more should've been done first, or it should've been done in a different way. However, you respect the viewpoint of the board and are willing to execute the decision.
- **You disagreed and are unable to commit to the board decision.** You didn't have a legal or ethical objection, but maybe you're too close to the executive or disagree with the direction the board is taking the organization. This moment is a difficult one, but it's the reality of serving in a board context: You won't always agree with every strategic decision. In this circumstance, your resignation is the only responsible path forward.
- **You disagreed because of a serious legal or ethical objection.** You feel the termination was discriminatory or retaliatory or that the board acted in bad faith. In this case, you should resign and consult your own legal counsel about your liability and obligations.

REMEMBER

The one thing that's never appropriate is staying on the board while actively undermining or relitigating a decision. After the board has decided, you either get on board or, if your objection is significant enough, move on or engage legal counsel.

If the vote fails or the board is split, in some ways you're in a worse position. A divided vote itself is a signal that confidence is fractured, and the working relationship between the board and executive is unlikely to recover fully. From here, you have a few options: table the discussion pending more information, bring in a neutral third party to help facilitate or provide guidance, or discuss other options such as the negotiated exit we cover earlier in the chapter. What you can't do is simply move on without a plan. If the board ends up stuck between two camps, that division itself is a crisis that can paralyze the board and do lasting damage long term.

Boards really struggle when faced with the decision to terminate, and it's not because of dysfunction or negligence. Performance issues are difficult to catch and assess when you meet only every other month or once a quarter. The board president and executive committee are often the first to see a problem because they have more frequent touch points, which is why having them communicate openly with the full board and maintain consistent documentation throughout is so important.

REMEMBER

When your board finds itself revisiting the same concerns without any material shift in behavior or outcomes, that's the signal that it's time. Somone will always be able to make a case for more waiting or that more can be done. One or two directors will always be unable to overlook their friendship with the executive and will push to delay. But at some point, continued patience starts becoming a major liability.

Firing Your Executive Leader

Making the decision to terminate your executive leader is just the first step of what's likely to be a year-long transition. Termination has a lot of moving parts, many voices with many opinions, and no shortage of risk along the way. How the board plans for that and conducts itself really matters.

Planning for termination

The window between the vote to terminate and the actual conversation is high-stress, and some board directors struggle to act normally while holding sensitive information. Move decisively. Take the time needed, but don't delay unnecessarily. Delegate authority to the board president to complete the following steps quickly and with dignity and legal durability.

Gathering documentation

Documentation is the foundation of your defense if the fired executive sues. Make sure you have a paper trail that demonstrates the problems you're encountering with your executive, including things like performance reviews, notes detailing verbal warnings, written feedback or warnings, and copies of policies violated (if relevant). You also need to collect employment documents like contracts, offer letters, and amendments.

Consulting legal counsel

Always confer with a lawyer before terminating. They review your documentation and talk through your termination to ensure legal compliance. They also can help with strategy for the termination by drafting severance or separation agreements, sitting in on the conversation, and handling communications in the case the executive ends up contesting the departure.

TIP

Call your directors and officers (D&O) insurance provider, who will assign you legal counsel at their expense and make sure you've taken all necessary steps to protect the organization. This situation is what that coverage is for, so use it. Flip to Chapter 17 for more on D&O and other recommended insurance policies.

Confirming the succession plan

Ideally, an interim leader is ready to step in the moment termination is complete. Your best option is an outside interim executive who has experience in navigating the complex challenges that are common after sudden leadership departures.

TIP

We advise against an internal interim in a termination scenario. If you inform them in advance, they're left navigating the uncomfortable reality of working alongside someone who is about to be let go. If you wait until after, they're going to be blindsided and handed major new responsibilities with no runway and an organizational mess to manage. Either way, it's an unfair position marked by high stress and low trust. We talk interim leadership in "Bridging the gap: Interim leadership and continuity planning" later in the chapter.

Forming a communication strategy

The board needs a communication plan that covers the entire stakeholder ecosystem. Consult those on your board with communications expertise or consider bringing in external support to draft messages along with talking points for everyone involved in the transition. In your plan, the board should identify who gets communicated with, by what method, with what message, and at what time. In the first round of communication, keep it short but detailed enough to stop rumors. Table 20-1 provides a communication matrix.

TABLE 20-1 Executive Termination Communication Matrix

Stakeholder Group	What to Say	Who and How	When
Executive/senior leadership team	Who's in charge and vote of confidence Why the change (the public narrative) What to tell downline staff (with written talking points) What priorities are for the next 30 days What you don't know (be honest) and that you welcome questions That you reaffirm commitment to the team and mission	The board president, ideally in person	Right after termination/ within 24 hours; call an emergency meeting

Stakeholder Group	What to Say	Who and How	When
All staff	Similar to the message to senior leaders but less detailed: Who's in charge Why the change, and appreciation for outgoing leadership (if appropriate) What to expect over the next 90 days When they'll hear from leadership next about the state of the transition and search Who to direct questions to (their supervisors)	The board president, in partnership with the interim executive	Within 24 hours
Major donors and critical funders	Who's in charge Whatever your narrative for the change is What the next steps/upcoming priorities are	The board president and/or interim executive	Depending on the sensitivity or critical nature of the partnership, anywhere between 24 hours and 30 days
General public	Who's in charge Whatever the public narrative for the change is What the priorities for the upcoming year are When to expect a search Where to send questions	The board, either by newsletter, web news, or press release	Anywhere between 24 hours and 30 days, as long as it's after you've notified your critical donors and funders

Understandably, some stakeholders may be caught off guard by the termination news. Keep the following in mind as you form your communication plan:

- Senior leaders will be most concerned with how they're going to manage their teams, what the termination means for their jobs and responsibilities, how strategy may have to shift, and when they should expect a new long-term leader.
- Staff members are likely worried about their jobs, what the change means for the organization and the programs, and how it will affect their day-to-day work. You won't be able to answer every question, and you shouldn't make any promises, but don't lose sight of these concerns when considering your messaging.

- The key with major donors and critical funders is to inspire confidence. Donors want to know that the organization is in good hands, that the board is aligned, and that a plan is in place for the year ahead. ***Note:*** This doesn't have to be every donor; work with interim and senior leaders to figure out who needs an advanced personal touch.

Dividing up the duties with an interim leader

When working with an interim, explicitly deciding who is going to lead on messaging is critical. In general, have the interim serve as the internal facing voice and the board as the external voice. This division of responsibility prevents crossed wires and keeps the organization is clear in its communications.

Regardless of who is delivering the message, here are a few final tips:

- Speak with one voice; the board and interim leadership need to agree on the narrative around any changes and be aligned on who says what.
- Acknowledge the emotion, remembering that transitions affect people personally, and a little grace can go a long way.
- Tailor the message to the audience. Staff members and funders and program beneficiaries all likely need to hear something slightly different.
- Don't make promises. Avoid committing to timelines or outcomes.
- Communicate early, and often . . . as rumors will fill the silence.
- Keep the focus forward. Gather up what lessons you need from the past but center the message on stability and what's next.

Devising an access and asset revocation plan

You need a plan on how to handle revoking access to facilities, and digital systems like email and financial accounts. It can be a bit tricky, especially when staff typically are the primary points of contact for these relationships or access management and may require advance notice to select staff overseeing operations or IT. You must handle this piece with absolute care and confidentiality. You also need a plan in place for how you're going to manage your executive retrieving personal items and turning over organizational assets like credit cards and keys. Have a deadline in writing for when the executive needs to return organizational property, and by what means.

Informing the leader of the termination

Delivering the news to an executive you're letting go is one of the hardest parts of the transition. The following can help you navigate this sensitive moment:

- **Who does it:** The board president should deliver the news, joined by at least one other individual to serve as witness and notetaker. That can be the vice president, legal counsel, or an HR representative.
- **Where to do it:** Pick a private and neutral location that guarantees you won't be interrupted and allows the executive to depart without having to engage with other staff. If an in-person meeting isn't possible, you can do it over video, although ensure privacy on all sides of the screen and refrain from using any recording or AI notetaking tools.
- **What to bring:** Have all the paperwork printed out and ready to share, including a termination letter, severance agreement, and plan for separation.
- **What to say:** Respect for your outgoing leader means showing up prepared with what to say and delivering it professionally. Bottom line? A clear, short meeting is more dignified and respectful than a long confusing one.
  - **Be clear on the why.** Don't sugarcoat or over-explain the reason for termination. Stick to the approved narrative and get to the point.
  - **Use plain, decisive language.** Remember that this isn't a conversation. The board has made a decision, and the decision is final. Ensure you leave no room for misinterpretation or debate.
  - **Keep the meeting short and end with next steps for the transition.** You don't have to dive into all the details, but you do need to provide just enough detail so the executive understands what's expected of them next.

WARNING

And here's what you shouldn't say:

- **Don't add your personal commentary.** This meeting isn't the time or place for your observations, opinions, or reflections.
- **Don't make promises.** Don't float ideas about references, consulting, or public messaging if it isn't confirmed or part of the terms of separation.
- **Don't pile on details.** Resist the urge to offer additional examples or stories to validate your decision. Doing so only leads to defensiveness and debate and can seem even more disrespectful and hurtful for the executive.
- **Don't apologize.** That signals doubt about the decision.
- **Don't serve the decision in a compliment sandwich.** People often recommend delivering negative feedback with positive feedback to soften the blow.

But trying to cushion the news by telling the leader you enjoyed working with them (or similar sentiments) undermines message's clarity.

- **Don't make it about you.** Resist saying things like "This is hard for me, too." We know it is, but this is their worst day, not yours.

REMEMBER

You can never predict how someone is going to act when they're fired, even if you've known them for a long time. Your responsibility as the person delivering the message is to stay calm, stick to the talking points, and resist debating. If things escalate to the point where they're hostile or you feel unsafe, it's time to end the meeting.

If the termination is effective immediately, be sure to collect keys, credit cards, and any other organizational assets they have on them before they leave. You'll need to have someone ready to escort them off site, if you're in organizational facilities, and be ready to revoke access both physically and digitally.

- Appoint interim leadership and ensure they have clear direction.
- Create and manage the cascade of internal and external communications.
- Form a committee to lead the executive search.
- Determine the transition timeline, including whether you're going to immediately launch a search to use the interim period for other strategic work.
- Stabilize critical donor and funder relationships through personal outreach.
- Audit the current leadership team to identify any gaps in capacity or institutional knowledge and make a plan to address them.
- Review and affirm near-term organizational priorities (those for the next 30 to 90 days).
- Review the organization's financial position and make sure the interim leader has full visibility into cash flow, upcoming obligations, and decisions that can't wait.

THE FIRST 30 DAYS

The first 30 days after a termination can feel uncertain. Here are the most important tasks to see to during this period.

Remember: Feeling like you need to launch the search for a replacement right away is normal, but taking the first 30 days to assess the moment and align allows the board to move forward more confidently.

Bridging the gap: Interim leadership and continuity planning

When an executive leader departs, the question that rises up is "Who leads now?" Rather than rushing into an executive search and cobbling together some sort of stopgap for executive responsibilities, nonprofits are increasingly turning toward a more strategic and thoughtful approach for navigating their transition: interim leaders.

An *interim* leader is someone who temporarily leads an organization during the transition time between long-term leaders. Some transitions call for only a short-term bridge, but others require someone with specialized expertise in turnaround, restructuring, or crisis management. It all depends on the nature of the transition.

Choosing an interim leader

When selecting an interim leader for your organization, the board has two options: handle the interim period internally or hire an external, third-party professional. The following sections look at some things to consider in each of these scenarios.

Opting for internal management

Internal interims are best reserved for short-term, planned absences (such as personal or medical leave) where the scope is defined, the timeline known, and the organization relatively stable. With the right support, this opportunity can offer meaningful professional development, though it requires a much higher level of board engagement and coaching to be successful.

Elevating a staff member into the interim role during a leadership transition is a different matter entirely. Turnover creates a stressful environment and demands more objectivity and bandwidth than internal candidates can offer. Internal candidates also carry biases that can complicate decision-making during an already difficult time, on top of the demands of their usual role. For example, elevating the CFO into the interim CEO seat creates an immediate gap in financial leadership that you also need to fill. Distributing responsibilities across multiple senior leaders is equally problematic because it leads to confusion and power struggles that can destabilize the organization further.

WARNING

Sometimes boards place internal candidates into the interim seat in turnover situations because they think doing so will save them some money. This move is a misjudgment. Executive leadership is the last place you want to cut corners, especially during transition. You also still need to be prepared to additionally compensate the interim for the added responsibility and likely pay for backfill support to cover their vacated role. Without that, you'll likely burn out a valued leader.

TIP

If a senior leader is interested in the permanent executive seat, you may be tempted to appoint them as interim and treat it as a test of their abilities. But this approach is risky. If it doesn't work out, the organization will likely lose a valued senior leader or create tension with whoever it ultimately hires. Instead, go with an outside interim (an option we cover in the following section). That person can help assess the internal candidate objectively, coach them, and facilitate honest conversations about readiness if the fit isn't quite there yet. Similarly, if you're looking at an internal candidate whom you wouldn't also *very* seriously consider for the permanent position, you should probably pass and go with someone outside.

Working with an external interim leader

An external interim leader is a seasoned executive who specializes in stepping into transitional leadership roles on a temporary basis. They're available quickly, require little ramp-up time, and come with the experience to lead on day one. If your organization is facing an unplanned or difficult exit or some level of distress or dysfunction, an external interim is a better choice than the internal option we discuss in the preceding section. They can be honest in ways that long-term leaders and internal candidates often can't. They ask hard questions, uncover uncomfortable truths, and help the organization make difficult calls.

What sets external leaders apart is that they're rarely just static placeholders. They give the board time to prepare for the search, offer objective insight into the state of the organization, and can conduct restorative work that sets the next long-term leader up for success, often leaving the organization better than they found it. They can also be invaluable in helping you find your next long-term leader, as we explain in the later section "Partnering on a search."

Outlining an interim leader's role

During a transition, a balancing act needs to happen: Your interim leader needs to advance the mission without independently committing the organization to major decisions, significant expenses, or long-term obligations that rightfully belong to the board or the long-term leader who follows. It's a similar but distinctly different relationship from a traditional board-executive relationship, requiring a greater degree of oversight and, in some regards, a greater degree of trust.

Your succession plan should have a section where you detail what authority you grant the interim leader. (More on that document in the earlier section "Sketching out what's in a succession plan.") It answers key questions like the following:

- What strategic work do we need this person to accomplish during this transition period?

- Should any strategic decisions, initiatives, projects be put on pause until a long-term leader is in place?
- Does the interim leader have authority to sign contracts or make financial commitments that outlast their tenure?
- What should their role be with key external stakeholders such as major donors, funders, or partners or the media?
- Can they hire or terminate staff, and if so, at what level?
- Can they apply for the permanent role?

Partnering on a search

No one is a better partner in your search for a long-term leader than a professional interim executive. During their tenure, they assess the state of the organization and work closely with staff to guide change and stabilization. They can help the board understand what will be required of the next person, assist with writing a more accurate position profile, and work with your search committee or hiring consultant to find a good fit. And because professional interims have often been through this process many times, they can lead onboarding, helping new leaders integrate faster by providing professional plans, assessments, and onboarding tools.

WARNING

The jury is out on whether you should allow interim leaders to apply for the permanent position. The most common concern is that their leadership creates a conflict of interest or may cloud judgment. An interim who wants the permanent job may make decisions to impress the board or start to lean into organizational politics instead of advising and acting in the organization's best interest.

On the other hand, if someone steps up and earns the board's trust, wouldn't hiring them for the permanent role save the organization money and time? The key here is to decide before you place your interim leader and make sure to say so clearly. Chapter 19 has more on executive search.

IN THIS CHAPTER

» Understand healthy ways of working in partnership with your nonprofit's staff

» Communicating respectfully through appropriate channels

» Appreciating staff for the work they do

Chapter 21
Working with Staff

Cultivating and maintaining a healthy and respectful relationship with staff is foundational to good governance. It sustains the trust and transparency necessary for the organization to function at its best and strengthens both your chief executive and boards ability to lead.

In this chapter, we share practices for building and sustaining a high functioning board-staff relationship. We cover appropriate behaviors, communication practices, how to show your appreciation, and give you tips on how to navigate the unique power dynamics inherent in this relationship.

TIP

If you have yet to hire your first full time employee or are operating a nonprofit without any staff, we recommend revisiting this when staff is onboard. This is not a chapter showing how to anticipate managing staff, but rather, how to be effective with the staff you have already.

Respecting the Lines between Board-Staff

The board and staff operate in two different worlds. The board governs from a 10,000 foot strategic view and asks: "*Are we doing the right things?*" Staff operate closer to the ground, driving day to day execution of programs, fundraising, and operations, asking: "*Are we doing things right?*" Both questions are valuable, and neither group is more important than the other.

The board and staff need to trust that each side has an important but distinct purpose and function to fulfill service to the overall mission, bringing expertise and perspective that the other does not. When directors wade into the operational weeds or staff feel pressure to be involved in board politics, things start to breakdown.

Ensuring that staff reports to the executive, not the board

The board does not direct or manage staff — full stop. That is the job of your executive leader, who is responsible for day-to-day operations, hiring, and performance management. If the board inserts itself into that role, the confusion is immediate: staff cannot serve two bosses at the same time.

- **Don't assign work to staff.** Don't ask staff to pull a report or prep materials or do research without the explicit OK from your executive leader.
- **Don't tell staff how to do their jobs.** Unsolicited guidance undermines the executive hierarchy and puts staff in an awkward position.
- **Pass feedback to the executive**. Compliments are fine but concerns about performance go to the executive. They have a more complete picture of their assignments and expectations and have first and final authority on all performance related matters.
- **Redirect staff if they come to you for advice.** Unless you've both gotten the green light from the executive, staff should be seeking direction from their supervisor, not the board.
- **Don't fill staff roles unless explicitly asked.** If the executive wants your help with something operational, like reviewing a grant or assisting with bookkeeping, they will ask. Volunteering yourself into the function, or worse, pushing in, creates serious problems downline.

Communicating thoughtfully

Consider your executive leader to be the Chief Vetting Officer, a role that your ideas, partnerships, and opportunities should always go through them first before being passed on to staff. If either side has requests or directions for the other, it should flow through the executive. By going directly to staff, even with good intentions, the board risks undermining its leader, creating competing priorities and confusion about who is in charge.

As you learn where the line is drawn and begin to navigate this dynamic, keep in mind the three 'P's of communicating with staff:

- **Process.** What is the process I should follow to communicate with staff? Most organizations have a protocol for how the board interacts with staff. If you're not sure what it is, ask the board president or executive leader before reaching out. This isn't meant to add unnecessary bureaucracy. It ensures the executive is kept in the loop and protects staff from competing demands. Remember, staff report to the executive, not you.
- **Purpose.** Before reaching out, ask yourself: why am I doing this? A purposeful request is clearly connected back to the organization and your duties as a board director. Maybe you wish to make a connection to a potential donor, or you have a question that can help sharpen your governance knowledge, or you need information to better represent the mission. However, if the reason you're reaching out is just out of curiosity about why a program is operating a certain way or out of a desire to feel more connected, maybe pause. Staff time is finite and every request has a cost. Make sure what you're looking for doesn't already exist in your board files or can be answered by a fellow member of the board.
- **People.** Nonprofits are all about people helping people, and that starts with how the board thinks about and treats people inside the organization. Staff are not a line item, nor a resource to be managed. They work day in and day out on the front lines, doing the hard work that brings the mission alive. In all your interactions, extend grace. Don't read too much into a redirected email or a delayed response. Respect the organizational process and the line between your job as a board and theirs. And remember, everyone is doing their best.

REMEMBER

Your title as "'board director'" can be intimidating to staff. You have the power to change this. Show up as a partner and that you are there to support them and the organization. The more visible and consistent you are, the more trustworthy you will become. There can be scenarios where direct communication between staff and board becomes essential. See Chapter 21's Cheat Sheet online at `www.dummies.com/nonprofitboards`.

Respecting staff expertise

Nonprofit staff bring deep and specialized expertise in the mission and programs, fundraising, community engagement, and finance. Many hold advanced degrees and/or bring years of direct experience working in the sector tackling their issue areas and serving their communities. They are smart, hardworking, and just as qualified as for-profits in similar industries.

REMEMBER

For example, just because you have a background in finance, doesn't mean you know more about finance than a nonprofit CFO. Being a successful entrepreneur doesn't mean you know how to run a fundraising campaign better than the Director of Development. Having built a successful brand doesn't mean you are an expert on how to reach the communities the organization serves. Instead of reaching into staff work, reach *out* to help bring your expertise into the boardroom, assisting with risk management and oversight, and channeling your ideas through your executive leader.

Educating Staff on the Role of the Board

Having the staff understand who the board is and what they do is essential to a healthy relationship. When staff lack this understanding, they may feel like decisions are being made by unknown people or come to develop a distrust of leadership in general. Education can help demystify this situation and build trust. Here are some ways an organization can go about educating staff about the board:

- Include information about the board when onboarding new staff. Make sure to explain governance versus management on day 1.
- Include FAQs about the board and its role it plays in achieving your mission in your employee handbook.
- Have the executive leader provide brief updates after board meetings, either about key decisions or major discussions that are currently underway.
- Share the strategic plan, as developed by the board, so staff understand where the organization is going and what the board is thinking about.
- Invite senior staff to present to the board, or to a committee.
- Invite board directors to speak at an all-staff meeting once a year about their role and commitment to the mission.

The goal is to make the board feel less like the mysterious hand behind the curtain and more of a known and trusted part of making the mission happen. Small things can go a long way. When staff regularly hear senior staff reference the board in a positive light, the board starts to feel like a normal part of life.

Showing Up When Staff Need You

Board service will come with requests beyond the boardroom. When there is a major fundraising event or a donor to call and thank; a community moment that needs a spokesperson or project that could use a volunteer . . . raise your hand and show up. Staff notice who leans in and works alongside them. And, when you do show up, come as both an ambassador and ally. You represent the values of the organization and the board in the ways you communicate and collaborate. Introduce yourself as a board director, get to know the names and work of the staff you're with, and support in the ways they need you to. Avoid taking over or critiquing.

REMEMBER

Follow through matters. Staff work hard to build event plans and call lists and volunteer schedules around board commitments. When you say you'll show up, be there. A last minute no show tells staff exactly where they and the organization actually rank on your priority list. Give as much advance notice as possible and offer to make it right.

Understanding When Friendly Is Fine, Familiar Is Complicated

The boards' relationship with staff should be warm and professional, but it should stop way short of familiarity.

Friendly means greeting staff by name, expressing appreciation for their efforts, and remembering the human side of every interaction. You can ask a staff member about a project they're proud of or celebrate a team win. On the whole, directors should strive to be approachable, and all interactions should leave staff feeling respected and valued.

Familiar dips into the less professional, and the power dynamic is the reason why. A director who texts a program director asking for information or invites staff to a private event at their home or develops a habit of grabbing drinks with certain employees may feel like they're just being friendly. But the staff cannot easily say no to the board director. That's the reality of the power imbalance. Employees can be put into an awkward position where they don't feel comfortable saying no or reinforcing boundaries and can't comfortably exit the dynamic.

Situation	Friendly	Familiar
You need information	Asking the executive, who routes the request if needed, and engaging through the channel, the communication is issued.	Texting a staff member directly because it's faster.
At an organizational event with staff	Staying to chat, asking about sometimes work, expressing appreciation for the team's work.	Pulling a staff member aside to ask about team morale, probing about the executive's performance, or asking overly personal questions about their life outside work.
A staff member raises concerns	Listening briefly then directing them back to the executive or their supervisor and then letting the executive know the conversation happened.	Engaging at length, becoming a regular sounding board for their frustrations, or signaling yourself as an informal ally or outlet.
Social contact outside of work	Attending organizational events or community gatherings, or public celebrations where other staff are also present.	Inviting staff to your home for personal/private social events, or to 1-1 social outings like dinner and drinks.

WARNING

One bad apple left unchecked on the board can cause long lasting damage to your organization's culture. Toxic behaviors, such as controlling tendencies, unchecked criticisms and unkind words directed toward staff not only cause harm in the immediate moment but can linger long after that director has moved on. Be mindful of the behaviors of the board and remember what you permit is what you promote.

Celebrating and Appreciating the Staff

The mission cannot exist without staff. While the board is up in the air, at that 10,000-foot view, the staff are in the trenches. . . and often goes unnoticed or underappreciated. Nonprofit work is known to be thankless at times, and can be especially so for staff, who are consistently asked to do more and more with less and less. A kind of work can go a very long way when it comes to creating a culture where people want to stay. Here are a few easy ways to celebrate and appreciate staff:

- Pay them more. As soon as the budget allows, advocate for salary increases, expanded benefits, and annual cost of living adjustments. Don't make staff ask. If your people are taking care of the mission, taking care of people is taking care of the mission.
- Champion rest. Work with your executive to find a slow period where the entire organization can take a fully paid week off. Over the holidays at the end of the year, during the summer slow season . . . or both!
- Host an annual appreciation event where board directors and staff can mingle like a holiday party, or happy hour, or a site visit.
- Feature staff stories in donor and organizational communications, making their work visible to the people who fund and benefit from the mission.
- Recognize staff by name in board meetings.
- Write LinkedIn recommendations for staff or amplify their professional profiles, when appropriate and honest.
- Approve a realistic professional development budget, and support staff attending conferences or training, or finding mentors.

REMEMBER

Consistency and authenticity in celebrating success humanizes the board. It shows that the people governing the organization care about the people delivering the mission . . . and that leads to the type of collective trust that keeps great organizations together for the long haul.

6 The Part of Tens

IN THIS PART . . .

Discover the ten most common myths currently limiting the nonprofit sector.

Recognize and correct the most common problematic board director behaviors, from confidentiality breaches to bad actors.

IN THIS CHAPTER

» Identifying common misconceptions that undermine nonprofit work

» Understanding how investing in infrastructure and staff is an act of stewardship

» Recognizing the true costs of volunteers

Chapter 22
Ten Myths of Nonprofits and Their Boards

Whether you serve on a board in the nonprofit sector, engage with a nonprofit as a donor or volunteer, or simply admire nonprofit work from the outside, chances are, you've heard or believed one of the myths in this chapter. They shape how donors give, how volunteers show up, and even how leaders and board directors govern their organizations. In this chapter, we bust ten of the most common myths and misconceptions about nonprofits and give you a clearer picture of how this sector really works.

Nonprofits Are Not Allowed to Make a Profit

We start with one of the most damaging myths in the nonprofit sector: that nonprofits shouldn't — or don't need to — make a profit to be successful. In truth, both nonprofits and for-profit businesses need to make money. The difference lies in what happens afterward.

REMEMBER

- **Revenue goal in for-profits:** Profit is distributed to owners or shareholders for personal financial gain.
- **Revenue goal in nonprofits:** Profit (referred to as *surplus*) is reinvested in the organization to advance its mission and benefit the community.

If your organization chronically breaks even or runs a deficit, that isn't something to be proud of. It's a sign that you're fragile and operating in survival mode. Underpaying your staff, cutting corners on systems or technology, and lurching from crisis to crisis aren't signs of good stewardship.

So, what should you do with a surplus? You can reinvest it in the following ways:

- Pay your people well, with competitive salaries and benefits that attract top talent.
- Invest in systems and technology that help you work more effectively.
- Make targeted investments to grow program impact or capacity.
- Build up your reserves to give yourself the breathing room to say no to funding that doesn't align with your mission.

At the end of the day, a surplus is a critical tool that allows you to build and lead an organization aligned with its mission. It also signals that the finances are being stewarded in a healthy manner and you're likely fulfilling your core financial oversight responsibilities.

Nonprofits Are Easier to Run than a Small Business

A lot of people assume that nonprofits aren't "real" businesses or they're easier to run than for-profit companies, but neither assumption is true. Starting a non-profit requires the same paperwork as any other business, including registrations with your state and the IRS. You'll have to comply with layers of regulations and meet certain structural requirements, such as setting up a board. On top of that, nonprofits have to manage every function a typical business does, from human resources to finances to systems and technology. Add to that the extra layers of public accountability, grant funding, and donor relations, and you'll find that nonprofits can be *more* complex and difficult to manage than their for-profit counterparts.

The Board Is the Executive Leader's Boss

The board-executive relationship is a partnership. The executive director runs the day-to-day aspects of the organization, managing staff and operations. Meanwhile, the board governs the organization, collaborating on setting strategic priorities, representing public interest, and monitoring outcomes and impact. It's less like a supervisor-employee relationship and more like the system of checks and balances you see in government. Learn more about how to build a strong relationship with your executive leader in Chapter 19.

Overhead Is Bad

Overhead is defined as the costs needed to operate an organization, outside of program delivery and fundraising, and includes things like financial systems, human resources, office equipment and technology, legal services, and even professional development for staff. Historically, overhead has been misunderstood and villainized when, in fact, it's what makes mission delivery possible. An organization that tries to minimize overhead ends up underinvesting in the very things it needs to function, which leads to real negative impacts such as higher staff turnover, slower or lower-quality program delivery, and greater risk to organizational health.

Nonprofit Employees Accept Low Salaries Because They Love Their Work

Nonprofits tackle some of the most complex social, political, and environmental challenges people face. It's serious work that requires skilled and experienced professionals. An organization that cannot pay its employees a competitive living wage isn't ethically fulfilling its mission. Instead, it's balancing its budget on the backs of the people doing the work.

When looking at staff compensation, boards should apply the same standards they would expect of any business. This means assessing the organization's competitiveness in the following areas including:

- Salaries at all levels of the organization (including executive compensation)
- Health insurance, retirement benefits and matches

- Vacation, paid time off (PTO), sick, and/or wellness days
- Flexible or hybrid work arrangements
- Paid parental leave, mental health support or employee assistance programs
- Cell phone or home office stipends, transportation subsidies, professional development stipends

REMEMBER

Hiring and setting staff compensation is the responsibility of the executive director, *not* the board. Instead, the board can establish the HR policies and metrics that guide hiring decisions and approve the organization's *overall* salary budget for the year. The one exception is setting the executive director's compensation, which is solely the board's responsibility . . . and it's important to get it right. Your executive director will be the voice of your organization, chief strategist, lead fundraiser, and financial steward, all at once. Strong leadership is critical for the success of your mission, and you must compete with other organizations to attract a strong leader. As they say, you get what you pay for.

Volunteers Are Free

Volunteers are a major asset to your organization, but viewing them as "free labor" is a mistake. Here are some of the investments, in time and money, you'll have to make when running a volunteer program:

- **Recruitment and screening:** Finding volunteers is a time-consuming endeavor that includes community outreach, an application process, background checks, and vetting.
- **Training and onboarding:** All volunteers need training, and someone must take the time to develop training materials and instruct volunteers on their duties and the organization's expectations.
- **Management:** Someone must develop volunteer policies and guidelines, create a volunteering schedule, and communicate with and support volunteers when they work.
- **Uniforms and equipment:** Depending on their role, volunteers may need branded clothing, name tags or some other form of ID, or various supplies and equipment to facilitate their work.
- **Stipends or reimbursement:** You may have to cover transportation costs, meals, and other out-of-pocket expenses for some volunteers to ensure their participation.

» **Appreciation:** To retain great volunteers, you must acknowledge their contributions and commitment through special events, awards, or other gestures of appreciation.

Every nonprofit is different, and the costs associated with volunteers will vary according to the organization's needs. But keep in mind that when you invest in your volunteers, you strengthen your programs and community relationships.

Board Directors Are "Just" Volunteers

"I'm just a volunteer" is an excuse some board directors use when things go wrong, suggesting that they shouldn't be held accountable because they aren't getting paid for their work. While it's true that board directors are typically unpaid, their privileges, responsibilities, and liabilities go far beyond those of a typical volunteer. When you join a board, you become a fiduciary of the organization with real legal and ethical responsibilities. You will be called on to help shape the organization's strategic direction, hire and fire the executive director, and set organizational policy. Serving on a nonprofit board involves a serious time commitment and requires you to be informed and engaged, as well as prepared to be held accountable if things go wrong. So, yes, you're a volunteer, but not *just* a volunteer. Read more about this in Chapter 2!

Only Fundraising Staff Raise Money

Fundraising is a team effort, divided across different groups throughout the organization. Everyone, from the volunteers to the executive director to the board president, represents the mission, vision, and values of the organization, which inspires people to give and support the cause.

Boards participate in fundraising by monitoring donor growth and overseeing strategic fundraising goals and donation policies while partnering with the fundraising director on donor cultivation and stewardship initiatives.

REMEMBER

Even though everyone plays a part in fundraising, not everyone is a solicitor, or someone who directly asks for money. Board directors can become solicitors based on their level of comfort with reaching out to their networks for financial support or their experience with asking for funding or donations. Check Chapter 13 to learn how to engage your individual board directors in fundraising efforts.

You Must Be Wealthy to Serve on a Board

It's easy to understand why this myth persists: Nonprofits need funding, and appointing board directors with money seems like an obvious solution. But building a board around wealth alone can be a real mistake. A board entirely made up of wealthy donors may end up with gaps in professional expertise, lived experience, and community connections that would greatly benefit the organization.

The most effective boards seek a mix of time, talent, and treasure when building their membership. That means recruiting people with the capacity to show up and do the work, subject-matter experts who bring legal, financial, marketing, or other operational knowledge to the table, and people with a deep understanding of the factors that drive the mission. Financial giving is just one way a board director can support the organization; it should never be the only expectation or qualification. Check out Chapter 6 to find out more about recruiting a diverse board.

A Bigger Board Is a Better Board

Tempting as it may be to try to recruit a large board, the reality is that a bigger board can work against you. As your board sizes up, it will get harder to reach a *quorum* (the minimum number of directors who must be present at meetings) and to have meaningful dialogue, and become easier for individuals to disengage or fall into groupthink. The general rule is to seat 9–15 directors on your board. This is large enough to bring diverse perspectives to the table and support a few working committees, but small enough to allow real discussion and debate and maintain accountability. It's also worth noting that the board's composition matters as much as its size. You need the right blend of professional expertise, lived experience, and stakeholder representation. And you need depth in critical areas like financial management and legal compliance so the board can absorb normal turnover without losing function. At the end of the day, the question isn't whether there are enough people on your board, but whether you have the right people, whether they're engaged meaningfully in the work.

IN THIS CHAPTER

» Identifying problematic behaviors by boards — both as a whole and as individual directors

» Managing a positive board culture

» Addressing when strategic progress is blocked (and how to fix it)

Chapter 23 Ten Dysfunctions of a Nonprofit Board

It's common for boards to experience dysfunction, with directors struggling with things like micromanagement, poor communication, and erosion of trust . . . especially during stressful times. But fear not: rarely do board directors' dysfunctional behaviors come from malice or bad intentions. Instead, they often stem from a lack of information, awareness, or context about the conduct that disrupts healthy board culture. Once you recognize what's going on, there are solutions to get you back on track. In this chapter, get a better understanding of some of the common dysfunctions of nonprofit boards, along with practical strategies and tips for how to avoid or address them.

Rubber-Stamping

Rubber-stamping happens when your board blindly approves decisions and executive requests without having discussion or debate. Your board might be suffering from this if everyone is nodding along, no one asks questions, and votes happen quickly. It isn't always intentional either. Directors may not have enough information to engage meaningfully with an issue, or information may arrive too late to allow for a real discussion. Either way, the result is the same: the board says yes to everything without real scrutiny, which puts you as a director, and your organization, at risk. Here's how to prevent rubber-stamping:

- **Educate your directors.** Make sure everyone understands their governance role and responsibilities, and the importance of speaking up.
- **Engage in team building.** Fostering personal connections between board directors can create the trust needed for candid conversations. Allow time for team building at least once a year, either during board meetings, social outings, or retreats.
- **Create a personal connection to the organization.** The more invested board directors feel in the organization's mission and programs, the more likely they are to speak up. Set up group volunteer opportunities or schedule experiences to engage directors in the nonprofit's programming.
- **Encourage board leadership to ask questions.** Model curiosity and ask questions. This gives other directors permission to share their thoughts and opinions. Leave time for reflection and questions before votes are cast.

Micromanaging

Micromanaging occurs when a board gets involved in every little detail of staff's work that they cannot act independently or lead. Examples include a board director telling the executive leader how to write a grant, revising policies that staff are responsible for, sitting in on staff meetings, wandering the halls asking staff to explain what they're doing, or needing to monitor every expense receipt or request. Anything that crosses over into doing the job of staff tiptoes into micromanagement territory and blurs the line between governance and management. This will ultimately expose the organization to increased risk and lead to increased employee turnover due to confusion, anger, and lack of direction or support. Here's how to avoid micromanaging:

- **Keeping your agenda at the right altitude.** Focus on strategy, oversight, and big-picture decisions. The board is responsible for the *why*, not the *how*.
- **Clarifying roles and division of responsibilities.** Create job descriptions for board directors and correct micromanaging behavior as you see it occurring.

» **Optimizing reports with summaries instead of detailed reports.** Ask for high-level performance metrics from management rather than reports on day-to-day activities. Try to stay focused on results instead of the process.

Disengaging

Maybe you recognize the signs: Half the board shows up for meetings unprepared; some directors don't show up at all. It's like pulling teeth to get volunteers for work that needs to be done. Meetings are driven by one or two people, with the rest sitting in silence. Emails go unanswered and events are underattended. This type of disengagement is a failure of the board's legal duty of care. Directors that either don't care about their service or don't recognize the weight of their responsibility are a risk to you and the organization itself, and leave management and staff without critical support. To better understand why your board might be disengaged and to figure out ways to get your group back on track, flip to chapter 7.

Breaching Confidentiality

Board service regularly puts sensitive information into your hands, from organizational strategy and individual donor data to HR matters and more. When a board can't maintain confidentiality, it creates a culture of low trust and exposes the organization to serious legal and reputational risks. Another cost that's easy to overlook: the inability of the board to speak *in draft*. This means directors are reluctant to speak up and share opinions with total freedom, and to debate important issues off the record. A healthy, functioning boardroom depends on people freely debating and dissenting without fear of public exposure. When confidentiality breaks down, board directors begin to self-censor or stop talking, and then you lose the value of their expertise. You can read more about how to establish group expectations, write a confidentiality policy, and navigate breaches in Chapter 16.

Power Blocks

A *power block* is a clique — a small group of people on the board who talk to each other before meetings and agree on decisions ahead of time, ultimately steering the direction of the board rather than maintaining the order and formality of the process. Instead of directors having healthy debates and candid discussion *together*, decisions in the boardroom feel settled before the meeting even starts. Eventually, other board directors quit speaking up because it's clear who's really in charge, and the board stops functioning as a true governing body. To combat this, we recommend:

- **Naming the problem.** Sometimes cliques endure because no one directly calls out their behavior. A skilled facilitator or board leader can bring attention to the problem and guide the group to a healthier dynamic.
- **Mixing up meeting dynamics.** Does your agenda leave space for discussion? Try having small group breakout sessions with intentional variation in each group's makeup. This can introduce people to each other outside their cliques and help build stronger relationships.
- **Switching up assignments.** Make sure your board rotates committee directorship and officer positions, ensuring that new perspectives and ideas are being considered.
- **Onboarding with intention.** As you bring on new board directors, try partnering them with veteran directors. Find opportunities for directors to engage with one another socially outside formal meetings and functions.

Power Tripping

You know the power-tripping board director. They have an opinion on everything. They tell the organization's staff how to do their jobs. They talk over other people in meetings and push every decision toward what they want. There is no room for other approaches. The most common culprits are board officers, long-term board directors, and major donors — people who really know the organization and feel a deep sense of ownership over its mission. This is one of the most difficult dysfunctions to address because dismantling it requires direct communication:

- **Reestablish boundaries publicly.** Don't single anyone out. Instead, use board training or a governance discussion to clarify roles for the entire group. If you set clear expectations about boundaries, everyone will understand where the line is. Then, in the future, if someone crosses it, other directors have the confidence to redirect the power tripper.
- **Have a direct conversation.** If setting boundaries doesn't work, someone with authority will need to speak with the power tripper privately and clearly. This won't be a comfortable conversation, but it's critical to have it. Power trippers rarely self-correct without being confronted.

Avoiding Conflict

Conflict avoidance is part of human nature, so it should be no surprise that it's one of the most common dysfunctions on a board. The problem is, avoidance doesn't make conflict disappear. It just shows up somewhere less productive. Important decisions may be delayed. Frustrations that should be aired in the boardroom find their way into side conversations and gossip. And, over time, this chips way at transparency, breeds resentment, and erodes the trust and communication that a high-functioning board depends on.

REMEMBER

Asking tough questions and raising concerns is part of your duty as a board director. It can feel uncomfortable to speak up when everyone else seems to agree or if you think you'll upset someone. But don't let an unfounded fear of rocking the boat or being a troublemaker stop you. Speaking up is how you protect the organization and help it succeed.

Making It Personal

Bias is a very powerful influence that can creep into your decision-making without you recognizing it. It's easy to champion the programs you personally connect with or dig in against the things you don't particularly like, but letting personal preferences drive board decisions is a fast track to losing sight of the mission. If you don't like a certain program, or even a certain staff member, check your ego at the door and remember your duty of care, loyalty, and obedience. Your job isn't to govern based on personal taste. It's to govern in service of the mission.

Remaining Stuck in What Works

One of the ways boards lose their effectiveness is by becoming complacent. A "this is how we've always done it" or "we tried that and it didn't work" mindset will erode your board's ability to innovate and grow. Just because something worked before doesn't mean it always will. Complacency shows up when the same directors serve year after year, without term limits, difficult conversations are avoided, data is sidelined, and blind spots go unchallenged. Stay open to questioning what has and hasn't worked, be open to new information, look for ways to improve, and make room for new voices in the conversation.

Lacking Decisiveness

Have you ever found yourself frozen when facing a difficult choice? Or perhaps you end up revisiting the same conversations repeatedly without making any real progress? Decision paralysis occurs when the desire to be careful and make the "right" choice prevents you from acting in a timely fashion (or at all!). A fundamental aspect of serving on a board is having to make hard decisions, from setting the organization's strategic direction and making budget tradeoffs to hiring an executive. These complex conversations can leave boards stuck . . . overanalyzing, over discussing, and pushing decisions off until "next time." In the moment, you may feel like you're fulfilling your duty of care (see Chapter 2) when you delay decisions because you want to delve deeper into the issues, but in reality, you're avoiding your responsibilities and eroding the trust your organization has placed in you. Here's how to avoid hesitancy and indecisiveness:

- **Define how the decision is getting made beforehand.** Will you make this decision by consensus, or will one person be delegated ultimate decision-making authority? If so, who? Be clear about how you'll reach a decision before you begin deliberating.
- **Put time limits on deliberations.** Setting a figurative timer for any major discussions — for example, "We have an hour for input" — can help people focus. Including a brief pause for reflection — "Take one minute to think before we share" — can dramatically improve the quality of your board's conversations.
- **Set a specific deadline for the decision.** Deadlines such as "in the next few months" or "by the end of the year" are too vague and too easy to later override. Set a specific date by which a decision/deliverable must be complete.
- **Make provisional decisions.** You don't always need a perfect or permanent answer. Sometimes you just need to get started. Making a *provisional decision* (a temporary solution that you'll reevaluate in, say, two months) can get the group moving and allow you to gather valuable data or feedback.

Index

E

F

G

H

N

O

P

Q

R

S

T

U

V

W

Z

About the Authors

Jackson Cooper is a nonprofit educator, professional fundraiser, and experienced executive with 15-plus years, having served as executive director and in senior fundraising roles with Pacific Northwest Ballet; the Arboretum Foundation; the Town of Cary, NC, Museum of Art; the American Genre Film Archive; and Chamber Music Raleigh. He has taught nonprofit leadership and arts administration at UNC-Greensboro and Seattle University. His leadership in nonprofits has been recognized by *Puget Sound Business Journal*'s 40 Under 40, *Musical America*'s Top 30 Global Arts Professionals, UNCG's Young Alumni Award, and the *News and Observer*'s Tar Heel of the Week. He has served on a variety of nonprofit and government boards, most recently as Board President for ARCADE NW and as a governor-appointed Washington State Arts Commissioner. He currently serves as an assistant professor of arts administration at Elon University. You can contact him at `jackson@jcooperarts.com`.

Caitlin Pontrella is a professional interim CEO and nonprofit governance expert who has served as the executive leader of 8 organizations, the board president for 4, and a consultant on more than 40 client engagements supporting governance, executive transitions, crisis management, and strategy projects. She has worked directly with organizations ranging from $250,000 to $19+ million, with mission spanning arts and culture, parks and recreation, conservation, agriculture, STEM, education, and human services. Beyond that, she is an adjunct professor, teaching governance in Seattle University's arts leadership program, a fellow in the Global Arts MBA 2027 cohort, and the author of Nonprofit Field Guides (`www.greatergovernance.com`), a reader-supported publication offering free, practical, field-tested guidance for nonprofit boards and executives. She loves hearing your board stories and questions, so please reach out at `caitlin.pontrella@gmail.com`.

Acknowledgments

Nothing is ever done alone. This book is a culmination of the incredible support that helped shape the journey to creating it.

An enormous thanks to Greg Scully and Hannah Grannemann for being incredible friends and brilliant nonprofit thinkers who helped shape the ideas in this book from good to great. My family for their patience (and joy) during the writing process as well as my students for their commitment to challenging and creating new ideas around boards and governance. The Wiley team: Tracy, Shannon, and our champion, Alicia! Finally, I couldn't have asked for a better co-author throughout this process. Thank you, Caitlin, for your friendship and collaboration on this journey!

—Jackson Cooper

There are many people I wish to thank who helped me to this moment. The many exceptional executives and board members I have worked with over the years in the pursuit of good governance. The good folks at Wiley Publishing, including Tracy, Shannon, and Alicia, who each helped push this project across the finish line. My co-author, Jackson, who served as a fantastic thought partner, problem-solver, and collaborator.

But most importantly, my family, who taught me what it means to live with integrity and a care for others . . . And in doing so, set me on a path to nonprofit work. I would not have had the courage to do what I have done so far in my life without their support and encouragement. And my partner, Don, who has shown me what it means to put service above self, lead with humanity, and win others over to a cause.

From all these people, and more, I have learned what it means to live and lead well and hope it is reflected here in this book.

—Caitlin Pontrella

Publisher's Acknowledgments

Acquisitions Editor: Alicia Sparrow

Project Editor: Tracy Brown Hamilton

Copy Editor: Kelly Brillhart and Megan Knoll

Managing Editor: Murari Mukundan

Production Editor: Tamilmani Varadharaj

Cover Image: Tshidzumba/peopleimages.com/stock.adobe.com